Clamdiggers and Downeast Country Stores

Florence "Flossie" Vasquez of Steuben, Maine

# Clamdiggers and Downeast Country Stores

## *Eastern Maine's Vanishing Culture*

### by Allan Lockyer

with an introduction by Sanford Phippen

Illustrations by Linda Lockyer

Northern Lights • Orono, Maine • 1993

Published by Northern Lights
493 College Avenue
Orono, Maine 04473




ISBN 1-880811-11-1 (cloth)
ISBN 1-880811-12-X (paper)

Library of Congress Catalog Card Number: 93-84637

In Loving Memory
Of My Father
CLIFFORD ELLIOT LOCKYER
1 June 1918 Newark, New Jersey
9 July 1966 Steuben, Maine

*Acknowledgements*

The author wishes to thank Harrison Bell, Nuna and Ted Cass, Michael Fournier, Harlan Hawkins, Linda Lockyer (the most loving wife, critic, listener, and traveling companion I could ever hope for), Sanford Phippen, Eileen Kurley Tallon, Carroll Terrell, The Francis Marion University Foundation, and the kind people of Downeast Maine.

# CONTENTS

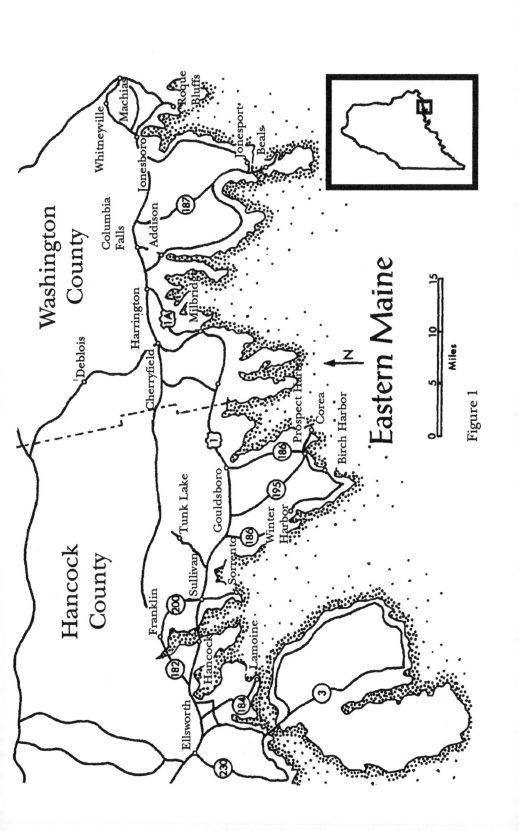

Figure 1

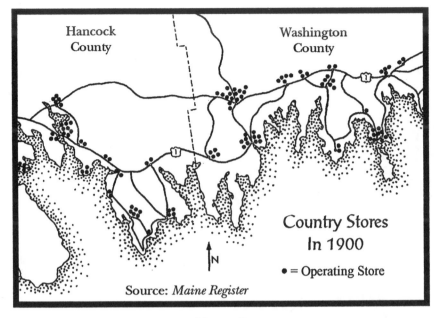

Figure 2

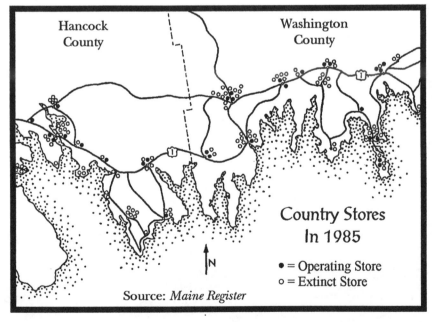

Figure 3

# INTRODUCTION

When I was around eleven years old, I helped my Uncle Bob Clarke deliver milk, cream, and eggs around Hancock and Hancock Point. It was only open summers, but it was typical of many Maine stores of the time. It had a full-length front porch with a deacon's bench where people (mostly men) would sit and chew the fat. There was an adjoining post office, so there was a lot of human activity by the time the mail was being sorted. There was also an apartment upstairs where various families lived over the years.

Uncle Bob would park the milk truck to the rear of the store, so I almost always entered by the back door where I would help deliver the dairy products to the ice-box area (the only form of refrigeration). The store was dark, poorly-lighted, musty smelling; and even in the early 1950s still sold staples such as flour and molasses in barrels and in bulk. As a young boy, I would be drawn chiefly to the penny candy section where I'd buy gum, licorice, "squirrels," "Mary Janes," and all-day suckers. I also discovered Zag Nut candy bars at the Hancock Point store.

The store, now torn down, was originally owned and operated by Herbert Young, a local Hancock man; and in my time there was a succession of local owner-operators that included George Marsters (who also ran a year-round Hancock Corner grocery), Albert Lounder, and Joe Tufts. Whoever was the proprietor at the time would wait on you, usually attired in a long white apron bloodstained from the meat cutting. There was no self-service, no adding machine, people's bills were totaled on pads of paper or on the brown wrapping paper, and the meat was hung on hooks. Pull-poles, or long poles with clamps on the end, were used to snag packages off the top shelves. Almost everyone on Hancock Point visited the store at least once a day.

The Hancock store where my parents kept our weekly tab was Leon Smith's at Hancock Corner off Route One, now the Village Store; and before Mr. Smith owned it, it was the Pamela Grange Store, one of two in Hancock at the turn of the century. In the Hancock Historical Society files, there's an old ad for one of these stores in 1907 which reads: "Dealers in General Merchandise of Every Description . . . The People's Favorite Place to Trade."

In all of the Hancock stores, there would be many sticky fly catchers hanging from the ceilings; and my mother remembers when they had shredded newspapers hung on the outside of the screendoors to help keep the flies out. There were usually spittoons, too, in those days for the customers who chewed tobacco; and there was always a store cat to take care of the mice. During the summers, the stores would stock fancy labels like S.S. Pierce foods for the summer trade. In some stores, the proprietors would reserve "the pick of the crop" for the summer customers. After Labor Day, the fancy goods would be sold at half-price to the locals.

On his way home from work on Saturday night, my father would always stop at Smith's Store, pick up our groceries and supplies, and also some beer and cigarettes for himself, and pay the tab. My mother would call in our order on Saturday morning.

Smith's Store was a hang-out, too, just like the Point store. There always seemed to be the same people in there, some just joshing and having a smoke with a neighbor, or passing the time of day with Donna Smith, Leon's good-looking daughter who took over the place after he retired. There was a stove around which some characters, including my step-grandfather Harold Dow, would be sitting gossiping. In the summertime, Harold would gravitate to a cooler spot behind one of the new-fangled refrigerators. A true general store, Smith's carried everything. I bought my first pair of new jeans (Wrangler's) from Smith's.

Of his Hancock stores, Allan Lockyer mentions only two on Route One:

Tide-Way at Franklin roads, which I remember as Butler's and Sawyer's; and the Hancock Grocery, which used to be called The Fleetwood. Both establishments are fancy new far-cries from the old days; but I never frequented them as much as I do now.

When I was growing up, there were six such stores in Hancock, a town of only 750 or so year-round residents. In my mother's growing-up years from 1915 to 1942 when I was born, there were twelve stores. Now, Hancock has over 1400 residents and the stores are down to three.

My late uncle Leroy Nason probably owned the smallest store in town, Nason's on the east side of Hancock. Only about three regular-sized customers could crowd in front of the counter at a time. I went in Nason's to buy mostly pop, ice cream, and candy. They had a most impressive glassed-in candy area; but there was usually a cat sleeping on a counter and often in the meat cutting area, so there would be cat's hairs in people's hamburger and with the slices of meat and store cheese. However, the canned goods were safe to buy, free from cat's hairs.

I remember a store in Gouldsboro where they used to keep a pot of beans simmering year-round on the stove and people could take a dipper and help themselves from the bean pot.

For thirteen years, Shayne Cobb and I have worked together at Orono High School; and Shayne has entertained me with stories about her aunt's store, Abelli's Fruit Store in Winthrop, Maine. Shayne's late aunt Helen Kempton was born upstairs over the store and lived there all her life. Shayne says the penny candy was a big draw at her aunt's store, too. "It was kept on low shelves a few inches from the floor. It got all the dust and dirt every time the floor was swept." Shayne remembers that there was very little room on the counter. there would be an ash tray for the smokers, open boxes of cigars, packages of Slim Jims for sale, and a fly swatter handy. Her aunt gave away free bags of candy on Halloween.

Shayne says, "Our store had been in the family since 1909. All the regulars frequented our store at a predictable time of day. In and out, all day long, eight a.m. to midnight. When the locals would ask, 'is it O.K. if I pay you next week?' My aunt would write up the charge on a piece of cardboard she had ripped from a cigarette package. She kept a pile of such charges with a fat elastic band around them. Our store was supposed to be an Italian fruit store with Bread, milk, and necessities; but translated into Downeast rural, it's a beer, cigarette, and candy store."

All I'm doing with this introduction is corroborating Allan Lockyer's thesis for this wonderful book. He's doing more than just telling stories and retracing his doctoral dissertation. This is a valuable sociological resource—but a most entertaining one—and not just for those of us who grew up here in Maine. For me, it's delightful reading, because I know several of the stores, their proprietors, and clientele well; but I'm sure the country stores, with or without clam diggers, in Maine are more of less like their counterparts in other rural parts of the country. They are social institutions, of course; and while the pot-bellied stoves and deacon's benches have given way to fast-food snack bars and video display racks, neighbors still pass the time of day at the Tide-Way and Hancock Grocery, as well as Dunbar's in Sullivan and The Trading Post in Franklin. People still keep tabs, too, and the gossip is as good as ever.

# P R O L O G U E

## SEEDS OF CURIOSITY

I remember the cloud of black flies that seemed to thicken as the warm May sun burned away the fog. It was Memorial Day weekend in 1960. The scent of lilac permeated the humid air, while down the road that was then U.S. Route 1, I could hear, despite the distance, muffled sounds of people's voices. The voices echoed in a strange way, perhaps because the bay was so near, bordered by overgrown fields with thick woods behind. And off in the distance, at a bend in the road, a tall, yellow building began to emerge from the fog and haze. My father told me it was a general store—a place where you could buy groceries, ice cream, soda, clothes, hardware, and tools. I was nine years old then, and the previous day we had driven more than five hundred miles from New Jersey to Steuben, Maine, where my parents had bought an old farmhouse.

My father gave me some money that morning and suggested I walk over to the store and buy a candy bar or some ice cream. "Maybe they still sell penny candy?" he had said, trying to arouse my curiosity. My father was always talking about penny candy, pickles in a barrel, and old fashioned store cheese. He had worked in a neighborhood grocery store as a teenager—it had been his first job—and apparently had acquired an affection for small general stores that remained with him over the years. My father must have worried about the traffic on Route 1 that morning though, because he insisted I cut across the fields. The going proved rougher than he had anticipated; I slogged through chest-high brush, crossed a shallow stream, and arrived—pants wet, feet muddied—at the big yellow store. "The store closed early today," a woman said, as she got into her car and drove away. Disappointed, I began the long trek back across the fields.

**************

Country stores—especially real general stores, the kind that sell clothing and hardware in addition to groceries—are disappearing. I remembered country stores that had closed. The abandoned relics dotted the landscape of eastern Maine. I instinctively knew there must have been more of these stores years ago—nearly everyone I talked to insisted there were—but didn't know how many, or why they had closed. Was it competition from supermarkets? Had their locations become obsolete over time? Had they simply gone out of style? The odds seemed to be stacked against small grocery stores. I eventually turned the question around. How had these relics from another era managed to survive?

I wanted to know the answers to these questions, but I also wanted to better understand the character of eastern Maine. I had gone away to college in 1969, had lived in several states in the South and Great Plains, and now, in my late thirties, was searching for that sense of place that rootless people crave.

When I lived in Maine year-round during the 1960s, my world seemed to range from Ellsworth to Machias, the respective seats of Hancock and Washington Counties. I took my driver's test in Ellsworth, and registered for the draft in Machias. My home was in Steuben, the western-most town in Washington County, and since 1973, I've summered at our camp in Gouldsboro, the eastern-most town in Hancock County. So as a graduate student of geography at the University of Northern Colorado in the early 1980s, it had seemed natural for me to adopt the region between Ellsworth and Machias as the study area for a doctoral dissertation on the survival of country stores in eastern Maine.

The small grocery stores in Ellsworth and Machias were omitted from my study because their populations exceeded 2,500, the U.S. Census Bureau's definition of an urban place. I was interested in country (rural) stores and they had to meet certain criteria. They had to be in the country, or in small towns and villages, but not in urban places. They had to be grocery stores, but they didn't necessarily have to sell clothing, hardware, or anything else. That was a distinction I later made. General stores—as opposed to just plain country stores—sell hardware and clothing in addition to groceries and snacks. General stores sell a little of everything. Country stores are simply small, rural grocery stores. And while country stores themselves are slowly disappearing, bonafide general stores are nearly extinct. When I completed my dissertation in 1986, there were 29 country stores in the area between Ellsworth and Machias. There had been 109 in 1900!

After extensive research, I found answers to most of my questions about Downeast country stores. But, had I become so obsessed with the survival of these stores that I overlooked some of the more interesting aspects—their social function, for example—of the whole country store milieu? Furthermore, had I written something that could be readily shared with other people who wanted to learn about the character of Downeast Maine through its country stores? Dissertations hardly evoke feeling about places, so I decided to write a travel book.

I began my journey in Ellsworth in the spring of 1988. My plan was to take a circuitous tour of country stores, all the way down the coast to Jonesboro, the last village with a store, west of Machias. I would raise many questions along the way, then allow the proprietors and patrons to provide the answers. Occasionally, I would deviate from the route—both in time and direction—in order to capture the flavor of the area.

It seems natural to begin this journey where the idea was conceived and where much of the book was written—at our camp on Jones Pond in West Gouldsboro. The camp lacks all modern conveniences, and over the years, I've got into the habit of going to the local country stores, for ice, kerosene, and other necessities. Admittedly, the need for camp supplies has given me an excuse to patronize rural stores, but the habit also seemed to come naturally—I LIKE COUNTRY STORES! And while I've always had the urge to see what is in them—my curiosity has yet to be satisfied since that very first encounter in 1960—I eventually became more interested in seeing who was inside, and hearing what they had to say. So, the establishment that once provided me with candy, ice cream, and soda pop, acquired greater meaning over the years. I came to view the rural store more as a social than as an economic institution. Country stores are places where rural folks go for advice, information, and companionship. It has always been that way—perhaps even more so in the past.

That's the way it was with Bob and Helen Morris, our neighbors, and summer residents of Jones Pond since 1938. They used to row a boat from their camp to Chan Noyes' General Store in the village of West Gouldsboro, about a half a mile away. The store has been a pottery shop since 1972, but Chan, now ninety-three years old, still lives across the road. The front of Chan's house faces the village green with Jones Cove and Frenchman's Bay beyond. Fields extend from the back of Chan's house a hundred yards or so to the shore of Jones Pond, a shallow, fresh water lake of perhaps a square mile, where ice was once cut and loaded on coasting schooners at the bay.

Chan had an old ice box at his store, Bob and Helen explained, and they used to row over and buy it in blocks. The ice, which had been cut from the pond that winter, was sold all year. "You could buy groceries there, of course," Bob said. "Then if you wanted overalls, or mittens, or gloves, or shoes, you could get those there too."

"Chan also had the village post office in his store," Helen said. "It was a wonderful thing to get in your boat and row down to get the mail."

"West Gouldsboro must have really changed when Chan closed his store," I said.

"Yes, I remember Phil Tracy saying, 'When they take your post office away, you've lost your identity,'" Helen explained. "Sure, people get a lot of their news at the post office. You'd stand around waiting for the mail and talk. And if someone is sick you usually find out about it in the post office."

Chan's Store had been a real general store. He sold nails, roofing, tools, shoes, and dry goods (clothing, fabrics—a term slipping into obsolescence), in addition to groceries. I wondered what had ever become of that stuff.

"Oh, he changed it into a so-called supermarket," Helen explained. "In other words, where you went around and picked up your own goods instead of standing around there as we used to, and we would say, 'I want this and that,' and they would bring it to us. (Too bad all that has changed, I thought.) And gradually he closed off the left side of the store and did away with the shoes and the clothing and household things, and it became more of a regular store. And then, finally, he closed the store and he kept a few antiques in there—just second-hand things to sell."

Helen was describing a process that I had witnessed throughout eastern Maine—the gradual transition from a general to a convenience grocery store, and in some cases, the demise of the business altogether. Tuttle's Store, which is also in Gouldsboro, is the only store in the area where the proprietor still waits on you. In most country stores, you get your stuff and go. In others, the proprietor gets your meat and deli goods, but everything else is self-service.

Helen said, "I remember one time when we were having breakfast at camp and my nephew was visiting and we ran out of maple syrup. So we said, 'Well, let's go down to the store.' So we stopped production of pancakes, went down to the pond, got in the boat and went to the store, got our maple syrup, came back and finished breakfast."

There had been many changes in West Gouldsboro since 1938. Bob and Helen told me about an Indian named Louis Jeremy who lived on the north shore of the pond, not far from where our camp now stands. "He was always here in the summertime and he'd have some little wooden baskets that he sold," Bob said. Louis Jeremy had left shortly before Bob and Helen first came to West Gouldsboro, but they learned about him from Fred Ashe, the man who owned most of the land on the north shore of the pond. "Fred was the kindest man," Bob said. "He allowed the Indian to camp on the shore. He also allowed another family to build a house on his land along Route 1."

Fred Ashe had also owned a country store in West Gouldsboro. He had a large delivery service, as did Chan Noyes. Indeed, Chan once told me: "I used to run a peddler's cart all the way down to Winter Harbor." Here was yet another aspect of the old country store that had died out before World War II.

When Bob and Helen first came to West Gouldsboro, Fred Ashe was out of the store business and made his living primarily off his blueberry land. It is hard for me to imagine, but the four-tenths of a mile of mostly second-growth woods that now stand between our camp and Route 1 had been blueberry fields in 1938. Bob and Helen used to leave a milk box on Route 1 and could look across the fields to see if the flag was up or down. Now it is alder, aspen, beech, birch, maple, pine, and poplar—good cover for partridge, porcupines, rabbits, and woodcock, and a black bear I've named Fred, after Fred Ashe, who died in 1957.

There is a small cemetery in the overgrown field just below Route 1 where Fred Ashe is buried. A trash heap lies next to the stream we call "Fred's Brook." And across Route 1 is the old foundation where Fred's house had stood. It burned several years ago, but the purple and white lilacs have taken over and bloom profusely each June. I wondered what it had been like back in 1938, with the general store, the blueberry fields, and the Indian making baskets beside the pond. The changes made me a little sad.

And there had been other changes in West Gouldsboro over the years. "I can remember the old saw mill that was on the brook that runs back of Chan's store," Bob said. "We used to go down and there was an old dock, and we caught flounder off the dock."

"What do you suppose happened to the fish?" I asked.

"During the war they were short of bait," Bob explained. "They caught flounder and used them for bait."

"George Potter, an old fisherman we bought our boat from told us they just fished them out," Helen added.

We found an old photo album in our house in Steuben when we bought it in 1960. And I remember looking at pictures of men holding up huge flounder by the wharves with Steuben Bay as a backdrop. All these years, I had wondered where the flounder had gone.

"The village once had a shoemaker and a blacksmith named Gouldsboro," Helen said. "Someone in the area found a baby on their doorstep, and they gave him the name of the town—Gouldsboro. The people who found him brought him up. And he became a blacksmith. Sam—I think was his name."

Back in 1938, there were carpenters, farmers, lobster fishermen, and sardine factory workers in West Gouldsboro. Clams were worth twenty-five cents a peck; lobster, twenty-five cents a pound. Still, I had gotten the impression that West Gouldsboro had always been a little more upscale than the other Gouldsboros. Was that true?

"Definitely," Helen said. "Another thing, right where Chan Noyes' present house is—that's where the Wayside Inn was. It burned in 1937, the year before we came. Nathaniel Hawthorne visited there. We have a letter at the Gouldsboro Historical Society describing his visit.

"This is where the Joneses settled, and they were some of the original settlers. General Cobb was the land agent here in Gouldsboro. And the people who visited here, and came up to Maine to see what it was all about, and tried to buy great chunks of land, came here—West Gouldsboro."

"And, of course they had entrance by boat at high tide," Bob added. "And of all these places in the 1800s, this is where the boats were built, and where the sea captains went out of Jones Cove, and went around the world—lots of them."

Obviously, geography had had much to do with West Gouldsboro's relative prosperity. The town is on the west side of the Gouldsboro Peninsula, facing Bar Harbor; whereas the other side of the town faces eastward, toward Canada.

"It was West Gouldsboro that started the Historical Society," Helen explained. "They have a sense of the past. That harbor down there (on the pond, not the bay) was a very active place in the 1940s. It's dead now. We used to get our ice at the store, and you were welcome there. And everybody not only congregated at the store, they also congregated at the dock. And you could go down and rent a boat from Chan at the store."

Chan Noyes used to have a motorized launch that he cruised across the pond for picnics every Saturday night, Helen explained. She described the boat, but I already had an idea what it looked like. I had seen an oil painting in Chan's house of him in his boat.

He had an oar over his shoulder in the painting, and in that pose resembled a lifeguard in an old movie. Chan was a handsome young man then, with thick brown hair combed back.

There were other camps on the pond in the 1940s that were only accessible by boat from the dock near Chan's store. It was an old Maine tradition to spend one's summer at a rustic camp on a remote pond. The whole family would go and live out a sort of frontier existence. But like the old general stores, traditional camps are also disappearing. Camp is now a place to escape to on weekends; that is, if the property hasn't already been sold to an out-of-stater. And so much for rustic living: Maine camps these days are apt to have all the comforts of home. Indeed, our camp may be the only one left on Jones Pond without any modern conveniences, and that's one thing about West Gouldsboro that's not about to change.

# Part One

## Ellsworth-Gouldsboro
## Hancock County

# CHAPTER 1

## A TURN AT THE CROSSROADS

E leven thousand cars a day pass by here," I once heard a man say. He was referring to High Street (U.S. Route 1) in Ellsworth. It's one of the busiest stretches of road in Maine during the summer. Ellsworth, the crossroads of Downeast Maine, lies about 150 miles east of Portland, on the way to Bar Harbor and Acadia National Park.

I opened *The Ellsworth American* one summer day, and found inside, a booklet entitled "Out & About in Downeast Maine—A Seasonal Guide." On the cover was a picture of a man wearing a Trenton, Maine baseball cap. He was smiling in a goofy way that made me think of Deputy Barney Fife of Mayberry, and Ernest, the funny-looking man in the Mellow Yellow commercials, simultaneously, as he held up two large lobsters towards the camera. I leafed through the guide and found an article entitled: "Prepare yourself for 'Grand' Entertainment in Ellsworth." The story was about the Grand, an old downtown movie theater dating from the 1930s. The article suggested that because of the increasing popularity of television, the theater's audiences slowly dwindled during the 1950s and 1960s, until finally, it was "forced to close its doors."

The old movie house had been scheduled for demolition in 1974. But a group of concerned citizens and members of the Downeast art community banded together and fought to save the "art deco gem."

It was in front of the Grand Theater that I failed my first driver's test in 1968. Perhaps the roots of my Ellsworth, Maine—BIG CITY!—anxiety can be traced back to the moment the police officer said, "Okay, Allan, I want you to parallel park." We were on the hill in front of the Grand. It was February; clumps of dirty snow and ice stuck to the curbs here and there. Main was a quiet street then; still, I unwittingly threw the car in reverse, instead of first, and nearly slammed into the parked vehicle behind me.

In those days, they had amateur boxing in the Grand Theater. And a few months after failing my driver's test, I was on stage in the Grand; bare to the waist, pacing nervously, my heart pounding—I can close my eyes and still feel the fright—while my opponent, a muscular paper mill worker, several years older than I, stood calmly in his corner. I still have the clipping from *The Ellsworth American*.

### TKO's Dominate Weekly Fight Card

> William Woodrow of Belfast walked off with the top boxing award last night at the Grand Theater after his bout with Allan Lockyer of Sumner High School was stopped because of an injury to Lockyer's shoulder.

It had lasted less than a round. I came out swinging; I felt my shoulder dislocate; it's never been the same. I never boxed again. But on warm summer evenings, when we need a diversion from life at the camp, we trundle down to the Grand. These days, it is sort of an "avant garde" theater (it seems especially popular with ex-hippies, yuppies, transplants, and back-to-the-landers) where you can see good films not ordinarily shown at typical shopping mall theaters. The 536 seat auditorium also features live entertainment and is said to rival the University of Maine's Center for the Arts.

In a way, the Grand Theater's renaissance is representative of Ellsworth's remarkable growth, from a sleepy coastal town in the 1960s, to the frenzied crossroads of the 1980s. At times, I hardly recognize the place. You can go to Ellsworth and forget you're in

Maine. Especially during the summer, you sometimes have to listen long and hard to hear a genuine Maine accent. Between the convenience stores, fast-food franchises, motels, outlets, specialty shops, real estate agencies, and automobile dealerships, it's not hard to imagine the day when the Bangor-Brewer-Ellsworth-Bar Harbor axis will finally coalesce. It's already happening.

Indeed, a summer drive to Ellsworth can try your patience, especially when you've grown accustomed to stopping at the nearby country store for a block of ice or a bottle of pop. But like everyone else who lives between Ellsworth and the Canadian border, I come to town out of necessity—to shop and to do other things not possible in the countryside. Small villages like West Gouldsboro cannot survive without the nearest central place. And Ellsworth is that central place—the node around which eastern Maine revolves.

But the increasing homogenization of Downeast Maine has been hard for me to accept. When I went away to college in 1969, eastern Maine seemed a long way from the Megalopolis to the south. The buffer of distance still insulated us from encroaching urbanization. Whereas Bar Harbor and Acadia National Park were attracting a growing number of tourists, any place east of Ellsworth still seemed way Downeast, beyond the reach of the "rat race" below. It was a comforting, but even then, erroneous idea. While the rest of the Northeast was being paved over, we were still safe from that madness in eastern Maine. "Unspoiled" was the word I always heard. The Downeast area was still unspoiled.

Now, twenty years later, all that has changed. Distances have shrunk; Boston seems to be coalescing with Portland; Portland with mid-coast towns like Rockland and Camden, which seem to be pushing towards Ellsworth; which seems to be extending its trade area all the way down into Washington County. And when *The Ellsworth American* was the subject of *Time* Magazine's "American Scene" column on January 18, 1988, it finally dawned on me that what I had feared all along was really happening: that a whole way of life—a unique culture—was vanishing.

### In Maine: A Town and its Paper

Ellsworth has reason to be wary of outsiders, who come
here seeking tranquillity and disturb what tranquillity

there is. They clog streets, drive up land prices and bring with them some anxieties they hoped to escape. And they talk funny. Not since the fire of 1933 swept down Main Street, consuming 130 buildings, has the character of the town and the region been so threatened. "We're getting a little class," says Victoria Smallidge, owner of the Pineland Diner, who moved here in 1970. Call it what you will, some locals are uneasy about a diner that offers a wine list and tenderloin with béarnaise sauce but holds mashed potatoes and meat loaf in contempt. *American* reporters discuss stories that straddle two worlds: a log-sawing contest in Brooklin, Me., and drug-awareness week at nearby Bucksport High. These days lawyers and real estate agents seem to outnumber clergymen and clam diggers. Even the lilting Down East accent, once spoken as if it were passing over a dip on a backwoods road, is losing its curls.

As real estate values climbed during the summer of 1988, I tried to console myself by thinking: Maybe, no, surely, this is the peak. These skyrocketing land prices will certainly discourage further development and population growth. Why would anyone pay two thousand dollars a foot for ocean frontage? Surely, they'll realize how much better off they are in, say, Massachusetts, Connecticut, New Jersey, or wherever they're now living, and leave us Downeasters alone. I was just beginning to get comfortable with that silly notion when I picked up the July 21, 1988 edition of *The Ellsworth American* and read:

### Multi-Million Dollar
### Shopping Mall Planned

A 250,000 square-foot mall complex anchored by major department stores may beckon Hancock County shoppers by 1990 if the plans of a group of Georgia businessmen come to fruition.

Another shopping mall? I wondered how local people felt about this latest assault on the Downeast area. They wouldn't have to drive all the way to the Bangor Mall. I heard that a lot. It would provide plenty of new jobs. Yeah, sweeping up, or flipping hamburgers for minimum wage. In the summer of 1988, Ellsworth's unemployment rate of two percent was the lowest it had been in more than twenty years. The baby boom had long since gone bust and there was actually a real shortage of teenaged and younger workers to fill the low paying service jobs the area already had. What were they going to do, import laborers as they did in Cape Cod? Finally, the new mall would draw Canadian shoppers who currently drive across Route 9 from New Brunswick to shop in Bangor. The traffic along Route 1 would increase significantly. That one really scared me.

Was everyone in favor of this mall? Why weren't people in the streets, protesting? Surely they had seen what gigantic shopping malls had done to other towns in America. And this was the summer of the devastating drought, the suffocating heat wave, the realization that the greenhouse effect was something to be reckoned with. Medical waste was floating up on eastern beaches, the ozone layer was imperiled, the world's rainforests were disappearing, and in Ellsworth, Maine, they wanted more pavement, more concrete.

Just east of the Ellsworth Auto Supply, along Route 1, stood a tiny gray cottage—naked, the trees gone from several dozen acres behind—the land that once framed it had been scraped to mud. It was here, I had learned, that the new shopping mall would go. Didn't anybody care what was happening? On August 4, 1988, the following letter appeared in *The Ellsworth American*.

### Homogenization of Eastern Maine

Dear Sir:

At first glance I was appalled by the concept of a giant mall in Ellsworth, as it only seemed to underscore the continued, widespread homogenization of Eastern Maine. Who needs more sunbelt anti-architecture in the midst of a blacktop desert, I wondered.

But as I read on my fears were quickly allayed. This proposed shopping center is to be called the Down East Mall, and will provide grateful shoppers with "the feeling of walking through a main street in one of the areas small towns." What a relief to know that as Down East Maine is being steamrolled, paved over, and boutiqued into oblivion, we'll be able to see a couple of bearded pensioners in oilskins, some scraps of buoy dotted fishnet, and a smattering of fiberglass gull droppings as we jostle for roast nuts and running shoes.

And our good fortune doesn't stop there: the developers have promised to save three trees and manufacture a pond. It's going to be fun for the entire family and I can hardly wait.

Joe Crary
Prospect Harbor

A year later, the proposed mall had been scaled down to a "theme-type village," which would include banks, hotels, restaurants, and factory outlets. Apparently, the major retail chain that was to have anchored the mall backed out; the developer admitted he had made some mistakes, but felt the revamped project, now called Acadia Outlet Village, would soon materialize. There were even rumors that L.L. Bean would locate an outlet in the village, but the Bean people insisted those were inaccurate.*

In any event, all signs seem to point to continued growth in Ellsworth and eastern Maine. And with record numbers of people in the Northeast reaching retirement (the "graying" of America), the deluge of population into the Downeast area may just be starting. Even the celebrated television show "Wheel of Fortune," was offering lake frontage near Ellsworth, Maine as one of its prizes during the summer of 1988. Good Heavens, I thought: It wouldn't be long before we had Vanna White, the show's hostess and letter-turner vacationing on one of the nearby ponds. Where was it going to end? So at the intersection of Routes 1 and 3, with the Maine Coast Mall and McDonald's to my right, I made a turn at the crossroads and headed Downeast.

---

*L.L. Bean opened an outlet store on High Stree in Ellsworth in 1990. Some locals felt that the Bean people left the good quality merchandise in Freeport and sent the rejects Downeast

# CHAPTER 2

# NUTBURGERS AND VEGETARIAN CHILI: LAMOINE GENERAL STORE

The advertisement in *The Ellsworth American* read: "Enjoy the quiet beauty of Lamoine Point. Visit us for breakfast, lunch, or light supper." In the ad's center was an abstract drawing of an awning, beach, clouds, park bench, and sunshine. It gave me the idea that the Lamoine General Store and Cafe was not your typical Downeast country store. I wondered if it was part of the "new" Maine. Not the Maine of hearty baked bean suppers at five o'clock sharp; rather, the Maine of "light" suppers, featuring healthful vegetarian dishes.

The new Maine is what the state is becoming—the trendy, what some would call "yuppie" place of the 1980s. It is a Maine enriched by creative, well-educated out-of-staters. Some of these people might have been back-to-the-landers when they first got here, but that trend has long since peaked. They're beyond that stage now—they've made it, so-to-speak, but more important, they've made it on their own terms. Many have started small businesses, others "do" crafts, or build things out of wood or stone. I'm not sure the new Maine is really what the state is all about. I'm not sure I even like it. But something's happening along this coast, and for lack of a better term, I'll just call it new.

7

There had been a country store in Lamoine in the 1970s, but I was unsure why or when it had closed. Lamoine is off the main road, and I had only been here once or twice, many years before. I remembered it as a quiet little village. Lamoine is only seven miles from Ellsworth, at the end of Route 184 on Frenchman's Bay. The schooner trade once linked villages like Lamoine, but when transportation was reoriented from sea to land during the twentieth century, many country stores on the ends of peninsulas lost their locational advantages and closed.

My wife, Linda, and I found the Lamoine General Store—that, frankly, looked like an old-time country store. Such a bucolic setting! To our right was Lamoine State Park, its fields and woods gently sloping down to the bay, while across the road, stood the old gable-front store building, with its wrap around porch. The day's newspapers were stacked on the verandah, while inside, the crisp morning air resonated with the soft sounds of classical music. We spoke to Becky MacQuinn, an attractive red-haired woman of perhaps "thirty-something," who was born and raised in Bar Harbor. "This is our first summer," Becky said. "The owner's name is Eric Hartman. Eric is originally from Ohio. His family moved to Orono when he was in high school, and he's been back and forth between Maine and Massachusetts and other places, and came back here in 1980. We live next door in a little farmhouse. These are neighbors from up the road."

Two young couples were eating breakfast at a table near the back of the store. Becky stood behind the counter which was also in the rear of the building. The day's menu was written on a chalkboard. Becky said, "We try to serve wholesome food. We don't sell beer or cigarettes. We are interested in giving people quality Maine products that are made locally. And we provide things for the campers and the campground like groceries, ice, and ice cream cones (Hancock County Ice Cream) and penny candy for the kids. And I think we're open to everybody."

A small boy pulled up in front of the store on what was obviously his new bicycle. Everyone inside promptly went to the front porch to express their approval. And I got the impression that considerable rapport existed between the store owners, clientele, and local children. The store's gentle ambiance sort of took me back in time.

"We pack picnics to go, and provide newspapers and Sunday papers," Becky added. "We're just trying to start slowly and find out what people want." I took note of just a sample of Maine-made products the store sold. There were many more.

—Illustrated Maine Maps
—T-shirts with maps of the Maine coast from Penobscot Bay to Frenchman Bay
—Mothbags and Orange Spice Potpourri from Ram Island Farm in Cape Elizabeth
—Indian Baskets by Micmac Indians
—Wild Blueberry Griddle Cake and Muffin Mix from Morgan's Mills, East Union
—Ployes de Boqouite (authentic French Canadian Buckwheat Pancake Mix) from Bouchard Family Farm, Route 1, Fort Kent

I had no idea there were so many small cottage industries in Maine. The number and variety seemed to reinforce what I had concluded about the new Maine—there were a lot of people out there finding creative ways to survive. But did these people really earn a living making mustard or blueberry jam? Surely they had other jobs; or, maybe they were what a friend Downeast had described as "trust fund babies." Maine's full of them," he said. "They really don't have to work." Indeed, I wondered if they worked at being poor. I wondered if they wore old clothes and drove old cars and trucks so as to look like everyone else.

Becky brought our breakfast order, and Linda and I sat at a table on the side porch. The porch was made of white cedar from the property, Becky explained. They had the logs milled and built the porch themselves. I thought of the time, creativity and energy that had gone into this little store. In an era of increasing homogenization, when one convenience store looks just like another, here was something built by hand out of real wood. If only the Mini-Marts and Seven Elevens could be built of cedar and left to weather a silver gray!

Eric Hartman, the owner, joined us on the porch. I would guess that Eric was also in his thirties. He was thin, athletic, with a brown beard and wavy brown hair. He seemed laid back, friendly, and knowledgeable about the community. I asked him why he had reopened the old store.

"It was adjacent to my house and we bought it, not necessarily to open up a country store, but mainly to protect the rest of our property. But then we decided it was a great opportunity— knowing it was a really nice old building and was in pretty good shape. So, to open the store we converted the rest of the building into some apartments so we could get some income coming in. We opened Memorial Day weekend. And as of right now we're planning to close in October. It's just as you can see, I'm on a dead end down here. This is pretty much of a bedroom community. There's not a lot of local industry. Almost everybody here goes to Ellsworth, Bar Harbor, Bangor, or Orono to work. We have university professors that commute to Orono or College of the Atlantic. We're not on the way to anywhere and they all go to Ellsworth to do most of their shopping. They don't spend their days here."

"Is there any indigenous industry such as clamming or worming in Lamoine?"

"Clamming is really on the wane. The flats are not very productive. It's really been dug out. There's actually quite a bit more boat traffic coming in to the state park now than when I first moved here. There's probably twelve to fifteen boats moored down there. Most are pleasure boats, but there's a few lobster boats. And we've got some wormers. At least the worms are still there. That seems to be fairly good. There's a couple of places that do crabs—pick crabs—but not much besides that."

Eric paused and then added, "There's sixty-five sites in the state park. There are no showers in the park yet, but apparently they're on line for next year. When that happens they think the park will probably be close to full in the summertime. So we get a lot of park business. And we get a lot of cottages and camps, especially right down on the point here."

It was a familiar story along the coast of Maine. Traditional marine industries—lobster fishing, clamming, worming—were imperiled and local people were struggling and trying to hang onto their land. Meanwhile, tourism and service industries were growing as people from out-of-state bought land and houses for seasonal use or retirement. And out of all the towns I would visit, the process was most advanced in Lamoine. It had become a suburb of Ellsworth. I wondered how the town was dealing with the recent growth.

"We put a moratorium on subdivisions for nine months," Eric said. "This gave the planning board time to make some new ordinances. You have to have specific reasons to stop growth. There will have to be some building, of course, but I'm pretty much a no-growth person."

"How do most people in Lamoine feel about growth?"

"There was quite a bit of controversy at the town meeting. People who have lived here most of their lives have this attitude that people ought to be able to do what they want to with their own land. And I understand that feeling. And to a certain extent agree with it, but hold a view that the world is just too small—you know, we all make too much of an impact. We all need to learn lessons from Cape Cod and Southern Maine.

"I think there's people in Lamoine that want growth. The other industry in Lamoine is gravel extraction. Oh, the trucks are just pounding out of here and it's not getting any better. And the town, apparently—legally—there's not a whole lot we can do to stop them. It's their land, and until the state steps in—which the state is—some people in Lamoine are actually in court with the town and the state. There's a big pit a mile from here where they're taking a whole hillside. You don't see it from the road, so people aren't very aware of it."

Actually, I had noticed several gravel pits on my way into Lamoine. And for years, I've witnessed the gradual scarification of land along Route 1 between Ellsworth and Hancock. It may be Downeast Maine with its views of Cadillac Mountain in one direction and Schoodic Mountain in the other, but it's as ugly as a West Virginia strip mine. Several large pits lie adjacent to the Hancock Heights Mobile Home Park. Trailers and gravel pits side by side: It's tempting to classify this dehumanizing landscape as "native;" while the tranquil image of seaside dwellings in Lamoine village might be associated with "transplants" or "summer residents." I'm generalizing, of course, but the sad fact is that in eastern Maine it is often the people who have lived here the longest, and in many cases, have worked the hardest—in industries like clamming, fishing, logging, and worming that are seasonal and endangered—who occupy the trailers.

The Maine coast was glaciated during the Ice Ages, and the glacial debris, which is left in large mounds of gravel known as moraine, is a valuable resource that is easily mined. The people who mine it are locals, and in an area where traditional marine industries are not faring well, it is easy to understand the side of the gravel industry.

I came up against the same argument when I discovered the destruction of my favorite trout stream in Gouldsboro several years ago. There, loggers had used the stream as a skidder track and left empty oil cans and heaps of brush along the path. And worse, they cut the stands of hardwood trees from around the pools. The previous year I had caught several nice brook trout, but when the loggers had finished, I caught nothing. The trees that once shaded the pools had allowed insects to drop from their branches to the fish below. But the trees were gone now; the stream silted up; the fish disappeared. It is privately owned land, but still, the stream's destruction weighed heavily on my conscience. It had been a special place to me since I was a child, and now suddenly it had been ruined. So I wrote a letter to a journalist, and made plans to take action.

But then I thought of the friendly logger I had met along the stream that June morning. The man was doing an honest day's work; he was trying to earn a living. I tried to convince myself that trees are renewable, that they would eventually grow back. I tried to think of the logger, not as a reckless destroyer of wilderness, but as a human being with a family to support. The exercise of letter writing had diffused much of my anger. I mellowed with the passing days. The letter eventually wound up in the woodstove; but more than ten years later, the fishing still isn't any good.

"When I first moved here, it was pretty much people living in the woods and back-to-the-land type people and then your regular Maine people," Eric continued. "But now it has become much more of a bedroom community. The property values have gone up so much."

"Can you still buy a house in Lamoine for under a hundred thousand dollars?"

"Yep, one right up near the end of the park just sold for eighty-seven thousand. The homes down this end are getting prohibitive for the average Maine person, though. And we still have people coming here and putting in trailers. But it seems to be slowing down on the trailer end of things and the more suburban or family-oriented professional types are moving into town."

"Are local people being priced out of the market?"

"Certainly no local people are going to be buying any shorefront property they don't have now. It's a double-edged sword, I guess, in that it's good for local people to have some people with money come in. They spend money here (in the store), and they spend money on other things. But, of course, the other thing is—who wants the town to become just a haven for rich people? Then the town really loses its character."

Lamoine was no longer the sleepy little village I once knew. It had been discovered, got caught up in the exurban migration that is changing the character of the Maine coast. And this country store—such a business would probably not have found a large enough clientele a decade ago—was evidence of that change. As Becky said, they tried to serve wholesome food; not the high fat, high cholesterol, high salt fare found at most country stores. Linda asked Becky about the special foods they prepared at the store.

"Well, we have blueberry muffins every day," Becky began. "Fresh blueberry pancakes are very popular. And, of course, we make it all from scratch. And let's see, we have the standard light breakfast—eggs and French toast. And the lunch things we do—we do nachos. And we use a corn chip that is made from organic corn and no salt. So it's a little different chip to start with. And then we grate up the cheese and we make the salsa. So that makes it kind of nice—a specialty. And we make hummus on a regular basis."

"What is that?"

"Hummus—which is a dip made from chickpeas and tahini, which is a sesame seed paste, and garlic and lemon juice. It's kind of a health food thing. We serve it as a dip with pita bread. Or we can do a sandwich—a vegetable sandwich with hummus or a pita pocket. We do tortellini salad, which we don't have all the time, only if the weather's going to be warm. (I wondered how one "did" a salad. The "do," rather than "make" or "prepare" a salad, I accepted as part of the speech of the "new" Maine.) Today we have chilled cucumber soup with herbs, crabmeat salad with fresh crabmeat, and crabmeat rolls. We have quiche normally, and we have vegetable lasagna.

"We normally have a vegetable quiche," Becky continued. "Sometimes it's chicken and broccoli, but usually it's mushroom. And then we have a good grade of turkey breast that we make turkey salad out of and sliced turkey sandwiches. We use a sliced alpine Swiss cheese that's good. We have grilled cheese and hot dogs, submarines—sub-sandwiches—that are a little different in that, there again, they're kind of home-grown. Oh, we also make a vegetarian chili."

"What do you put in that?" Linda asked. "I've never heard of vegetarian chili."

"It has no meat in it. It has mustard seeds, a teaspoon of cocoa, and, of course, it has tomatoes and basil."

"I've heard of putting in coffee," Linda said.

"Well, this calls for cocoa. It's really good."

"Out west, it's not real chili unless you have day old coffee in it—a Texas chili," Linda explained. (Linda knows her chili—she's from Arkansas. But I had never heard any of this before and was wishing we had come for lunch or supper, instead of breakfast!)

"But it has meat and everything in it," Becky said.

"Oh yes, it's rot-gut chili," Linda laughed. "You'd die if you ate it!"

"This is spicy, but not too spicy," Becky continued. "Our bent is toward meatless dishes. I make that twelve bean soup which we sell. It's very good. You can vary that depending on what you have on hand. I add to it a can of tomatoes and celery and onions. And it keeps forever."

They also make desserts which emphasize the locally grown fruits—blueberry cake and strawberry pie, for example. Becky said, "One thing we're going to do this weekend, again, is nutburgers. We love them. They're made out of cashews, walnuts, cheddar cheese, and a couple of eggs, cooked brown rice, and onions, minced up. And then you put chili powder or hot sauce in it—but not real hot. And we just grill them."

I wrote the first draft of this chapter in South Carolina. It was early November and still warm—low eighties—the leaves had not yet fallen. When I got around to revising it in late May, Linda and

I were back in our camp in West Gouldsboro, Maine. I worked in the loft by the soft light of a kerosene lamp, while outside, the May dusk resonated with the shrill sounds of frogs—peepers—a sure sign that spring had finally come to eastern Maine.

I had first heard the peepers while running in South Carolina on a warm evening in late January. I stopped twice, just to listen, to make sure they were frogs I was hearing, before continuing past the tin-roofed shotgun houses and their patches of turnip greens, past the barren fields with their rotting tobacco barns in the distance, across the highway by the Piggly Wiggly supermarket and into the town of Marion. The peepers—which always seem too early in South Carolina—had made me dream ahead to May, when we would leave our Southern community of live oaks and Spanish moss for our humble camp in Maine.

And in the loft that spring night, I thought: new Maine, old Maine, what does it matter? Those peepers have peeped every spring night I've ever been in Maine. Who is to say they won't just go on peeping forever? And with that thought, it was time to leave the new Maine and go seek the old. My next stop was Card's Tideway Convenience Store, a place where the clam and worm digger was still king.

# C H A P T E R 3

## DIGGER'S PARADISE: CARD'S TIDE-WAY MARKET, FRANKLIN ROADS

C ard's Tide-Way Market stands at the intersection of Routes 1 and 182 at Franklin Roads, just four miles east of Ellsworth. The gray, shingled two-story building, with its large Irving Oil Company gasoline island out front, seems to dominate the landscape from either direction. And there is always traffic here. Indeed, Franklin Roads may be the busiest intersection, and Card's the busiest country store, between Ellsworth and the Canadian border.

I first took notice of Card's back in 1985 when I heard it advertised on a local radio station.

> Card's Tide-Way Market in Hancock just put in a new canopy to eat your lobster under. Yep, now you can enjoy lobster at Card's Tide-Way. This week only, you can have lobster, steamers, corn on the cob, potato salad, and an ice cream cone for just $5.95, and you get free popcorn while you're waiting. Beer, wine, gas, fishing supplies, and Royal Chews—Maine's number one dried or smoked fish. Thurston believes in being friendly too. That's why he just built you the best two-seater in all of Maine.

You won't find any signs saying FOR EMPLOYEES ONLY
at Card's Tide-Way Market and Take-Out, open every day
at 5:00 a.m.
By the way, you might want to ask Thurston about that Caddy
or motorcycle he's got out back. Heard they're for sale, too!

"We haven't been doing too much advertising lately," Thurston
said. Thurston Card was an engaging fellow with a twinkle in his
eyes, a bushy gray mustache and long gray side whiskers that stuck
out from under his baseball cap. "We're so busy. This summer I
have three grandchildren coming up from Pennsylvania to work.
It's kind of a family business. Even though I'm not married, my
two sons come up and help work. This is my sixth year. I was born
and brought up here. I spent twenty-two years in the military.
Then I spent ten years working in Boston."

"I get the impression this is pretty much of a clam and worm
diggers' store," I said.

"Oh yeah, boy, when we do two tides a day it's really busy
around here. And I cater my hours to the diggers. If they go out
at four o'clock, we're open at four o'clock."

"How are the clammers doing this spring?"

"They're getting off to a slow start. Of course, the weather—the
whole month of April has been just like this. We've had one good
weekend." It was the end of May. We had had fog, drizzle, or rain
nearly the entire month.

"Yeah, that doesn't help at all," Thurston continued. "And the
clams are getting hard to come by. You're lucky if you can dig a
bushel a day. You used to get three or four bushels a tide. All the
lobster pounds are opening up on the Trenton Road and they're
dying for some clams. There's people that call me up two or three
times a day, because they know we deal with the diggers. I've got
a lady—she's opening up her shop this morning and she has no
clams. I've got a couple of diggers going down this morning to sell
them to her. That should improve as the summer goes on. The
tides get longer, and guys can get out in their boats and get some
decent clams."

Spring comes late to eastern Maine. The trees are just beginning to leaf out in mid-May, then the black flies arrive, and finally,
the tourists. The Fourth of July has traditionally been the begin-

ning of the summer tourist season as June tends to be a cool, rainy month.

I asked Thurston what he liked about running a country store.

"The people. We have loyal customers—three or four of them over here every morning waiting for me. They'll throw the newspapers on the steps and the guys will help me bring them in every morning. It's a nice, working relationship. And they're here every day. Never miss a day."

"Does it slow down much in the winter?"

"I still have my regulars. People work every day."

"Do you think you'll be here five years from now?"

"I have no reason not to be. I can't think of any other place I would rather be."

"So you've got a coffee shop here now?"

"Yup, a little place for them to sit down. And I'm keeping that small. And Bobby does a good business with his lobsters in the summertime."

"That's your son?"

"Yes, he's been doing that business four years now."

"Is it still $5.95 for a lobster dinner?"

"He went up to $6.95 last year and he'll probably have to go up a little this year. Lobsters are so unpredictable."

A worm digger came in to look at hats while we were talking. Thurston had hundreds of baseball caps hanging from the ceiling.

"It's time to buy a new hat, ain't it?" the digger said, holding up his old one with holes all through it.

"Quite a selection there," I said.

"Got some," he said. "This one's got bird-shot through it." He showed me the holes in his old cap.

"Were you in it when it got shot?" I joked.

"I don't think so."

"Good thing," I laughed.

"I don't think there's a store around that sells as many hats and gloves as we do," Thurston said. "I probably keep a stock of about five thousand gloves."

"Do you sell the clam boots too?"

"We order the boots for people—the hip boots—the diggers' boots. But the gloves I buy by the case—two or three cases at a time, twelve dozen to the case. Sometimes they use one pair of gloves to a tide, pulling clams."

"Yeah, I saw a guy doing that down in Steuben," I said. "He was right out in the middle of the channel, down to his elbows, pulling them. But, I guess that's where they get the big ones?"

"Sometimes that's where they get the only ones! Of course, they're worming too. It's a real good business. I've been told that out of that little bay right there (Thurston pointed towards the bay across the road), they take about three to four thousand dollars a day!"

"In clams?"

"Clams, worms, crabs. It's quite a resource, isn't it?" Thurston said. "Just one little bay. The coast is full of them."

"Yeah, there's 3,500 miles of bays along this coast," I added.

"But there's very few that has the mudflats that Hancock and Trenton have," Thurston continued. "Stonington has a few flats, Wiscasset—."

Back in 1968, when I was a junior in high school, I bought a commercial digger's license from the state, borrowed a hoe from a neighbor, and went worming. Once. I had heard all those stories about the big money that could be made digging. People told me I would like it; that as an athlete I'd be good at worming and worming would be good for me. "It helps your arms and your legs and your back," a friend told me. He didn't say that it would make you bowlegged like him and his brothers, or that it would ruin your back like it had done to other diggers I have known. But those were the words of youth. He was only sixteen, a good age to be a wormer.

I remember getting up at four in the morning, arriving on an Addison mudflat before five, and digging some 381 worms during that tide. We then went to the basement of the worm buyer's house to count the worms. I hadn't minded pulling the blood-worms out of the mudflats one at a time, but when the worm buyer expected me to reach barehanded into my pail of wiggling worms and count them, I got queasy. A few days later, I was offered a summer job doing maintenance at a campground. I took it! Had I stayed with worming, however, I might have earned more money over the years than I have as a college professor. Good wormers can make a few hundred dollars a day, but the supply of worms, the market, and their backs are often unreliable.

Once viewed as one of the lowliest jobs, digging—either for clams or worms—became respectable in the 1970s and 1980s. Feature articles appeared in magazines and newspapers depicting clamming or worming as "wholesome," "respectable," appropriate for the back-to-the-lander, or the native Downeaster. Indeed, some diggers' cars were adorned with bumper stickers that read: MAINE CLAMMERS DO IT IN THE MUD, while T-shirts appeared in local country stores bearing the inscription: AMALGAMATED MUDPOUNDERS OF MAINE. And as the prices for clams and worms have steadily risen, diggers have become consumers.

"Most clammers live in trailers." This was what one former digger told me who is now in the mobile home parts and service business. Diggers also seem to like things new and NOW! After all, they get paid every day. Theirs is a lifestyle of immediate gratification, so the mobile home, with its appliances built-in, appeals to diggers. And diggers are free spirits. They get paid for what they dig. They don't punch time clocks; they simply go out when the tide is low, be it five in the morning or six in the evening. So if the clams or worms are plentiful, and the price is high, it is easy to understand how one would be tempted to become a digger.

But it hasn't always been good for diggers. There have been periods when few people dug clams or worms—times when the flats just weren't productive. And the way the flats are currently being dug up, those days may soon return.

When I was growing up in Steuben in the 1960s, the clams were available, if not exactly plentiful, but there were few diggers. The price was only about ten dollars a bushel then, and there were many other productive flats further south and nearer to large markets. Steuben Bay had one steady clammer in those days, and he went out each day in a handmade ten foot cedar skiff. He was an elderly man, and he'd row his skiff out the channel with the outgoing tide, dig two or three bushels of clams, then row back with the incoming tide.

I used to jog past the old clammer's house on summer evenings. A nineteenth century gable-ended Maine house, clapboarded and painted white; it had an unpretentious, yet distinctive Victorian façade. The image was always the same: at dusk a tame brown rabbit sat on the front lawn, while inside, a light was burning, the television was on, and there was the back of the old clammer's bald head visible in the parlor window. A faded globe of the world rested on a pedestal next to the clammer's easy chair. And when I contrast this image—twenty-five years old—with the mobile homes that many present-day clammers live in, I can't help but think that clamming had less of a boomtown mentality back then. The old clammer, with his handmade cedar skiff had lent a certain orderliness to the wharf. Such a contrast from today's clammers who use powerboats, and even all-terrain vehicles to get about on the mud.

Billy, a Steuben boy, taught me how to dig clams. We walked out on the mudflat in rubber boots and Billy said, "Look for holes." Billy pointed out the tiny holes in the mud through which the clams breathed. You simply stuck the tongs of the short-handled clam hoe into the mud around the breathing holes and pulled up the clams. You had to be careful not to break the clams with your hoe. Whereas in the channel, and farther out on the flats where the mud was softer, you could reach down into the mud and pull the clams up with your hands. I was always getting cuts in my fingers from the razor sharp edges of the clams. These days clammers use rubber gloves for "pulling."

Worm digging is simpler still. With a similar short-handled hoe, but with blades perhaps three quarters of an inch in width, you simply turn over the mud. Diggers leave long trails or strips. The worms are usually only four or five inches down, so the diggers just go right along. I stood on the shore and watched a wormer in Jones Cove in Gouldsboro one day. He never saw me. He wore a Sony Walkman radio and seemed totally engrossed in his labor. And what labor it is! You can always tell diggers by the way they walk. It's a gait actually: even on solid ground diggers walk as though they're still pulling mud. Many are bowlegged; some are hunched over; most diggers seem to have bad backs, among other ailments.

I've seen diggers come off the flats, reach into the beer cooler, pull out bottles of "Bud" and exclaim "pain killer!" I've known diggers to strap six-packs of beer to their belts, tear off a can, toss it out on the mud, dig a strip to it, drain it, and start another strip.

I asked Thurston if he thought the clammers and wormers who patronized his store ever thought about the future—the time when they would no longer be physically able to dig.

"No, I don't think they do."

"I've seen some of them pretty close to your age and they look like they've had it."

"You would too if you were bent over like this (Thurston imitated a digger) all year. My son has tried it a couple of times, but he's back working here."

"Do you extend credit to the diggers?"

"Yeah, I have to. It's difficult to carry them, but it's tougher not to. It's tougher to turn them down when they come in here all the time. They're my bread and butter. And when I think of the dozens and dozens of diggers that come in here, I can't think of any one of them that has screwed me out of a dollar. Not one of them. Every bad check that's bounced has been within a five mile radius. And there's never been a digger."

"I guess if you're good to them they'll be good to you."

"Yeah, so they're entitled to some consideration."

Thurston's oldest son, Bob Card, who was twenty-eight, joined us, and added, "Plus a lot of your diggers travel a long ways to come around this area. We had a couple of diggers that stayed in our motel the other night from Augusta. They come down because—at certain times—they can get in three tides." (The days are long during Maine's summer, and if low tide is, say, between five and seven in the morning, they can get in a second tide that evening, and one more the following morning before heading home. Every two weeks, the earth, moon, and sun are aligned, which results in additional gravitational attraction or "spring tides," where high tide is higher, and low tide lower, exposing more mudflat.)

"They can make themselves up to two hundred and fifty dollars, and they pay fifty dollars for the room," Bob explained.

"Twenty-five dollars; we give them a break," Thurston said.

"And another twenty-five for beer while they're here?" I joked.

"Yup. There's a couple of guys who come up from around that nuke plant (Maine Yankee in Wiscasset)," Bob said. "That's quite a ways—about a three hour drive. It's like a carload, and they pitch in for gas—four or five in a station wagon. Last summer they were here every other day."

"How do the local diggers feel about them coming in?"

"Sometimes there's a little friction there," Thurston explained. "And the friction isn't because of the diggers. It's because they may be paying a cent or two more a worm in Wiscasset than they are here in Hancock."

"They're taking those worms all the way back there?"

"Yeah, they'll come down here and dig 'em and shoot 'em right back and get two cents a worm more for them. You're talking a lot of money if you dig a thousand worms a tide."

"Sure, I guess they get about ten cents a worm," I said.

"That's a bit of difficulty there," Thurston continued. "There's a guy that comes down here from Wiscasset—a nice guy—and we figured out one time what he spent for coffee in the store during the three months he dug. He'd get one cup of coffee before he dug, and when he came back, he'd get two more cups—somewhere like 520 dollars! I like those guys."

"What about Italian sandwiches? Do you sell them?"

"Oh, we sell them," Thurston laughed. "We figured up one day that in one year we go through about eleven thousand!"

"I guess the diggers thrive on them," I said. "That's their staple."

"And they're not called Italians anywhere else," Bob added.

Indeed, Italian sandwiches—pronounced "eye-talians" by Downeasters—are as much a part of the Maine landscape as Cape Cod houses and lawn ornaments. In the July 7, 1989 issue of *Maine Times*, David D. Platt suggests that Italian sandwiches are: "The real thing."

> SOMEWHERE OUT THERE a substantial, middle-aged woman in a print dress is making up Italian sandwiches—batches and batches of them, filled with salami and tomatoes sliced in a certain way, with lettuce and onions and pepper and peppers, wrapped in what passes for waxed paper these days, encircled with rubber bands.
>
> The wood countertops in her spotless kitchen are piled high with boxes of fresh buns from some Downeast bakery. Her husband delivers the sandwiches to mom 'n pop stores in an old car. The customers who buy them may or may not want them "oiled" at the moment of purchase. I know my mental picture's not wholly accurate, but that's how I envision the creation of the "Italians" that sustain me when I'm on the road.

Italian sandwiches have been part of my Maine existence ever since I can remember. They always taste better
when they've been pulled from a cooler in the back of a
store in Jonesport, Dexter, Greenville, Jackman, Rangeley
than they do when bought at an Irving Big Stop or ordered and eaten at a restaurant table. It must be the
waxed paper. The important thing about them, however,
is that they're a part of the scene that hasn't changed in a
long, long time.

A friend from out-of-state once told me: "I was driving down
from Bangor and I saw this sign—FRESH ITALIANS! What kind
of a place is this?" The befuddled woman had no idea the sign
meant sandwiches. I once asked a digger why the sandwiches were
so popular and he said: "You drive an Italian, and you've got the
energy to go!" What he meant was that the foot-long sandwich is
a balanced meal—just what a digger needs to dig a tide's worth of
clams or worms.

Downeasters also like to eat dried or strip fish. I've known locals
to keep dried fish on the dashboards of their cars and pickup
trucks. It does stink, but it sure is tasty. And as some folks have said:
"If there's a maggot or two in it, that's even better!" I asked
Thurston if he sold strip fish.

"Yeah, they should be coming out soon. And the other that we
sell a lot of—that should also be coming out soon—are the wrinkles.
Have you seen them yet this year?"

"No. I usually see them on store counters. Who buys those
anyway?"

"People like yourself. They're pickled and they go good with
beer. I've had people come in and order a gallon. They were
afraid they couldn't get them anywhere else."

"Or they buy ten of the little containers and they walk out of
here with wrinkles spilling all over their shirt," Bob added. "It's a
riot. And they're awful tasting. It's like a snail. They get 'em on the
lobster pots. You pull up a trap and you might get a whole bucketful."

I asked Bob if people in Hancock had accepted him when he
first came from Boston.

"Well, here I was, a store owner's son, coming down to make
money off the local area," Bob said. "At first, they'd come in at
night after the tide and dump a bucket of clams and half of them

would be rocks. I'd give them the money. I'd just trust them and they'd snicker and walk away. You had to win their confidence. The more you get to know a certain culture the less the distinctions stand out. Like I just spent a winter in Boston. They don't seem too much different there. People all have the same hearts and souls and go through the same trials. That commonality comes through."

Bob mentioned that his father seemed to have a good eye for business. "In running this store, we hash out possible decisions on what to do and what not to do. A lot of times I disagree, but we end up doing what he wants and that's the right thing to do. He really has a good business sense."

The store had a large inventory. Stuff—junk, mostly—was hanging everywhere. It sort of beckoned you to buy something.

"Yeah, all these little trinkets and things under the counter," Bob said. "Silly little things that sell like crazy! And those little roach clips with the feathers on them—they were the rage for a while."

"What are they?"

"You know what a roach clip is? It's what they used to use on the end of a joint (marijuana cigarette). It's just a little clip and it has a feather on it. You clip it on your car visor."

"Who buys those?"

"Clammers' wives."

"So that's kind of a local status symbol?"

"They were for a while, but I haven't been selling so many lately. All those vendors that sell those strange things to us. . . they're interesting. People show up in trucks and they open them up and they have all this crazy stuff. My father dickers with them. If you ever want to see the color, just sit at that table for a day. (Bob pointed towards the coffee shop.) It's unbelievable the people that pour in here."*

---

* A couple of years later, Thurston sold the Tide-Way Market. The building was destroyed by a fire during the fall of 1990 and was replaced with a modern-style convenience store. I stopped during the summer of 1991 and bought an Italian sandwich. It was a pretty good sandwich as far as Italians go, but not the "Real Thing" described by David Platt in his *Maine Times* essay. The new store was big and clean, and had an area for customers to sit and eat and socialize, but the hats and boots and clamming gloves, if there were any, weren't hanging from the ceiling anymore. The store had lost its charm.

# C H A P T E R  4

## LIKE SOMETHING GETTING RIPPED OUT: HANCOCK GROCERY

I wondered what it was like to live above a country store for ten years, to gradually win over the hearts and minds of your customers, only to walk out the door one day knowing you're never coming back. Barbara Vittum had run the Hancock Grocery, an immaculate little store that specialized in wines, cheeses, and gourmet foods on Route 1 in Hancock for ten years. The store was owned by Barbara's parents, but every time I stopped in, she was there. The Hancock Grocery was then—and still is—very much a people-oriented store. "The mood of the store is upbeat," Barbara had told me in 1985. "Down people don't come into the store. The clientele has really changed over from negative to positive people. Getting to know the people is the best part of the business. A lot of people come here just to talk with friends and neighbors." I had always looked forward to stopping at the Hancock Grocery, but when I came back in the spring of 1988, Barbara was gone.

Evelyn and Gil Page, the Hancock Grocery's current owners, told me that Barbara had wanted to try something different. "She has another business in Bucksport now," Gil said. "It's called the Vineyard, which is wine, gourmet foods, and cheeses."

We hadn't seen Barbara in two years, so on a rainy day in May, Linda and I drove to Bucksport and found the Vineyard in an old Victorian house along Main Street, near the paper mill. Barbara, and Martha Ohrenberger, who had worked with her at the Hancock Grocery for five years, were out back, unpacking boxes. Shasta, Martha's golden retriever, came out wagging her tail. The dog had always slept behind the counter at the grocery store. "You two are about the last people in the world I expected to see this day," Barbara said. She was just getting the business started. It had been quite a task, renovating the thirteen-room Victorian house, and getting the Vineyard off the ground. Martha, meanwhile, was just helping out. She was now a nurse in Bangor.

"I really felt sad about it," Barbara said, when I asked her how she felt about leaving the store. "It was tough. I suppose that's why I went back into business. I've got to have that contact." I would guess that Barbara and Martha were in their early thirties. Both had straight hair when I had last seen them, while now, both had short, curled perms—sort of like Shasta's pretty waves and curls, I thought.

"So your father decided to sell the store?"

"Well, it was my mother's and my store to begin with. And we got so busy that he had to quit his job and come down and work. And we just kept adding people as we went. He wanted to retire and take it a little easier, and I ended up getting a divorce. I didn't really want to run the store myself. It was too big. It grew too quick—like a golden retriever—all paws."

Barbara waited on a customer; Martha came in form the back room. Shasta padded in behind. I asked Martha if she had undergone a similar withdrawal.

"I was originally from Hancock so it was quite a treat for me to work at the store. I knew those people from my past. You know them in a different context. You learn more about their lives. It was an experience for me—a real growing experience. From there I learned that I wanted to work more in depth with people. I went into a new career—nursing. I went through a withdrawal in that I went back to work at the store every other weekend; so I kind of weaned myself away gradually. So that by the time the store sold—it was in January—and we took the final inventory—at that point when we were driving away it was like something was getting ripped out.

"I missed the daily contact. And you see people and they all say, 'Gee, it's so different not having you there.' After ten years of having Barbara there—it's like a solid rock. I can't imagine how traumatic it must have been for Barb—one day you're in your home upstairs—to just pack up and leave. It must have been hard."

"Do you ever go back to the store in Hancock?"

"Yeah, whenever we go through, we stop. It's a different atmosphere altogether. The whole place, when you go in, you look around and there are things you never have seen before. You want to go in and face the shelves. Should I do the meat case and rearrange? It's weird. It's like you're going home. It's like—I went back to Hingham, Massachusetts, where I'm originally from, and asked the owner of the house if I could just see—go in the backyard just to reminisce a little bit. It's a very strange feeling— an alienation that you feel. You see people that used to stop in every day. 'Well, how are you doing?' And then you walk out the door."

The feeling or sense of belonging to a particular place, that Martha had described, is what people are often looking for when they buy a country store. This yearning for small town security seems particularly strong among those store owners originally from out-of state. Evidently, that feeling of community was missing from their lives in the cities or suburbs they came from, and at some point they just decided to "chuck it all," and buy a country store. By the mid-1980s, approximately one-third of the country stores between Ellsworth and Machias were owned by people originating outside of Maine. More than once I heard proprietors whose stores were for sale say that if they could only find another "sucker from out-of-state" they could unload their faltering business. Indeed, a teacher who moved to Maine more than twenty years ago told me that out-of-staters bought country stores out of desperation. "They get so fed up with that rat race down there, that one day they just decide to quit and come up here," he said. "It's an emotional decision. They believe in the myth that you just sit around the old potbellied stove. They don't realize there's only a few cents mark-up on a gallon of milk."

Unfortunately, many would-be store owners never find what they're looking for, and this may explain, in part, why country stores are always changing hands. Barbara came back and I asked her why she didn't stay in Hancock and open up another store there.

"I didn't feel right about being down there after selling out. I sold them the store and they have to carry on. It would have been sort of weird to sell them the store and start another store right where I was. It would have been unfair, because I'd met so many people and had so many friends down there I just didn't think it was morally right."

"How do you like it here?"

"Good. I've met all kinds of nice people and I'm having a great time. I just drove through one day—this house was for sale and it looked intriguing. It had a yard sale going on so I came in and gave the old look around. That's how I happened to settle here. I think my challenge here is that this is unusual. What I'm doing is selling foods and wine and things that aren't commonly found around, or that people have never heard of before. So it's been fun to talk about food and wine and to be with people."

"You kind of got into that in the other store," I said.

"Yeah, that's the part I enjoyed the most. I'm going to have an all-Maine room here. I'm going to have all Maine products—probably thirty or so different companies that I'll be doing business with—wines, jams, jellies, flour mixes, green beans, carrots, herb vinegars, etc. There's a lot of stuff out there. I want to do that because I think it's great that people are doing stuff. People in Maine got guts, anyway. You've got to, to survive. It keeps you free. When you're not dependent on some major corporation's decisions, you could say, 'I've got to make a good vinegar if I want to still make it, or I've got to make sure my carrots are all perfect.' Whatever it is you're doing, you put more of yourself in it."

"But Maine sure is changing. How do you feel about all this growth the last couple of years?"

"Oh, sad. I don't mind growth, but when you cut down all the trees, that certainly isn't growing. And condominiums don't do anything for my blood pressure. And it's sad that the people who live here can't afford to live here anymore. You make eight or ten or twelve or fifteen thousand a year—you can't afford to own a piece of property because the property taxes go up. You live on the coast and some guy wants to put in a condominium or what have you. He can make his tax payments easily and all the property values are driven up by that. But it's a free country and anybody who can buy the land can have it, so you really can't—you asked me how I felt— that's the difference from what I feel. What I feel—I don't like it! Sad, you lose all that. And the other thing I noticed about people from away; they come here to escape, and whenever they get here, almost right after they get their houses built, almost the first thing they do, they want to change it like to where they came from . 'Well, where I came from we had this. We did this.' And you feel like saying, 'Well, what in the heck you doing here? You came here because you liked this.'"

When I first met Barbara, I marveled at her drive, her competence, her knowledge of the store business. But then I met her father and realized that common sense runs in the family. Ken Vittum bought the Hancock Grocery in 1977 after twenty-six years as a sales representative. He had definite ideas about how a store should be run. He did not extend credit to customers and felt that was one reason why small stores often failed. When Ken bought the Hancock Grocery, it had a lunch counter where locals used to loiter for hours over coffee. He found, however, that women rarely patronized the store. They apparently felt uncomfortable walking past the counter occupied by unkempt men. And although Ken was advised by some of his customers not to remove the counter (they said it helped his business), he decided to take it out anyway. The women started coming back, and the clientele changed over, as Barbara had said earlier, from "negative to positive people."

Evelyn and Gil Page, the current owners of the Hancock Grocery, seem to share Barbara's and her father's values. When I asked the Pages what they thought was the key to succeeding in the store business, Gil said: "I am thoroughly convinced that cleanliness is number one. I think personalities have a lot to do with it—and a fairly decent variety that you specialize in. You can take an old building such as this one, and keep it clean, and it's attractive."

The Pages had been in the grocery business all their working lives. They had owned and operated a supermarket. But they decided over the years that running a big supermarket wasn't for them.

"It's still a country store," Gil said of the Hancock Grocery. "This is what we wanted."

"And the customers come for the wines and cheeses and the gourmet foods which a lot of your little stores don't carry," Evelyn added. "It's just a very unique little store."

"The kids are grown up and we can work all the hours we want to work—and you can in a small store," Gil said.

One change the Pages have made has been to add video rental. Gil said that movie rentals have become part of the convenience store situation all over the country now.

The conversation changed to small town politics, and here Gil talked Yankee common sense. "You hear both sides of every story," he said. "From town politics to whatever is going on. It's difficult to choose or to take sides. You've got to be a clergyman, a public relations person. Of course, you have your own opinions, but don't often voice them."

I didn't see a Megabucks machine in the store and this rather surprised me, since the state lottery, like the movie rental, is another function of country stores that in recent years has become increasingly important. Gil said that he had gotten a lot of calls for Megabucks, but had mixed emotions about it. "It's something on a Saturday afternoon," he said. "It ties up your store terrible." I had heard this from other proprietors too. And as we talked about Megabucks, I also got the feeling that those proprietors who were perhaps a bit uncomfortable with gambling, were more likely to point to its inconvenience, rather than just say they opposed it. "There's a big jackpot and everyone's rushing in on a Saturday afternoon between three and five o'clock to get their Megabucks ticket and absolutely nothing else," Gil explained. "It ties up your whole operation."

Gil told me that for him and Evelyn, the country store was as much of an avocation as a job. "If we can get upstairs at seven o'clock at night and sit down and watch a little television, then we're happy," Gil said. Like Barbara, the Pages live above the store. "It has its pros and cons," Gil explained. "You can't get away. And I think Barbara felt that way too when she had the store. See, her mom and dad didn't live above the store. And eventually, we will move too."

It was common years ago for proprietors to live above their stores, but this practice has pretty much died out, especially among native Maine proprietors. As I traveled Downeast, I found, however, that store residency was experiencing a small resurgence, especially among younger owners from out-of-state. "It helps keep the overhead down," I was told, again and again. And with the area's skyrocketing housing prices, store residency was becoming more of a necessity than a choice.

# CHAPTER 5

## CALL ME WALT FROM ALASKA: SUNRISE GENERAL MERCHANDISE, SULLIVAN

I once knew it as Trader Don's, a rickety, false front building that specialized in discount boots and clothing. It was now the Sunrise General Merchandise, and judging from its patchwork exterior, the store building might have been a Downeast example of folk architecture; that is, building done by common folk—ordinary people like you and me—with no professional training in architecture. A new room was being added to one side to house the returnable bottles and cans—the Sunrise Redemption Center.

But it looked to be a slow process: board by board, nail by nail; the new construction reminded me of the area in Latin American cities that urban geographers call the zone of in-situ-accretion. This zone is still under construction, but here the building is often done by the residents themselves—little by little, brick by brick, as they get a few dollars ahead. At one time this area might have been a shantytown on the city's edge, but its inhabitants, recent arrivals from either inner city slums or perhaps the rural hinterland, have stayed on—persevered—and gradually they have become productive citizens of the city. Meanwhile, a new generation of shantytowns is already under construction on the city's edge. People building their own cities; people creating their own jobs: It's a long way from Sullivan, Maine to Latin America, but the landscape of human aspirations and ingenuity is easily recognizable.

The Sunrise General Merchandise is on Route 1, less than a mile east of the Sullivan Bridge. Not a bad location, I thought, since there is no longer a grocery store nearby in North Sullivan. Still, it is hard to get a new country store off the ground, especially the first few years.

"You've got a little of everything in here," I said to Richard West, the owner.

"Well, soon as we've got it made around the way we want it, there'll be more. We're trying to do it out of our pockets."

Richard was a middle-aged man, short, stocky, a couple day's growth of whiskers, graying cropped hair, and clad in a well-worn coat. He seemed like an independent character, but I also detected a compassionate streak. I thought: Here is a man who would give you the coat off his back.

"So you're building slowly?"

"Oh yeah. We tried to get help everywhere. Tried to get help from the bank to buy it. Couldn't get help from the bank. Same old story everywhere, I suppose: They don't believe in stores, hotels, restaurants—that stuff."

Richard said he only gave credit to a few people he knew and trusted. But then he said, "I give a lot of stuff away. I give away one hundred and fifty two-hundred pound bags of potatoes. I keep giving them away to people."

"Generosity, huh?"

"Little kids come in and I'll give them a lollipop. I'm going to go broke if I don't get out of here. A lot of good people out there."

I wondered if Richard's benevolence extended to out-of-staters. How did he feel about people moving here from away?

"The flatlanders come in and ruin a town. And then they move out. The first thing they do, they get one of them in the town office. They just totally destroy the town. And then they pack up and they move out. I've seen it so much and in so many towns around the state. It's pathetic. And you've got your old Maine people back in town—they're moving back, sure. But there's nothing to offer them. There's no jobs, there's no nothing."

Richard spoke from his own experience. He had lived out-of-state for twenty years. He was back home now, he said, because he had made his own job—the store. But like so many Downeasters of his generation, he had left Maine for greener economic pastures. He had started out as a woodcutter up near Tunk Lake when he got out of high school. "An old man took me on," Richard explained. "I broke my bucksaw one day in the woods and I had a power saw too. I said, 'This ain't for me.' I said, 'You can have the wood I cut, I'm going to Massachusetts.' He said, 'You're not serious?' I said, 'You give me ten dollars and I'll show you how serious I am.'"

"Did you go to work in a factory?"

"Yeah, I worked in just about every factory there is."

"Well, I guess if that was in the fifties, there wasn't a whole lot of work around here other than cutting wood."

"Well, mostly it was cutting wood. You made a dollar and it meant something. We used to could go down on the beach here, dig clams, roast 'em up and eat 'em—everything. At least there used to be plenty of clams."

"Now there are no clams," I said. "I guess if they can get a bushel they're doing well."

"Yep."

It was hard to make a living in the area when Richard was a young man. It was still hard; and he empathized with the younger generation. He said, " I try to give out a couple of scholarships to kids, trying to get them interested in some law thing." He hoped they would return to Sullivan after college and use their education to improve the community.

"They've grown up in the town and know what it's like," Richard said.

There was a thank-you note tacked to a post from a recent Sumner High School graduate who had received a scholarship from Richard. And while neither Richard nor his humble business seemed the sort to be endowing academic scholarships, the letter, addressed to Mr. Richard West, gave the proprietor and his store a newfound importance—made it seem like a bigger, more substantial enterprise—and forced me to see Mr. West in a way I hadn't seen him before.

And then my eye began to focus on a handwritten cardboard sign displayed on the wall behind the counter that read:

WARNING: 24 HOURS CAMERA MONITOR BY STATE PO-LICE. I said, "What about the camera? Is there any truth to that?"

"I'm not saying."

"Have you had any break-ins?"

"Oh Yeah, they smashed that window right there. I have to put a new window in here. I caught them going through there."

"You caught them?"

"My alarm went off. They got two out of four—that wasn't bad."

An article by Sandra Rappaport in the May 19, 1988 edition of *The Ellsworth American* told the story.

### STORE OWNERS FOIL BURGLARY ATTEMPT, TWO ARRESTED AT SULLIVAN

An unsuccessful burglary attempt at the Sunrise General Store in Sullivan last week ended in two arrests after store owner Richard West and his son Bob interrupted would-be thieves in the act of entering the building and Bob West pursued them to identify their getaway car.

The Wests, who live behind the store, heard suspicious sounds at about 2:00 a.m. on May 10 and came around a corner to find two men trying to break in. One of the intruders was already halfway through a window, according to Bob West. The men ran away into the woods and Richard West called the State Police, who contacted the Hancock County Sheriff's Department. While waiting for law enforcement officers to arrive, however, the Wests heard a car start up nearby and drive off down the road. Suspecting that the vehicle might have some relation to the incident at the store, Bob West pursued it in his Chevrolet Cavalier and was able to see the number on it.

The *American* article went on to explain that the driver of the suspected getaway car was eventually arrested and charged with operating a vehicle while under the influence of intoxicating liquor. Bob West identified the passenger as one of the men who had tried to enter the store. Dogs tracked the other would-be robbers, the article explained , but then lost the trail. Had they simply vanished into a nearby house? I asked Richard if the would-be robbers were local guys.

"Oh yeah."

"What do you suppose they were after?"

"Mostly cigarettes and beer. They have a long way to go to get by. They can't beat the alarm system—not the one I've got."

A cat without a tail wandered over. Richard said the cat was going across the railroad tracks and lost his tail. "He came to me that way. All dumb animals come to me. I've got dogs, cats, chickens."

I read another hand-lettered cardboard sign: STATE LAW— MUST BE 21 YEARS OF AGE AND HAVE A PICTURE I.D. TO PURCHASE BEER OR WINE. NO I.D. NO BEER OR WINE. PLEASE DON'T ASK TO CHARGE! THANK YOU THE ASSIS- TANT MANAGER AND MANAGER.

Richard's son, Robert (Bob), a quiet young man in his early or middle twenties, is the assistant manager. Robert was busy in the redemption center and was now sorting a candy order.

A big man—large frame, large hands—with thick, wavy brown hair, and wearing blue work clothes, the sort that mechanics often wear, came in. I assumed he was a regular customer. Richard said, "This guy here is from the land that is free—Alaska."

"What part?"

"I live in Anchorage. I work all over the state. I'm going back. I was raised here."

"And then you moved to Alaska?"

"Yeah."

"How do you like it there?"

"I love it. I want to tell you something—all the time I've been there everybody told me how expensive it was to live there. I didn't know what expensive was until I come back home. Every- thing costs more, including cars."

"Here?"

"Yeah. Milk costs you like three dollars a gallon. Two fifty to three dollars a gallon. Okay. A loaf of bread is the same price you pay there and potatoes are about twenty cents more a bag than you pay here. And that's it. Your lights are cheaper, your gas, cheaper—everything. Gasoline is twenty to twenty-five cents cheaper."

"Well, it should be with the pipeline."

"They don't buy that. It all goes to JAP-an. They sell it back to us. They take it over there and refine it and send it back. Same with the lumber."

"Well, how do you account for those stories then—that it's so expensive up there?"

"Well, you know—I lived in Barrow for three months. I was doing a job in Barrow. And, of course, you take way out in the middle of nothing, they have to ship stuff eight hundred or a thousand miles. That's expensive. But in Anchorage it's different. One hundred and fifty dollars a month—you can't do it here. (He was referring to the monthly rent on an apartment.) Then you get them with a Jacuzzi and a hot tub, heated parking, and all that, for about six (six hundred dollars a month)."

"Well, what do you like about it. The fishing?"

"Well, I like the fresh air for one thing. Which, you know, the air here is alright. I've got nothing against that, but that's about all that it's got going for it. I like hunting, fishing—the outdoors. I like being able to get in my plane and fly back in the bush and go pan gold—stuff you can't do here."

"You've got your own plane?"

"Yeah. A friend of mine and I, we bought one together. Here, you're so hemmed in by state rules and regulations. Like this man here (Richard). He opened this store and had to go to the state and get double licenses that's hanging on the wall. That's bullshit."

"You know, like in Alaska, you want a license, you go into the city hall and you fill it out and you hand it to them. And twenty-five dollars and there's your license."

"So they don't have the government regulations they have down here?"

"Well, they do, but it's not so as a man would want to commit suicide in the process of getting his paper work. You know what I mean?"

Richard said to me, "You ought to go up there and write a book."

The man from Alaska said, "Anybody who'll want to write a book about Alaska will have anything you'd want to write a book on. You know—any subject. They've got country stores. Up there, the stores are just like stores in the 1800s. Except they have electric lights and refrigeration. You go in and see the old miners, the old timers—they're sitting there chewing tobacco and spittin' in the can. You know what I mean? They're not all like that, but there are a lot that are. And you'll see things that'll just blow your mind."

"Like what?"

"Anything—like I lived downtown Anchorage. And, uh, we've had moose come out our lawn. You drive south of Anchorage a couple of miles and you'll see all kinds of ducks and geese. And you go another two or three miles and there are cliffs and there are Dall Sheep up there and mountain goats. You don't see that stuff here. My kids ask me all the time, 'Dad, when are we going to see a moose?' And I say, 'Christ, I don't know.' You know, you might see a moose one day when you're here. Chances are you won't.

"Now Anchorage is a big city. It's not like a big city, though. It's not like New York City. It's not like Boston or Portland."

"How do you mean?"

"If you need something, you just drive downtown and pick it up and leave and you're in the country. It's not all suburbs. I've had to stay here now about a year and a half, but my time is up now."

"So you're going back?"

"I go back in a month. I don't know, it's all what a person wants in life, I guess."

"Have you had any problems finding work in Alaska? There's a glut of oil right now."

"I don't have no problem."

"What sort of work do you do?"

"I turn wrenches." And then he added, "Alaska is all one state and I want to tell you something, just about the wildlife and how the actual living is today. We get in my plane. My wife won't fly because I ripped the landing gear off it once, but I'm still here. And if I wasn't, so what? I enjoyed doing what I was doing when it happened, you know. Well, like I was saying, we'd fly over and see a whole rookery of walrus and seals. And we flew over Mount McKinley, and there were herds of Caribou, something like ten thousand of them at a whack. At Delta Junction, we flew over and we saw buffalo. There is buffalo in Alaska. You ask somebody, 'Is there buffalo in Alaska?' 'No, there ain't no buffalo.' Well, they've got pretty good herds, you know."

"If you know where to look, I guess."

"Yeah. and it's things like that. You go in and see the old gold mines. You see the old guys workin'. And . . . I don't know . . . it just does something to you. If you like the outside—the outdoors at all—and if you like being free."

I had heard Downeasters speak of being free many times before. To them, being free might mean being able to go out in the woods—right out the back door—and shoot their gun; to be free, say, from the restrictions imposed by the dense populations of Massachusetts or perhaps New Jersey. Compared to most places in the eastern United States, Downeasters have a lot of freedom. That freedom is disappearing, however, and this is evident from the growing number of NO TRESPASSING signs. Not only are clam diggers finding fewer clams, they're finding it harder to get down to the shore—the lands they've crossed for generations are being posted.

"Hey, let me tell ya—In Alaska you can dig clams and make a living. You can't do that here."

"People here seem to make a living digging clams," I said.

"I'm not a clamdigger, okay, but I can dig six bushels within just a very few minutes. That's how plentiful the clams are in Alaska. Salmon fishing, trout fishing, Dolly Varden, geez—cod fishing—you can't do it here.

"I first went to Alaska in 1965 when I was just a kid. I went with a friend of mine for a visit and liked it. So I came home, and my uncle is the youngest one, like five years older than I am. so I brought home pictures and books— and Jesus—and a regular goddamned fruitcake. I brought home all kinds of stuff. Jesus, my uncle, Phil, and Neal, and Ernie—they moved right up there."

"What's your name?"

"My name is Walt."

"Walt what?"

"Just call me Walt from Alaska and that's it."

We got on the subject of women. I had heard that women are scarce in Alaska, but Walt said, "You can believe that all you want, but the truth is they don't have a shortage of women. They've got some of the most beautiful women in the world there."

"Well, see, everything I've heard about Alaska isn't true then."

"Take a trip and figure it out for yourself. I'm going to tell you something right now, (I was beginning to get the feeling that this man liked setting people straight.), when you go, you're not going to accomplish nothing in two or three weeks. Go like June one and you stay 'til September one."

"Would you say, then, that Alaska is like Maine was, maybe thirty years ago?"

"A hundred."

"In Alaska, you're free," Richard said.

"It's not like here," Walt added.

"When you first went to Alaska, were you considered a flatlander?"

"There's no such thing as a flatlander in Alaska. It's not like here."

I thought that perhaps Walt had returned to Maine to help Richard and Robert in the store, but he said he had only known them for a few months. "They're good to people." Walt said. "Kids come in, and of course Dickie has the candy out. And if he doesn't, then Robert does."

Richard then told me a fantastic story about a wild man who had terrorized Sullivan years ago. "His body was nothing but hair," Richard said. "There's a book up to Franklin—in the library. It's got pictures of the wild man chasing someone down the road with an axe! He came down from the mountains. He had hair all over him . . . just like an ape!" (Was Richard pulling my leg?)

"Now if somebody wrote a book like that—even that old book right there—it would sell," Richard added. "I'm telling you . . . you'd make a fortune. People are interested in what happened years ago. They don't know what was here before they come."

# C H A P T E R 6

## NO BEANS IN EGYPT, MAINE:
## THE TRADING POST, FRANKLIN

O ne rainy July day, Linda and I drove up Route 200 to Franklin. We went through dense woods strewn with large granite boulders, then slowed to a crawl as the road curved into East Franklin. On the left was Johnny's Brook Children Center: an old school house with yellow paint peeling off its clapboards, surrounded by a chain link fence. The Franklin Historical Society appeared next—open Thursday and Saturday from two to four. I made a note of the days and hours it was open, but never got back for a visit. Perhaps someone in the historical society could have verified Richard West's fantastic story about the "Wild Man" of Sullivan. Was he pulling my leg? Sometimes it's better to leave great mysteries unsolved; it gives you something to ponder on those damp foggy nights at the camp, with the woodstove burning, and the dog resting at your feet.

A sign on a tiny wooden building read: EAST FRANKLIN POST OFFICE. Another sign read: HOG BAY POTTERY. So this was Hog Bay. I knew it was up the Taunton River from the Sullivan Bridge, but the coastline meanders so much here—I never thought of Hog Bay coming into East Franklin. An inlet widened westward to the bay itself, while on the east side of the road was a red house with a barn out back, then a narrow road going uphill into the woods. Somewhere around here is a road that leads to the top of Schoodic Mountain. I last hiked the mountain on Memorial Day in 1969. The trek was memorable for two reasons: I went with a high school girlfriend who lived in Franklin; we battled clouds of blackflies to the tree-line. Never again—at least—not in late May. Back on the road to Franklin—an old Dodge Dart parked on the roadside; its bumper sticker reads: LIVE AND LET LIVE. Gravel pits, blueberry fields—we're going up a steep hill now with views of Hog Bay in the distance. A large white pine on the hilltop probably hasn't many years left. The top is dying; its highest limbs are without needles. I had watched the same process on a white pine in Gouldsboro. Over a period of many years—little by little, limb by limb, it had died from the top down, until finally, it had turned into a silvery-gray skeleton. The big white pines, Maine's tallest trees, which once were cut for ships' masts, have slowly vanished like real country stores.

I made some notes as we drove into Franklin.

Cape Cod house, car with Pennsylvania license plates, large blueberry field out back. Quaint little cottage with granite wall.

Coming into the outskirts of Franklin now.

Lawn ornaments—fawns, deer, ducks. House trailer with butterflies, more ducks, a well with a well cover. A little sign that reads: ALL EYES THAT SHINE ARE NOT DEER. Farmhouses, blueberry fields in back. Woodpiles. Large white pines shading the road. Tamarack trees—many of them.

Going downhill now.

House trailer in the woods. Maple trees. Large gable-front Maine farmhouse with a red door, bay window with China plates in the window, woodpile out back, road going up into blueberry barrens. White frame house with attached barn, shutters, lots of flowers, sign reads: 1866 (date built). House trailer on the left. Lobster traps for sale along side a skiff. A new yellow house with marigolds lining the driveway. Birch trees. A little white house; a little red house; house that is sold—sign reads: COLDWELL BANKERS. An old car. A piece of an engine.

Coming to the village center.

An old Cape Cod House with a front porch. Sign in front of a house reads: HOG BAY BOAT STORAGE. An old lady working in her garden. Another sign reads: THE CRABTREES. Woodpile, flower boxes, Joe-Pye weed, old elms and a house behind. At the intersection of Routes 200 and 182—a little memorial in the center of town. An old Cape Cod house with verandah, swans, a deer, bird bath—all lawn ornaments.

Going over the railroad tracks, east on Route 182.

Farmhouses with barns attached. A large lawn, then a white colonial house with gingerbread trim. Silver maples, some willow trees. We can see the Trading Post.

It is pretty here in Franklin, a town that really doesn't look much different now from the town I remember driving to in 1969. And the former girlfriend's house? It was raining when we drove by, but the large green lawn was still freshly mowed, while the red, nineteenth century gable-front farmhouse appeared as immaculately maintained and timeless as ever. I might have pulled in, tapped lightly on the door, and expected a red-haired seventeen-year-old girl to appear.

The sign out front of the Trading Post read: FOOD, SOFT DRINKS, COLD BEER, ICE CREAM, STEAMED HOT DOGS, REST AREA, GAS, OIL, GROCERIES, SANDWICHES. This is Franklin's only store and restaurant. It stands on Route 182, about half a mile east of Route 200 and the village center. A large development was under construction across from the Trading Post. The sign in front read: FRANKLIN INDEPENDENT SENIOR HOUSING—18 UNITS FOR THE ELDERLY.

We read the posters and notices on the front of the country store: BLUEBERRY RAKERS WANTED, MULCH FOR SALE, A BLAST FROM THE PAST—SUMNER HIGH SCHOOL REUNION, TAYLOR'S WORMS AND CRAWLERS, EASTSIDE LANDSCAPING. Altogether, we counted four signs advertising for blueberry rakers. It as getting near that season.

We entered the restaurant through an entrance from the country store. The single room, with grill, lunch counter, tables in the middle, and booths in a row next to the front window, was noisy; but not in an annoying or threatening way, rather, the noise one might have associated with a backwoods Maine family at the kitchen table. They were passing around home-made fudge and pictures of grandchildren, and it was obvious that everybody here knew just about everything there was to know about everybody else.

We sat at one of the tables and I took note of some of the signs on the walls: BREAD PUDDING $1.25; GOSSIP WELCOME HERE; AS SOON AS THE RUSH IS OVER, I'M GOING TO HAVE A NERVOUS BREAKDOWN, I OWE IT TO MYSELF, I WORKED FOR IT, AND NOBODY IS GOING TO DEPRIVE ME OF IT. The last two were wooden plaques, while on the same wall, a handwritten paper sign read: COFFEE PRICES—FIRST CUP 40 CENTS—WARM-UP FREE—THIRD CUP 40 CENTS.

A waitress was bringing out food on a platter. She carried gigantic meatball subs; a bacon, lettuce, and tomato sandwich with real thick slices of what looked like garden fresh tomatoes; homemade biscuits; and muffins. It all looked delicious. We placed our order and I continued to read. A man's T-shirt read: ELLSWORTH CHAINSAW. On the back wall of the restaurant was a Fire Roads Map of Franklin, and then a yellowed newspaper clipping about the novel, *The Beans of Egypt, Maine.*

We settled down to a hearty meal of cheeseburgers, homemade biscuits, strawberry shortcake for Linda, and bread pudding for me. We were stuffed. It was some good!

"It's always like that when we have a really big special," the waitress said. She was a thin, energetic woman in her mid-twenties—the type of Maine woman whom you just felt would tell anybody—you included—exactly what was on her mind.

"Is everything made from scratch?"

"Everything. The muffins, the biscuits, the pies—everything is made fresh every day.

"Do you do the cooking yourself?"

"She does most of the cooking." She pointed to another, slightly older woman, with a slightly fuller figure—the woman who had been passing around the fudge. "Kay does almost every bit of the cooking. I only get roped into it a couple of days a week."

"You're the ones who asked about the chocolate bread pudding?" Kay asked.

Linda and I had tried some chocolate bread pudding at the Ship's Wheel Restaurant in Jonesport a few days earlier. It was excellent and we wondered if they ever made it here.

"Last week was the first time we've had bread pudding," Kay said. "We sold it out three times, I think, since then."

Kay wondered what they put in the chocolate bread pudding. We weren't sure. Chocolate chips? Linda said, "That's his (my) test for a good Downeast restaurant: if the bread pudding is good, then everything else is usually good."

I asked Kay if the restaurant was always so lively.

"This is calm. Honestly, this is calm compared to what it's usually like here. Breakfast-time is unreal. Sunday morning is a zoo. We open up at eight o'clock Sunday morning and they're out there at seven-thirty lining up so they can get their seat. Oh yeah, they've got their favorite seat and if they don't get it, it's like, 'You're in my seat! You're going to move yet?'"

Norma Albee, the owner of the Trading Post had told us she called one table the "Methodist Pew," because the same men sat there everyday. I said to Kay, "So this is really the place to hang out in Franklin!"

"Oh yeah. And when it rains it's unreal. They're here all day."

"We noticed your coffee prices," Linda said. "The free warm-up, and then the third cup you start paying again."

"That's why," Kay explained. "There were a few bad days this winter when you couldn't get out, so they'd stay here all day. And they were drinking coffee all day. The coffee was disappearing, and we said, 'We've got to do something.' But they don't seem to mind."

Norma Albee, the owner, whom we had last talked to in 1984, came in. She remembered us and said, "Time—when you're in here it means nothing—the years just run right into one and then the other."

I asked Norma about the faded newspaper clipping on "The Beans" that was taped to the back wall. She said that a lot of people in Franklin had really been offended by Carolyn Chute's novel, *The Beans of Egypt, Maine*. It seems that Carolyn Chute had no idea there really was an Egypt, Maine. She had wanted an exotic-sounding name for a typical Maine town, and while she knew there was a China, a Paris, a Peru, and a Poland, she'd never seen an Egypt on the map.

But there is an Egypt, and it is part of the town of Franklin. You won't find Egypt on the state highway maps, but this village appears in my 1962 Hancock County Map, compiled by the Prentiss and Carlisle Company of Bangor. And several years ago, I had seen the name EAST OF EGYPT on the front of an old country store building in the center of Franklin. It was the name of a local agricultural co-op, but I didn't know then what EAST OF EGYPT meant. I thought perhaps it was just some "far-out" name that meant some hippy or back-to-the-lander had come up with. But the name meant just what it said: the co-op was located east of Egypt, Maine.

The village of Egypt—what is left of it—is on Route 182, about four miles southwest of the center of Franklin. A paved road leads north into the woods—Egypt Lane. Then there's Egypt Bay, upstream on the Taunton River from the Sullivan Bridge. There is no village center, but people residing on the lane or along the bay are said to be living in Egypt.

Like many small Maine villages, Egypt once had a hotel, post-office, sawmill, and school—all gone now. Back in the schooner days—before the highway or the railroad—it would have been a nice long sail up this bay—sort of like going to Egypt!

Anyone who knows Maine and has read *The Beans of Egypt, Maine,* would realize the story takes place inland or perhaps in the western part of the state. Still, locals took it hard. Even those who hadn't read the book got the sordid details of illegitimacy, incest, and violence second-hand from those who had. Indeed, patrons of the Trading Post debated whether or not readers elsewhere would think Chute had meant to name the book after their town. And furthermore, there are no Beans in Egypt, Maine. Not a one—never have been! And while I'm sure folks in Franklin would admit there is incest, illegitimacy, murder, and mayhem in the Maine woods, *The Beans* is certainly not an accurate portrayal of everyday life in their town. Poor Carolyn Chute: she never found an Egypt on the map, and little did she know that one existed way Downeast. And little did she know how upset folks down here would get!

We left the Trading Post and drove back into the center of Franklin. The old F.P. Gott General Store building stands as an empty monument to the glorious past of country stores. It's a massive clapboarded gable-front structure with an elaborate side staircase dropping from the second floor to the ground. We also passed the old EAST OF EGYPT co-op, itself a monument of sorts to the back-to-the land movement of the 1960s and 1970s.

A big, black Labrador Retriever sat outside a mauve and beige-colored house. There were several large old houses here, including THE CRYSTAL PALACE ROAD HOUSE, a bed and breakfast place in a colonial house with an attached barn. The sign also read: DINING; ROTO-TILLING, and led me to believe the owners did a variety of things to earn a living.

A man with a metal detector rooted around out front of the Schoodic Grange as we passed. Nana's Crafts was open and had styrofoam models of sheep on the front lawn—they looked quite realistic! We passed Shoppe's Fly Shop (fishing tackle) and a sign that read: ELLSWORTH 11 MILES.

It was raining steadily when we turned onto Egypt Lane. The signpost at the entrance had a basket of flowers on it. I wondered if it had always looked this inviting, or had the negative image cast by Chute's novel prompted the residents to spruce up the country lane? Several gnarly old apple trees were on our right as we drove along—an old orchard, perhaps. I saw a stand of young pines and an underground house with solar panels. I said, "Here's an attractive, cedar shingled house on the right. You know, it's a beautiful road.

We're going up a thickly wooded lane—right up a steady incline—in the rain and fog, and yet . . . And there's another lovely house. So far, every house we've seen here has been very nice."

"Lovely," Linda added. "Nothing extravagant, but tasteful."

"It's no wonder people here got upset. Look, there's a nicely maintained vegetable garden. That's a pretty cedar-shingled house over there, too. Are we at the end of the road?"

Linda said, "No, it's just wet under the trees . . . Oh, we are! Well . . . it turns to dirt."

# CHAPTER 7

# A MILLION DOLLAR VIEW:
# DUNBAR'S STORE, SULLIVAN

"They say there are more pictures taken from this spot than from anywhere else in the State of Maine." That's what Phil Dunbar told me when I asked him how his store had survived for a hundred and six years. We were standing in front of a window in the back of Dunbar's Store, looking out at Frenchman's Bay and the "Sleeping Giant" beyond. Years ago, an old woman in Steuben told me that, growing up, they had always called the view of Cadillac Mountain and Mount Desert Island the "Sleeping Giant," because from across the bay, it resembled a large man sleeping on his back.

"I've got a million dollar view," Phil sighed. "I had a woman come last year asking for the sale price. I said, 'I'll take a million dollars for it.' She said, 'Ten years, you'll get it.'"

"I bet you will. The way real estate prices are going up around here, you'll be able to retire."

"Al, last September, I had a man drive up. I was out pumping gas. He says, 'This store for sale?' I says, 'I don't know—not really.' He says, 'I'll offer you two-hundred-and-fifty-thousand.' I said, 'No.' 'Two hundred-seventy five.' 'No.' 'Three-hundred thousand.' I says, 'No, it's not for sale.' And he says—he had a young fella with him—he says, 'If you want to sell it you let this fella know and he'll call me any time.'"

"Was he an out-of-stater?"

"Yeah, and then about a month and a half ago, a guy from Bangor stopped in and said, 'I've got a buyer for this store.' He says, 'Is it for sale?' I says, 'No.' And I asked him out of curiosity just how much he'd give for it. And he says, 'around three-hundred thousand, maybe a little more.' And yesterday I was here and Century 21 come in—asked if the store was for sale. I says, 'No.' So there's a market. And anything that's on the shore, you're going to be able to name your own price."

Dunbar's Store is a relic: It's a low, cramped, nondescript wooden structure with large picture windows in front, always pasted over with local notices, advertisements, and grocery prices. It's too close to the road. There's not enough parking, and it's on a dangerous curve. You back on to Route 1 and pray your engine doesn't quit. In another location, this store would have few takers.

But that marvelous view, and for that matter, any place with a view along this coast, is in great demand by people from out-of-state. But Maine people have been slow to understand this. "Years ago, nobody wanted to live down on the shore except lobster fishermen," a man had told me in Steuben. He still couldn't understand what all the fuss was about. And until the past two decades, shore property—especially way Downeast—wasn't worth much.

I said to Phil, "Well, what's the average person around here do for a home now? You look in the paper and they want a hundred thousand dollars for places you'd buy for nothing a few years ago."

"Poor people are either going to rent or live with their parents or move away. You see so many of them—well, they're moving away. There's nothing here for 'em. Well, you live here all your life—."

Phil and I were classmates at Sumner High School back in the 1960s. And while I had spent the past twenty years living in eight different states besides Maine, Phil had stayed right here in Sullivan, and eventually bought the family store.

"There's twenty-four new houses in Sullivan and they're all out-of-staters. They're either people who lived here thirty or forty years ago that have retired and come back—" He paused and said, "And Little Tunk Pond—that's been bought. There'll be five new places built there. An outfit out of Massachusetts bought it. They're trying to buy a chunk of Big Tunk. And they want to develop it."

Phil pointed to a bare lot on the shore—less than an acre—that was just sold for seventy-nine thousand dollars. "And over across here (he pointed to the shore again), last year a guy bought six hundred feet of shore property. He paid thirty-five thousand for it. Four months later he sold those two lots—six hundred feet— I think it was over eighty thousand."

An old country store that has survived the coming of the automobile, the paved highway, and the supermarket, solely because of its geography? I suppose we could leave it here, but there's more to Dunbar's than a view of the water. In a way, Dunbar's Store is unique. He doesn't sell sandwiches, pizza, or fast (takeout) foods of any kind; and at the moment, he didn't even have gasoline. His gasoline pumps were dug up, and had been for some time. "Strictly groceries," Phil said. "'Cause I was reading your article (The article suggested that the area's general stores were gradually becoming convenience stores that specialized in items that turned over rapidly like soda, beer, bread, and fastfood.), and I said, 'That don't fit me. Not at all.'"

"Do you have people that buy all of their groceries here?"

"Oh yes. Oh yes. You take every Friday and Saturday and Sunday—the same people—you can almost tell the time they're going to come."

"Are they primarily elderly people?"

"No, no, you know, some twenty (years old), some thirty, and then you've got the thing a lot of people are doing now, Al, they're living day to day."

"I'm sure you get a lot of clammers and wormers."

"No. None."

"Why is that?"

"Well, I don't have any fast-food. No sandwiches. No gasoline."

"Well, why would local people do all their shopping with you instead of going to, say, Doug's Shop 'n Save supermarket in Ellsworth?" (We are only about seven miles east of Ellsworth here.)

"Well, I've got a pretty good selection of everything. And you take Doug's prices. You go along and you take one item—they're apt to knock this one down to nothing. They'll lose twenty cents. And then they'll turn around and take three or four items and mark it up ten or twelve cents.

"You take, Al, the whole state—of course they're all computerized. And they can tell you how many of this they're going to sell. How many of that they're going to sell. How many of that are they going to sell. And they're so big; they can buy cheap.

"The big guy is going to kill us. But I don't worry about it. The only thing that would kill me is another store that would open up like one of these—well—medium-size stores."

Dunbar's Store fills a void. It is the only medium-sized grocery store between Ellsworth and Winter Harbor. There are small convenience grocery stores in Hancock, but it doesn't make sense to do all of one's shopping at, say, the Hancock Grocery, with Ellsworth just a few miles away. But Sullivan is a bit farther down the road; and Dunbar's is just big enough—to fill an entire grocery order—to spare someone the inconvenience of going to Ellsworth, especially in the summer when traffic is heavy, or in the winter, when the road is icy.

This idea, that consumers will try to cut costs by traveling to the nearest village carrying the goods they need, is an integral part of Central Place Theory, a location theory used by geographers to explain the spacing of settlements on the rural landscape. For Central Place Theory to work perfectly, however, the landscape should be a flat plain without any barriers impeding transportation. Ideally, then, consumers can travel in any direction—their travel expenses determined only by the distance to that village. It is assumed, therefore, that people will shop at the nearest village (store). And if the villages (stores) are too far apart to serve the rural population adequately? Then, an intervening village (store) will be established, so that ultimately, the distribution of villages (or country stores) is fairly even.

Altogether, I counted eight country stores in the twenty miles along Route 1 between Ellsworth and Gouldsboro in Hancock County, which represents an average linear density of one store per two and one half miles. Only nine stores were found in the forty mile stretch of Route 1 between Steuben and Machias in Washington County. However, if five additional stores are counted which stand less than one mile from Route 1, the average linear density of the Washington County stretch is one store for every three miles. Overall, residents of Hancock County have slightly better access to country stores than residents of Washington. And with the exceptions of those persons living in the woods or on the ends of peninsulas, one is seldom more than five miles from a country store.

Of course, certain functions of settlements are used more often—and by more people—than others. For example, a jewelry store will have fewer customers on a daily basis than a grocery store. The grocery store is said to be a "lower order" function—more apt to be encountered in the small village than the jewelry store, a "higher order" function, restricted to larger towns. The jewelry store must reach outward a greater distance (i.e., Ellsworth extending its trade area into Washington County and pulling in rural shoppers) in order to survive. The higher order good (jewelry) is said to have a greater "range," and this ensures that large towns be located farther apart than small villages. It also means that jewelry stores require a higher "threshold" or minimum population to survive than a grocery store.

Central Place Theory is a neat idea, but in reality, neither human or natural resources are evenly distributed; nor are settlements always evenly spaced. And as I learned from my own experience and observations, people don't always try to minimize costs and distances. Some folks just like to drive more than others. Some people shop in certain grocery stores because they feel welcome there. Others try one store for a while, get tired of it, and go on to another. In the academic world, there are those who treat geography as a law-giving social science, based on theories and models; and then there are others, known as "humanistic geographers," who believe that each place has its own unique character—that no two places are alike. And while I have tried to keep at least one foot planted in the "geography as social science" school of thought, I did not have to travel too far down this coast to get footloose—to realize that all places are indeed unique. And that's what I think geography is ultimately all about—discovering the character of places!

Phil and I talked about the local economy. It was getting harder for clamdiggers to get down to the flats, not to mention the scarcity of clams. "The only way the clammers are going to make it is to have a boat," Phil explained. "'Cause you take people with private land—they don't want anybody down their driveway. Well, one reason, of course, the clammers dump their trash out.

"Well, you take this musseling now. You wouldn't believe how big that's gotten. It's ruining the clam flats. It's a thing of the past (clamming). It's going to be. Unless something comes in and kills the mussels out. Then the clams will come back. My father said back sixty years ago you couldn't dig a clam. They came back."

"Well, what did the clamdiggers do back then?"

"Everything was in season then. They farmed—of course—in the summer. Or they worked for people. Of course there was a lot of carpentry work. And in the winter-time they'd cut wood."

"From what I've heard, lobstering was better then, too," I said.

"That could be. That could be."

"Do you think these clammers, twenty-four or twenty-five years old are thinking about the future?"

"No, the only thing that saves us, Al, is welfare. If it wasn't for welfare they'd be starving."

Phil told me a story about one clammer whose mother was living in a nursing home. But she hadn't been able to live there until she had gotten rid of her house. The system didn't allow it. So she gave her son the house. Well, he was on welfare and food stamps. But now that he owned property he couldn't get welfare anymore. It wasn't much of a house, Phil explained, but it came with several acres of land. The man sold it to the first person that came along, however, just so he could go back on welfare. And he sold it for next to nothing!

"Al, the biggest problem—of course you know it—the big thing now, I claim, is dope. You take these kids around here—stealing, breaking in, something that all leads to dope."

"You think so?"

"You go up to North Sullivan. We've got a dope dealer up there."

I said, "It seems to me there are more clammers now too—more than there were when we were growing up."

"Yes there is. There's about a hundred-some-odd licenses right here in Sullivan, out of a population of about one thousand."

"And most of them are young guys," I said.

"Oh, you'll see them going in their fifties—and, they don't claim it on their income tax either. A lot of them don't. They get cash. And you see they can still get their food stamps. And, they've got kids."

"From what I've heard they'll be lucky to get a bushel of clams," I said. "I don't know how you can live on that."

"Thirty to forty dollars a day," Phil said. "That's what they do. They'll come in and cash a check and buy very few groceries, beer, and then they'll buy pot."

"Mostly pot?"

"Yeah, mostly pot. There's some drugs. There's two in town going to jail. The court system's too easy. It's a different world, Al. Just stay here and survive—that's what I'm going to do."

I was beginning to see a relationship between clamdigging, the daily, rather than weekly, paycheck and pot. The drugs were habit-forming; the users needed them every day, and this took cash. So they'd dig a bushel of clams, and as Phil had suggested, they would have enough cash left over after buying a few groceries and some beer, to buy some marijuana. Living from day to day: Phil had mentioned that. But weren't these people the least bit optimistic about the future. Phil had three children, and I said, "What about your kids? Do you want them to take over this store?"

"Yeah, definitely. I don't want to see them move."

"Will you encourage them to go to college?"

"Yes."

"So they can come back and run the business though."

"Yeah. That is right. You can't get hurt getting a college education today. You need it. Computers—the big thing. I looked in the *Boston Globe* a few weeks ago—anywhere from twenty-five thousand to seventy-five thousand, job-wise."

Roots. The area was definitely undergoing rapid change—and not necessarily for the best—but it was home to Phil. His roots were here. The store had been in his family for one hundred and six years and now he had a family of his own. He looked to the future, and it was easy to see where he was coming from.

Phil pointed to the Sorrento side of Frenchman's Bay. We looked out the window at an unspoiled stretch of rocky coast—nothing but bluish-green pointed firs. And he said, "There's one thing that isn't going to change—you can't see a house and I don't think you ever will."

"Why is that?"

"It's owned by summer people—two or three families—and it's been in the family forever, and it's going to stay there. That's the only thing that's going to save this coast."

"Yeah, they've probably got enough money to hang on to it," I added. "That's the scary thing—native Downeasters don't have the resources to hang on to their land."

"And the people that do own the shore—unless they're quite wealthy—are going to be forced to sell. They can't afford to pay the taxes and upkeep. You take a man who makes twelve to fifteen thousand has a pretty good job up here."

"Well, what do you think these diggers can make in a year? Your average clammer."

"Six to seven thousand, maybe. That's a clam digger. A worm digger—a good worm digger might make fifteen thousand. Then they'll clam in the winter some. Or go mussel dragging in the winter—whatever they can find.

"The old Bluenose, she keeps running."

We watched the Bluenose, the ferry to and from Yarmouth, Nova Scotia, as it sailed between the Porcupine Islands-Sheep, Burnt, and Bald—and out into the blue Atlantic.

"I guess you watch it go out every morning."

"Eight o'clock sharp."

# C H A P T E R   8

## SPIRITS IN THE ROCKS: THE EVEN EXCHANGE, EAST SULLIVAN

T he old Hanna Grothers' General Store building at the intersection of Route 1 and Tunk Lake Road in East Sullivan, had been closed for eight years when Beatrice and Wilton Martin bought it in 1972. The last thing local folks could remember about the store was an old photograph of the building with a Cadillac sticking out its side. According to Wilton, Theresa Sutherland, a very prim and rather wealthy middle-aged woman, was the store's last owner. Miss Sutherland soon married one of the Wayland boys, who Wilton described as a handsome young man, some twenty years younger than Theresa and from the wrong side—an east side boy—of Sullivan.

"She eventually found out he was just there for the easy life, so she kicked him out," Wilton explained. "Well, the first thing he did, he got in the car—her car, a big old Cadillac—and he got coming up the road, and he put it right through that wall there! And it had mustard and ketchup and pickles all over it. This was a general store then, but it wasn't long after that she gave it up."

I was in the Even Exchange, an antique and used furniture business that the Martins operated out of the old Hanna Grothers'

Store. What began as a summer business for Beatrice—while Wilton was airport manager in Rockland, Maine and then Lakeland, Florida—became a year-round enterprise after Wilton's retirement. The old store was built in the 1890s, Beatrice said. There was an apartment upstairs that had been used all through the years. Beatrice said something about the unique way the rafters had been put in, but I wasn't paying much attention. There were just too many distractions—too many antiques and odds 'n ends to catch my eye. She suddenly had my attention, however, when she said, "We have a ghost. We call her Lucy."

It had all started about eight years earlier when Beatrice and a friend from Florida came up to spend the summer in the apartment above the store. Beatrice and her young son had previously lived there by themselves. But she had worried about a break-in, because in those days, teenagers would have their cars out front at night, drinking and hollering, their radios blasting. Beatrice said, "And I stood up in that apartment and I said to Janet, 'You know, for the first time, I'm not afraid to stay here anymore. I feel relaxed, and I'm not afraid of what's going on around here.' About the time I said that—it was eleven o'clock at night—I heard the front door just bang open and great big, heavy, booted footsteps—four of them—came and stopped right down here. I said to Janet, 'Someone has broken in.' And she said, 'No, it's up here.' And it resumed in the attic over our heads and went out through the end of the building. We couldn't understand it, yet we were terrified.

"It went on for three nights, doing the same thing. It would come burst through the front of the attic—great big heavy boots across those timbers—through the building out the other end."

"But you never found the front door open?"

"Oh no. No. It stopped right there—five feet from the door—and resumed in the attic. And for three nights, it went through the attic.

"Well, we tried some exorcism on it, through friends. And then this friend of mine said it was a bad spirit and she would get rid of it. It's a very involved story."

"Oh?"

"Anyway, my sister-in-law came in one day and said, 'I've just had my fortune told.' There's a spiritualist over here in Franklin.

She said, 'I had more fun. You should go over.' We decided we would. And I went to the woman's door—I had never seen her before—and she took one look at me and said, 'Ah, don't be frightened, it's just a spirit in your place that's trying to frighten you out of there.' And she told me everything that happened. She said, 'We will do something today, and when we're finished, you'll never be bothered by that spirit. But you must never tell what we did.' I never told. But from that time on, we were bothered in many different ways. She said there were several of them. We were tormented all summer long, one way or another, by these spirits."

"What sort of things?"

"I would be sitting here with my books (She pointed to several books on a table.) and the next thing I'd hear them fall on the floor. And footprints. All the stuff under the bed—there would be animal footprints on it. We would hear noises. And someone tried to push a friend downstairs—took her feet out from under her. Many things went on here, but for some reason it stopped when we remodeled the building.

"But there was a lot more that happened. A man came one day when they were doing a talk up at the Town Hall on ghosts along the coast of Maine. He came from Massachusetts, and he spent about three hours up in the apartment by himself and we had a long conversation afterwards. He told me about all the spirits he had found up there. He said that back in the days when this was first built, they used the apartment to live in, but they also gambled there. He told me about all the games and all the people who would sit around the table. He even gave me the names of them— and it's all local names that he didn't know. And he also said that up in our attic there was a man who knifed another man. He didn't die—it didn't kill him then—but later he died from the wounds. And he went on and told me all the things that were happening in this building all through the years with all these spirits. He said this is a commune for spirits."

"Were you able to verify these stories?"

"No, I never have, except that some of the people he described who lived in here, I could verify. He told me about a nice little old lady with a pug on top of her head, who lived here, and how she loved to make tea. Well, I knew the lady. I knew who she was. And often at night I would hear someone in the kitchen. When I was sleeping, I would wake up and hear someone moving around like they were making tea.

"He explained about the energy from the rocks and water. But we haven't been bothered for a couple three years now. But every once in a while something will disappear or something will happen and we'll say, "Oh, Lucy's back."

"Lucy, is that what you call it?"

"You know who Lucy is, don't you? The oldest human."

"Oh yeah, I read the story about the archeological dig. The remains are supposed to be more than two million years old."

"You know, I never went anywhere without my dog, Beaujolet. I never went anywhere without Beau. And the night we arrived from Florida—we always go down to celebrate my aunt's birthday on the twenty-fifth of June in Southwest Harbor. We always take a turn around the cemetery, always do. So anyway, we did this night too. And Beaujolet was thirteen or fourteen years old at the time and he just laid down in the back of the wagon and slept. We got to the cemetery gate and that dog stood up and growled this low growl, and his eyes were like fire and his hair stood on end. And he didn't stop. He kept it up all over the cemetery, and Beaujolet laid down and went to sleep and there was never a peep out of him. And everyone remarked that evening about how strange Beau had acted.

"When the man from Massachusetts came and told me about all those spirits up there, he said in that room over there is a man with a long jacket, long hair, and a lot of whiskers, and he was shell-shocked in the war. And he's walking around in circles, and he keeps saying, 'Where's my dog? I've got to find my dog. My dog's gone. Someone's taken my dog.' The man from Massachusetts said he's concentrating on a dog. He said, 'That dog of yours picked up this spirit from the cemetery and brought it back here.' He didn't know about all this going on. He sat and told me about it. I didn't tell him."

"He didn't know you had taken the dog to the cemetery?"

"No. He said, 'An animal, probably a dog, picked him up at the cemetery and brought him here.' Everybody says we're crazy, you know. So many things have happened, you just wouldn't believe.

We had one very angry spirit, he said was a very ugly spirit. And we did have one that was tormenting everybody. It tried to push someone downstairs and things like that. And he (the man from Massachusetts) said another man was also there. He keeps opening and closing drawers in a dresser, looking for pills. And he said there's a baby lying in a crib crying, and a woman is crying beside the crib. And she's saying, 'Oh, the baby is crying in the crib.' And the man is being very ugly to the woman. And then he (the man from Massachusetts) said, 'I see it again and the baby is gone and the woman is crying.' And he said that ugly spirit is still here, and that's the one we're having trouble with."

"When you think about it, a lot of history has crossed this threshold," I said.

"He said this place was a gambling den upstairs," Beatrice continued. "But how much of that do you believe, you know? But I believe what I saw, and I believe what we felt up there."

"You say someone lives upstairs now?"

"My son lives there. We have completely redone the apartment, and since then, nothing's happened. But it was when I was alone, and when Janet came back with me—and when the dog came from the cemetery that it all happened. And I believe that most of it happened when the dog came back from the cemetery. Years before that, I was alone up there and I heard noises and just thought they were noises. Someone touched me on the shoulder one night and shook me awake and I thought it was just my imagination. And I saw someone walk across the room one day and thought that was just my imagination.

"I was walking the dog one night and Janet came tearing downstairs. We had a stuffed tiger and she was carrying it. She said, 'Get out of this apartment! Its eyes are going just like this.' (Beatrice moved her eyes from side to side.) And she was terrified, and we wouldn't have that tiger back in the apartment. This spirit was in her room all the time. I had a very quiet one in my room. It would touch me on the shoulder. But he was violent in her room. Apparently, it all started when she came. And when she left—she doesn't come back anymore—it stopped. Whoever it was, didn't want her here. It just didn't want her in that room. That was the room where the baby was and the pills were, and that was where the ugly man was. I have another friend who is a spiritualist and he said, 'I wouldn't let my wife sleep in that room.' There's a lot of people that have been up there and feel the spirits and say the same thing. It's full. It's very frightening. Isn't it interesting, the stories about old buildings?"

It was May, and chilly. A bank of fog just seemed to hover over Hog Island in Frenchman's Bay. The day was dark and gloomy; it grew drearier still, and then it started to rain. I had never really given much thought to ghosts or spirits. And as I drove along Route 1 towards Gouldsboro, I thought: If ever there was a good place for poltergeists, it was here!

# CHAPTER 9

## HAPPY BIRTHDAY, RICHARD: YOUNG'S STORE, GOULDSBORO

Lucille Null had worked "on and off" at Young's Store in Gouldsboro for fourteen years when I interviewed her in May of 1988. Serious, yet always laughing; competent, but also compassionate: Lucille, a working mother in her early thirties, seems to possess all those qualities that a good country storekeeper needs. "I like this job," she told me. "I don't think there are many people who can say they like their job, but I do."

Lucille was standing with her back to a large rectangular window, a window through which you can look out across Route 1 to Frenchman's Bay and Mount Desert Island. The tiny, one room store, with a ceiling so low that tall people must duck their heads, stands on high ground along a wooded stretch of Route 1. And when you emerge from your car in the small, paved parking area in front of the store, there's a sense that your car is slipping downward in two directions: east is a long steady incline, while south, a sharp descent to the bay. So you get out of your vehicle and you walk slightly uphill, or north, to go into the store. There is a real sense here of gravity at work, of clamdiggers leaving Young's and dropping precipitously to the mudflats below. And you can see the store from a long way off. It just beckons you to stop, if for no other reason than to admire the view—of green spruce forests, and islands, and water, and on a clear day, of boats, some with sails!

Lucille stands behind the counter facing north towards the customers, the coolers, and the videos, while the patrons find themselves looking out the front window, towards the big bay, which for many of them is where they earn their living. Such a grand setting for this humble saltbox building, with its porch overhang, and its two gas pumps! A small electronics factory, Anderson's Hardware, the Gouldsboro Post Office, and an antique shop are just down the road, but everyone stops here. Young's is a landmark, and a community gathering place.

"I started when I was in high school and I worked for the State of Maine for a couple of years. Then I worked in a department store in Ellsworth, and when I had my daughter, I came back here," Lucille explained. "It's real convenient."

Young's Store is a family-owned business. "My mom ran the post office in Gouldsboro for thirty years and then they bought this business in the last year and a half," Lucille said. Mrs. Geraldine Havey, a sweet old woman in her eighties, had owned the store for many years when Lucille's family bought it. "Gerry was the daughter of Alton Young, and when I first came here, Alton and Millie owned the store, and then Alton died, and then Millie died, and then Gerry took over on her own," Lucille explained. But Mrs. Havey had grown old with the business and finally decided that even with plenty of reliable help she had to put the store up for sale. Lucille had worried that an out-of-stater might buy it and not really understand the local people. "If you haven't been in this area you don't realize that people like dried, strip fish," Lucille explained. "You have to know where to look for it. Last week we had twenty or thirty fish—whole fish—come in, which is very hard to find. And they were gone within a matter of three or four days."

Lucille was not exaggerating when she said that strip fish were getting harder to find. I had been in Young's on numerous occasions when people had requested it, only to learn there were none available. But why were strip fish so hard to find? There was no shortage of codfish. According to John Gould, the smell involved in drying the fish on racks or fish "flakes" as they are called, may be one reason for their scarcity. In an essay entitled,

"Environmental Sweetener, or no more 'Maine Ho!'" Gould explains that:

> A "flake is a rack for drying fish; the word derives from the Icelandic for some kind of wickerware. The flake was introduced into the Maine and Canadian Maritime scene when the Vikings drifted along from Greenland some five or six hundred years before North America was officially discovered.

Later, after the arrival of the English and the French, the flakes became quite commonplace, especially during colonial times. Gould suggested that:

> We had endless miles of them. Nobody had yet moved back from tidewater, and all endeavor was related to sea and shore. Every little community had its fish flakes and facilities for catching, curing, and processing—from the salted cod to the refinements of train oil and fish peas. When a vessel approached the coast of Maine, the masthead lookout could smell fish before he saw land. "Maine Ho!" he would sing out.
>
> As Maine coastal property has its newer emphasis, the fish flake has declined. I do not know of one. Where once the noble cod lolled in indolence with his vest unbuttoned and exuded his impelling thurification in all directions, there are tennis courts and gazebos, and rose gardens and summer people who do not forgive us our trespasses. The fish business is not what it once was. And now the true believers in a sweet environment have petitioned and demonstrated and prevailed.
>
> (*TheChristian Science Monitor*, 17 June 1988, p. 30)

"People like to keep the strip fish on the dashboards of their cars," I said to Lucille. I remembered riding to baseball games in the 1960s with a Steuben man who always had a dried fish on the dashboard of his pickup truck. He'd tear off a strip, chew, and talk at the same time. His truck stank of fish.

"Yeah, some have maggots in them," Lucille added. "We had one woman who always waited for those. She'd wait 'til the fish had maggots in it before she'd buy it."

"And she'd eat it?"

"Yeah, and then she'd eat it! 'Call me when it gets like this, okay?'"

I asked Lucille what she liked about working in the store and she gave me many of the familiar answers. It was convenient for her. She lived nearby and was able to work around her daughter's school schedule. She had made many friends the past fourteen years and felt it would be hard to leave them. She also got to know everything that was going on, but added: "You're going to have to weigh everything you hear. I've learned you have to shut your ears to a lot of things . . . you really don't want to know."

Young's Store has undergone some changes since Mrs. Havey retired. The two most obvious changes are the Megabucks (state lottery) and the movie rental. "One of the reasons we brought in Megabucks is that it's a drawing card," Lucille said. "We also know that movies are a big drawing card. We don't rent a lot. Probably between eighty and a hundred in a two-week period. But everything you add becomes a drawing card, and hopefully you can sell the things that make money, like soda, beer, wine, and chips. Those are all your money makers in a store this size. But you have other things that will get them through the door. Like gasoline— it's your biggest drawing card."

Country stores are changing as the countryside itself changes. And video rental has become the "in thing" at those country stores intent on keeping up with the times. But is there really such a thing as "country" anymore? Aren't the residents of rural Maine exposed to the same ideas, information, and products as the residents of large cities? In this age of telecommunications, there are people right here in Gouldsboro, Maine with access to as much information as, say, someone living in New York City. The reality is that highways and telecommunications have created a metropolitan culture where the distinction between rural and urban has become blurred. In a cultural sense, we can all be part of the metropolis if we choose to be. And judging from the way cellular telephones, satellite dishes, and video cassette recorders have diffused throughout eastern Maine, many Downeasters have evidently embraced this metropolitan culture.

"Country stores are always going out of business," I said. "How does this tiny store keep going year after year?"

"I think location has a lot to do with it," Lucille explained. "And as bad as I hate for the way it goes, a store of this size, in order to succeed, it's got to have credit, you know. You have worm diggers, clamdiggers."

"You mean you extend credit?"

"Yeah."

"Is it seasonal—pretty much the winter months?"

"No. It's year-round. For example, this morning I had three or four worm diggers come in and they wanted soda, cigarettes, and something to eat until they can go down and sell their worms and cash their checks. That happens a lot of the time. That's good stuff. In the winter-time we're lucky in this area because we have a wreath factory just up the road and we extend a lot through that. And then we have a lot of woodcutters come in for gas and oil, and that runs monthly. And then you have some you help get by through the winter."

"Do you ever have people who won't pay?"

"All the time I've been here there have been some, but it's not many. You always get it. The slip may be two years old by the time you get it, but eventually . . . there's some you just hold your breath."

"You're not in this store to rake in the profit then?"

"No, I would have hated to see this store just go. I mean, it would be hard on this area. There are some people who never set foot in a grocery store in Ellsworth. The secret to this is repeat customers."

"Does it really slow down in January?"

"This January, no. We had a very good January."

"How do you explain that? Cutting wood?"

"We didn't have a lot of snow to begin with. Which means people could stay clamming. They can cut wood. But there's a lot of money made in this area in November and December—trees, wreathing, cuttin' wood—there's a lot of money made. And they still have it come January. People think that as fast as they get it, they spend it. Well, they don't. They pretty well plan for January, February, and March. April has been our worst month. April and May are the worst. First of all, April is tax month. Anyone who is self-employed is going to pay a rate of thirteen percent social security."

Lucille also said that many of her customers were still scallop dragging in January; but by February, all that peters out. There's nothing left.

A clammer came in to pay off his slip. "Two ninety-nine, thank you," Lucille said. That was just two dollars and ninety-nine cents; not two-hundred and ninety-nine dollars. I got the impression from that transaction, at least, that credit at Young's was mostly "nickel and dime" stuff—a Slim Jim, a soda, an Italian (submarine) sandwich. The telephone rang.

"Young's Store," Lucille answered. "Hi, I need some ham. No, the big, boiled ham. Right. And salami. Right. I need some chicken salad. I need ten pounds of hot dogs—real small ones, please. Yeah. I need a couple more sticks of that pepperoni that you sent me last week. Yeah. And I also need six packages of Oscar Meyer bologna. I need six packages of Oscar Meyer cooked ham. Okay, send me three packages of that then. And I need six packages of Oscar Meyer franks. And that will be it. Okay. I've got plenty of that. Okay. Thank you. Bye bye."

Lucille said, "The tide just got over as you can see."

"Yeah, they're all coming in," I said. "I noticed by the boots."

"Or the mud."

The clammers and wormers had congregated around an old sofa and a worn chair at the end of the store. But one man seemed almost to be holding court. He was a fixture in the store. He had been coming to Young's as long as I could remember, and his father sat in that same chair many years before him. The man's name was Richard Wallace. He was in his fifties and had always reminded me of the actor, John Wayne, in his later films. Richard's eyes were slits. His weathered face and sturdy body had endured more than its share of hard labor, and, perhaps, hard living. "You were saying about the clams," I had worked my way over to his end of the store. "You don't think they're going to last much longer?"

"Well, it doesn't look good now," Richard said. "Places I've dug for years—always the most beautiful clams you'll ever see—and now they're showing like; a lot of black bellies and water bellies. And I understand it's happening all along the coast now. It happened quite a few years ago and the clams nearly went out."

"Showing." I had heard that expression used by other clammers and I took it to mean "appearance." It was an odd way to put it, I thought. I assumed it was an old expression, part of the folklore of this coast, an expression that would probably disappear with the clamming industry; if indeed the clamming was as poor as clammers said it was. I had asked Lucille about the clamming earlier and she had said: "Of course I've heard for ten years, 'There are no clams.' And I do know they have to struggle to get what they do get." Still, every year, they continue to dig clams, and as the clams get scarcer, the price per bushel goes higher. The clammers seem to get by.

"Do you think the poor clamming has something to do with red tide?" I asked Richard.

"No, I don't think it's red tide. It could have something to do with ice. I'm not exactly sure. I do know that when you dig now, that one out of about eight or nine or ten—something like that—are black or water belly."

"What do you mean by black belly?"

"Well, the belly actually shows black. The bellies look black. And, uh, the other ones look water sag. You touch them; they go to pieces."

"Not much in them then?"

"Doesn't seem to be. Not like there was. And of course the mussels are doing a lot of it too. Well, we used to have good clams up here and the mussel draggers are dragging and it's all holed in with the mussels and smothering them out."

Like other clammers I talked to Downeast, Richard didn't think the problem was too many diggers. This always surprised me, but it shouldn't have. Downeasters never seem to begrudge another person trying to make an honest living through hard work. If there is any bitterness—and I've encountered very little of it in eastern Maine—it's reserved for out-of-staters who sit behind desks and don't get their hands dirty—people like me, I guess.

"But it does help now that they put the two-inch law on," Richard said. "And if they enforce it, that would help. You see, they got away from that two-inch law for a while and they were taking everything. Wasn't even leaving the seed, and that wasn't good.

"But the good diggers can't get more than a bushel. When I was a kid you could get ten or fifteen bushels. When they took that two-inch law off, that hurt a lot."

"Do you dig worms too?"

"No, I used to. Well, a matter of fact, I don't dig too many clams now, either. My back's had it. But when I do get a mess, I see a difference in the meat right away. Now a half bushel of clams up here used to give you four quarts (of clam meat). Now I don't think I get three out of the same amount. You have so many black bellies. That's the difference in them."

Richard had been a fixture in Young's Store as long as I could remember, but he told me he had also lived for a long time in New York State and on Cranberry Island. Like many Downeasters, he had left as a young man to seek employment out of state. "I worked on a private estate," he explained.

I said, "It must have been your father I remember in this store about twenty years ago."

"My dad used to live right over here," Richard said, pointing up the road. "Well, I guess you can call it a family tradition. This is more like the old country stores—come in in the morning—sit down, talk and joke. You know, have their coffee."

"There aren't many like this anymore."

"No, I remember Small's Store up here used to have one place near the old stove, a nail keg. Everybody'd sit around and tell their stories. But that's going out now."

"Yeah, this is one of the last of its kind."

"Really. Well, a bunch of boys—like the Martin boys, that drive trucks out in the morning—gets together and has a big joke and a laugh—raise heck a little. Mostly the same crew. Everybody around in these little places knows everyone."

And then Richard said, "I don't do anything anymore. Can't on account of my back. I guess the doctor said my bones's worn out—the places between the bones. They're like stones rubbing. I started out when I was a young boy, working in logging camps— all that. That was hard lifting then. We worked hard."

"How old are you now?" I asked.

"Fifty-five."

"Well, you don't look fifty-five."

"Thank you. I feel it. Well, I've done hard work for years. Logging, clamming—always had to work hard—since I was a kid."

"What would be your advice to these young guys digging clams now? Would you encourage a young kid to become a clam digger?"

"No. I'd say, 'Stay in school and find something a little easier on your back.' This clam business and this shore business—it's going."

A customer came in and said, "Happy birthday, Richard."

"Thank you."

"Is today your birthday?"

"No." (He started to laugh)

Lucille said, "He says that so everybody will buy him a beer."

"You'd be surprised how many beers I can get. 'Let's help celebrate my birthday. Well, good. Let me get you a beer.'"

"A party every day!"

"Right. Three hundred and sixty-five days a year. You'd be surprised how many beers you'd get," Richard laughed.

Lucille said, "Remember that old ice cream man who would come in and you'd tell him that, and every time he'd leave, why we'd have at least two or three half-gallons of ice cream! He'd say, 'Oh, it's your mother's birthday today?' He was on that truck for twenty years."

I asked Richard what he did in the winter and he said, "Right there," pointing to the chair. He did a little deer hunting in the fall, and liked to go pickerel fishing up to Morancy Pond. I also asked him how he felt about the way the area is changing; about outsiders buying up shore frontage.

"Well, the kids ought to be able to get to the shore. First thing they (out-of-staters) do now, they'll get the land, then—slap! (He clapped his hands) NO TRESPASSING. You know? I don't like that part. Still, there's two ways of looking at it. They give you permission to go on. It'll only take one damn dummy out of the whole kit-and-kabootle to go down and make a mess. And that'll ruin it for everybody. You can't blame the people. If everybody'd leave it the way they found it, it wouldn't be so bad. When they get down there and start throwing their garbage out and breaking bottles and all that stuff—I don't blame the people (property owners). If they had a little respect it wouldn't be bad, but a lot of them kids are snotty. All the shorefront is getting the same. You can't go here. You can't do that."

Several clammers had come in and it was clear that Young's was still the community gathering place. "They'll discuss it all before the end of the day," Lucille said. "If all the world's problems could be solved over what's been decided here."

"So you don't try to discourage people from standing around and talking?" I said. "At some of these stores it's 'get your stuff and go.' They don't want you to linger."

"No, I think that's part of its charm," Lucille said. "That's the way it was one hundred years ago. Who would want to change all that? We don't. Some days it's difficult. I'll be honest with you. I'm a non-smoker and they'll sit over there and smoke cigarettes. And I don't drink coffee. But you just can't take it away."

A young man came in to cash a check. It was for eighty-two dollars—a morning's work digging worms. "Sure thing," Lucille said. "You have a three dollar slip here. You want to get it knocked off? Alright."

Back in 1985, I left questionnaires in Young's Store to find out certain things about the clientele: who they were (age, gender, occupation); what they bought; and where they lived. Clam or worm digger was the most frequently listed occupation. Altogether, sixty-seven percent of Young's patrons purchased cigarettes; forty-nine percent bought beer. Males (the average age was thirty-four years) accounted for seventy-nine percent of the patrons, eighty-one percent of whom lived within five miles of the store. So Young's is essentially a "diggers'" store, frequented by local men.

But if the store is heavily patronized by diggers, the women tend to stay away. I learned this by surveying customers at several stores. I found a correlation between beer sales, digger patronage, and male customers and a similar correlation between meat and milk sales and female patrons. The area is still traditional in that women buy most of the groceries; but I also think the perception people have of certain stores helps determine their patronage by gender. Further Downeast, I met a proprietor who was trying to change the perception people had of his store. He was a new owner, and in the past this particular store had catered to the local clammers and wormers. He said, "Oftentimes a car would pull up and the husband would come in while the wife would stay in the car. The women refused to cross the threshold."

Lucille said, "We try to cater to the diggers. It's a hot dog or a cheap meal for them—sixty-five cents for a hot dog. And we also try to keep the sandwiches in. Like an egg salad sandwich or a ham salad is a dollar twenty-nine. We keep a lower range as well as a two-dollar sandwich. Because they'll have a bad day. And when they go out and get absolutely nothing, you try to have something." Lucille told me that without a doubt, most of the guys who came into Young's got at least one—if not two—of their daily meals at the store. I asked her if she thought the diggers ever looked, say, ten or twenty years down the road.

"I don't think so. I really don't. Like we have one man who comes in here, he's close to seventy. and he's dug worms, clams, and cut wood all his life. I don't think they look ahead. Of course, a lot of them are young too. And I think a lot of them figure as long as their back will hold out they can take it. They can make a good dollar digging worms, especially if they can get into a market that's year-round."

Amos Kelley, Lucille's brother, told me he digs worms when he isn't working in the store. He evidently enjoys the freedom associated with worming. Lately, he had been digging down in Addison, about thirty miles east of Gouldsboro. "You can't get any worms around here?" I asked.

"Well, you can get as many here, but the price has gone so high on 'em this year. You see, the worms are so much bigger down there. Like the worms we're digging around here are this size (He opened his hand from thumb to index finger.) You see, this year you get ten cents for an average worm and you get twelve cents for a big one."

"These are blood worms, right?"

"Yeah, blood. Geez, nobody's sandworming 'cause the bloodworms' price is so much more. I think sandworms is only about five cents and that's a lot of difference for most people. I'd rather dig clams, but there just isn't any money in that right now."

"They're all dug up around here, aren't they?"

"They're coming back a little bit now. They've got that two inch law on. I think in a couple of years it will pick up. It's just like everything—the more they pay for it, the worse it gets. It went so high that everybody was diggin' 'em. I'd be surprised to see—like blueberry season's coming up—usually they (the diggers) shift over to raking blueberries. But geez, the worms are so high, I'd be surprised if they'd go. The fellow I go with, now he's a good digger, and he's making about a hundred and fifty dollars in three hours."

"Are you digging double tides?"

"Oh, I don't know if it's worth it. It's like—we can't live on what we make off here (in the store), with us just starting out. I have to pick up a few extra bucks."

Amos was twenty-nine years old. He had a mustache and dark brown hair that stuck out from under his baseball cap and fell over his ears. And like most worm diggers, he was stocky, or "rugged," as they say around here.

Amos got busy and I talked some more with Lucille. The Town of Gouldsboro was in the midst of a comprehensive plan, she said, and she had mixed feelings about that. "If you come in and you've bought your land and you've worked hard for your money, I don't think I should tell you what you can and can't do with it. That's what this comprehensive plan—it's scary. It doesn't want structures over thirty feet high. I don't think anyone's ready for that."

Lucille also felt that more people coming to the area would mean more business for the store. But then she said, "Except you hope and pray that the people who buy the land realize the local people have to make a living. I've heard a clam digger say he tried to walk down a path through the woods to get down to the shore. And the owner came out and said, 'I really wish you wouldn't walk by. You know, it makes my wife nervous.'"

"He's probably been using that path for years," I said.

"He had been. I also heard that same clam digger looked at that guy and said, 'You know, it's a very wise idea not to get the local people, especially the clam diggers, mad at you.'"

I said, "I've always heard: Never post your land. That is—if you want to keep your camp."

"I've heard those stories. They'd raise the hair on the back of your neck. It's like one guy stands there lighting matches and the other guy's blowing them out. Those are some of the stories I hear over in the corner. Somebody came in and bought one of these islands out here (she motioned to the islands out in Frenchman's Bay). Didn't want them huntin' out there. Boy—I guess they hunt now! A book of matches, you know, and you're standing there talking."

An out-of-stater could easily have bought Young's Store. "They have the money," Lucille said. Amos was only twenty-eight at the time the store came up for sale, and while he had the ambition, he lacked the money; and the bank wouldn't take a chance on him. "You knew this store was going to make it," Lucille explained. "Gerry made a profit. They (the banks) don't take into account someone's age. I mean, Gerry was in the business for thirty-two years. She must have gotten tired of it. And she was here every day. But the banks don't care about that The bottom line is the money." But Amos was lucky. His family had helped him raise the money. He now had his own business. His days were full.

"Maybe that's part of the problem," Lucille explained. "You walk in and say, 'I'll buy this general store and I'll work here and get this fun on the side.' There's a lot of hours in one of these places—a good fifteen hours a day. And that doesn't count what you do after the doors close. And we've got five sets of hands."

"And you're open three hundred and sixty-five days a year?"

"Yes, much to my dismay," Lucille laughed.

"We're open Christmas day and they all gotta come here," Amos said. "Last Christmas day we were so busy. They wanted to close up for two or three hours. I had to go down and buy just about all the milk Tuttle's (country store) had. We didn't have any left."

Lucille said, "I only remember two days this store has been closed, and that was the day Alton Young died and the day that Millie died . Alton died and Millie closed the store and then Gerry closed the store when Millie died.

"I remember the day that Alton died; that was Gerry's father. Gerry says, 'Well, Mom, I'll see if Lucille can work.' Millie goes, 'That store going to be closed all day?' That's the only time Millie said anything. She was ninety-something when she died. When I started here, she still walked over the hill with the boiled eggs. I can remember her doing that. Or sitting up there (in her house) in that window because she wasn't able to get down here. But she'd know whose car drove in. Or, she'd sit there and wait for someone to wave to her 'cause a lot of people would drive in and wave to her."*

---

*(Young's Store changed hands during the summer of 1990. The new owners are Downeasters who seem intent on preserving the store's homey atmosphere.)

# CHAPTER 10

## TUTTLE'S STORE, GOULDSBORO

A tall, thin man stood in the doorway holding a can of Lysol. There was a distinct scent in the room.

"I've heard to use tomato juice," I said.

"Tomato juice or vinegar, either one," Frances Tuttle said. "I'd rather use vinegar 'cause it isn't quite so messy."

"It really isn't so bad," the thin man said.

"I thought your dog might have gotten into it," Frances said.

"No, oh, no," the thin man said. "No, he's got it once, but he lucked out this time."

"Yeah! We can smell the skunk alright!" I said.

"You ought to come out to my house—you can really smell it!"

"Keep it over to your place," I said.

"Really!" the thin man said. "He's dead now anyway. He won't do it again." The man went out the door and I thought: That's one less Arkansas Polecat to wind up dead on the highway!

"I've had to deodorize this place once before, this morning," Frances said, as she propped open the front door. "He came in right after he tackled it."

We were in Tuttle's Store, a single cramped room full of groceries, snacks, newspapers, magazines, boots, shoes, hunting clothes—you name it—this general store has it. They sell medicines, kerosene, ice, fishing supplies, and, there are shoes from the 1960s. "Those on the top shelf are all out-dated," Frances said. "Lots of times they'll have parties on times way back. Did you look at the prices on them?"

"Yeah, eight dollars, three-twenty-nine, five dollars," I said.

"And they're leather," Frances added.

Tuttle's Store stands on a hilltop at the intersection of Routes 1 and 186 in Gouldsboro. And like many crossroads stores that have stood on the same site for decades, the yellow, false-front building, adorned with hanging flowering plants—begonias, geraniums, pansies, petunias—is a local landmark. The store is highly visible from either direction; there's a phone booth in the parking lot, and until Greyhound discontinued its service Downeast, Tuttle's was a bus stop.

The store's front door and two front windows, one with letters on the panes spelling TETLEY TEA, came from the original Tuttle's Store building which had stood at the bottom of the hill at West Bay Stream. Frances said they had a hard time bulldozing the old store down years ago because it had been built with big beams and wooden pegs.

Heading eastward along Route 1, you drop down a steep hill from the present-day store to West Bay Stream. The Gouldsboro Grange is on your right, while on the left side at the bottom of the hill stands the old post office and another old store building. The original Tuttle's had stood across the street. The two remaining structures are now the summer retreats of out-of-staters. I saw New York license plates in front of the old post office building one July evening as I slowed down to watch a doe and her fawn—still speckled—scampering on the rocks of West Bay Stream. The tide was low, exposing the rocks and mud flats, as the evening twilight showed brightly on the two deer, their rust red color framed by the green spruce and poplar woods. It only lasted a moment. The deer looked up and bolted into the woods, but the image of nature unspoiled, still pristine, has endured in my mind.

The original Tuttle's Store building was at the intersection of Route 1 and the Guzzle Road, a circuitous lane running from West Bay estuary, north several miles up to West Bay Pond. Frances Tuttle owns a house on the Guzzle Road, so I asked her where the name came from. I had been told that a bootlegger had once lived there and the name had had something to do with guzzling liquor. But Frances said, "No, that's an Indian name. It's an Indian name and it's Guzzle Brook. And a guzzle was a long drink of water. The Indians named the brook because that's where they went to get water. It's all springs, and the springs all join together to make a pond. I've heard that from the old people.

"But there could have been a bootlegger there. They were all around everywhere during Prohibition. One time I was playing hide-and-go-seek with a bunch of other children in the neighborhood and hid behind a bush that we called Snake Bush. And there I looked and saw this small, square can—one gallon—brought it down to the house, and my father said it was alcohol. He said, 'Probably came in on a boat and stashed it so they wouldn't get caught.'"

It is still hard for me to think of Tuttle's Store without thinking of Allen Tuttle, Frances's husband, who died in the winter of 1984 while trying to find a bundle of newspapers after a heavy snowstorm. Allen Tuttle was one of the friendliest people I've ever known. His sudden passing was a shock to both residents and non-residents. One of my neighbors on Jones Pond, an out-of-stater, was stunned. He said, "Few things have shaken me so much in recent years. Allen Tuttle was one of the most memorable characters I've ever known." My neighbor used to stop at Tuttle's frequently for items for his camp, but mainly because he enjoyed talking with Allen. We become so comfortable with country store proprietors; we depend on them for so many things; like the rocks on the Maine coast, we expect them to always be there.

I last talked with Allen Tuttle in July of 1984 and he had said, "We put in a sixteen-hour day. That's what keeps us going. Perseverance—stay at it day after day. We go to bed as soon after nine as possible each night and get up at four-thirty."

Allen told me he had been unable to persuade his daughter to take over the business. "She doesn't want the long hours," he said. Allen was an independent sort. He told me he had been a boxer and then described an encounter he once had with a would-be robber. The man had a gun in Allen's ribs; he was watching Allen's right arm; but Allen was left-handed and hit him with an uppercut to the jaw, disarming the villain with one blow.

I asked Allen, that summer, how he felt about the grocery chains and whether he had ever considered joining the Associated Grocers. Allen said, "No franchise—don't owe anyone anything. That drawer can pay all my bills. That's independence! They (the proprietors who belong to the Associated Grocers) think it's easier, but they own you. They send you a lot of stuff you don't want."

When I first wrote this chapter, I titled it "Rum Runners Up the Guzzle." Frances asked me to change it, however, because they've never sold alcoholic beverages at Tuttle's Store. And while they've refused to sell them out of principle—both she and Allen had always wanted to keep liquor out of the store—it also goes to prove that a well-run general store doesn't have to sell beer and wine to prosper.

Frances said, "I would like to sell the store very much, though, because the time has come for me to sell it. It's awfully hard here without Allen." But then she added, "I've never once in my life wished I could have it different. Not once. I love the store business and the people I see each day. But I'm sixty-six years old. And while I can do it myself, it's time the store went. And when it's all over and done with—what am I going to get out of it? What I sell it for—part of it goes for income tax. The government gets their share. And then, I've got to get a place fixed up to live in."

I asked Frances if she thought these old-time country stores had a future in Maine.

"I don't think they can get along without them. Even in your city places you find your little country store—your little 'Night Owl.' I think they (shoppers) go and they buy everything they think they need. Well, they forgot their sugar, or something. And, they normally buy their bread and milk daily anyway 'cause who has that size refrigerator? But we're so rural here, I think country stores have a very big place left. And if I was younger, we wouldn't be selling out."

I mentioned that the number of country stores between Ellsworth and Machias had stabilized at about thirty. Frances said, "Did you notice the new one over at Steuben?" I had. It's called Mathews' Country Store. "They're doing quite well over there," she added. "And they have a little lunchroom. This is what someone needs to do here. Now that back room would be a peach. But these old feet and legs don't need walking."

"What advice would you have for somebody starting out in the store business?"

"I'd say that there's no better life for a young couple. With the set-up I've got." Frances paused, and I said, "You live right in the store?"

"I live right in there." She pointed to her living quarters. "When Allen was alive, why he stayed out here, mostly, and I could go in and out. I could be getting my dinner and doing my housework. I had it all set up, anyway. I have a big mirror on the wall, and I can see if there's anyone out by the gas pumps. And I have a bell in there that tells me if someone comes in."

"It works perfectly," I said.

"For me, it's an ideal way."

"Did you ever wish you could take some time off?"

"No. Of course, not many people growing up don't have some parent or someone to come in for them. We did for many years—like she (Frances motioned towards the apartment where Allen's ninety-two-year-old mother was staying), you know. When we first started, we took turns on Sundays. She (Allen's mother) and Lee stayed one Sunday and then Allen and I would stay the next Sunday. And there aren't many families that wouldn't have the same set-up. (A bell went off in my head then, and I thought: This is the reason that stores owned by out-of-staters seem to turn over so fast. They don't have their parents or relatives here to lend them a hand.) It's only tiring when you become one. Completely tiring. So that's the best I can say. I've loved every minute of it."*

---

*Frances Tuttle eventually sold her store, but the new owners made some changes that might have contributed to its eventual demise. They took out the gas pumps, phased out the boots and clothing, started selling beer, then shortened their business hours.

For several weeks during the summer of 1990 they had a yard sale in front of the store as they tried to sell off a lot of the dry goods. It was as if they were selling off the old general store's soul—making it just one more mundane convenience store, like its rival down the road.

To be competitive, a country store needs to be open at six o'clock in the morning and remain open until at least nine at night. A friend told me the new owners didn't open until eight; and , they even took a vacation and closed the store for a week!

And if a country store is going to sell beer, the beer cooler needs to be near the front of the building so patrons can "get their beer and go." The new owners placed the beer cooler in the rear of the store, almost as if they felt guilty in breaking Tuttle's long tradition of not selling alcoholic beverages. I wondered, also, if by bringing in beer, they didn't drive off much of the older clientele that had stopped there just because Tuttle's never had been a beer store.

During the summer of 1991, Frances Tuttle would occasionally honk her car horn at me as I ran along Route 1 in Gouldsboro. She was finally free of the old store routine and out and about Downeast. The people who had bought Tuttle's Store were gone; bankrupt was what I had heard. Still, the perennials in Frances's flower garden at the store bloomed all summer as expected, almost as if they too were waiting patiently to greet a new owner. I sure hope so!

# CHAPTER 11

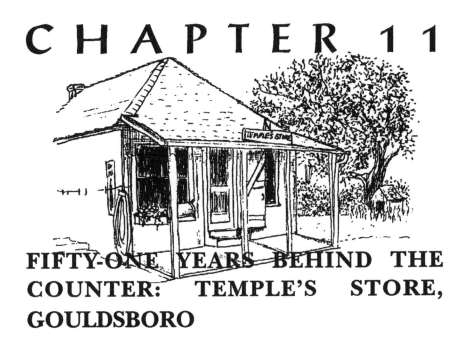

# FIFTY-ONE YEARS BEHIND THE COUNTER: TEMPLE'S STORE, GOULDSBORO

Temple's Store, a tiny, one-room building with green asphalt shingle siding, and a wooden porch with bare light bulbs strung along its roof overhang, stands on Route 1 in Gouldsboro. The store closed in 1981, but Leitha Joy, a trim, eighty-nine-year-old woman with a keen sense of humor, ran Temple's for fifty-one years from 1930-1981. Mrs. Joy is one of my links to the past.

I had been trying to get some idea what this stretch of the Maine coast was like at various periods in the early twentieth century, and by talking to people of different ages and generations, I began to get some sense of the World War I era, the Great Depression, the 1940s, the 1950s. And what did it matter? Well, I think we need that continuity. We need to know something of the past to understand the present. I'm not old enough to remember too far back, but the Maine I remember in the early 1960s didn't seem too much different from the Maine Mrs. Joy and others told me about. And according to an editorial by Davis Thomas in the January 1989 issue of *Down East* magazine, one only had to go back to the early 1950s to find a Maine that was "insular"—like an island, cut off from the rest of the country.

Thirty-five years ago when this magazine first saw the light of day, Maine was a far different place than it is today. Isolated, even insular, it lagged behind the nation's quickening pace of economic and cultural advance. There were those who liked it that way, of course. But for many Mainers, prospects were not encouraging. Heavily rural, Maine ranked near the bottom of the forty-eight state roll call in most social and economic indexes. The state's major cities which had flourished in the nineteenth century were languishing in decay. The leather and textile industries were headed south, leaving unemployment in their wake. More than 600 one-room schoolhouses still dotted the countryside, and less than $500 per student was spent annually on primary and secondary education. The brightest of the younger generation fled the state each year at graduation time. Rivers ran foul and the environment was seriously at risk.

If Maine really was as isolated as the *Down East* editorial suggested—and I believe it was—then it stands to reason that a very unique culture would have developed here. The use of the word "insular" in the *Down East* article intrigued me. It made me think of the hills, coves, and valleys of Appalachia—of eastern Kentucky and West Virginia—where linguists have suggested that the regional dialect is the closest one can  get in America to pure Elizabethan English.  The idea being, that back in the 1700s, indentured servants—originating in England's poor urban areas—simply ran away from Tidewater Virginia plantations and hid away for generations in the coves and valleys of Appalachia, allowing a unique culture to develop in isolation, as well as preserving the traditional dialect.

Could parallels be drawn between isolation in Appalachia and insularity in eastern Maine?  I think there could.  But, unfortunately, the homogenization that began in the 1960s threatened to erase all that was unique to the Downeast area by the late 1980s. The older generation was my link to coastal Maine's insular past, and I wanted to talk to some elderly people and grab hold of that vanishing culture before it was gone.

We were sitting at the kitchen table of Mrs. Joy's modest house, which stands just to the west of her old store building.  And as we talked, I could hear wind chimes sounding in the breeze, and occasional traffic on Route 1.

I asked Mrs. Joy if they used to make home deliveries from Temple's Store.

"My father, Billy Temple, did. He had a pickup truck in the 'forties and 'fifties. I remember way back when I was a girl and they had dry goods on wheels. They had big long drawers they pulled out, with all sorts of underwear—house dresses. They wore house dresses then."

Words falling into disuse; a whole way of life disappearing; an old store building falling into obsolescence: There had been many changes.

Mrs. Joy said, "I don't know our next door neighbors. In the old days we always used to be neighbors, you know. If I needed a potato I could borrow it. If anybody needed to borrow they'd come. We'd go to our neighbors, spend an hour or so. Possibly we had our children with us and we'd have lunch. We don't do that anymore. We have to go to Ellsworth or Bangor to get something to eat now."

"Do you still go to the baked bean suppers at the Gouldsboro Grange?"

"I went Saturday night."

"Those suppers seem to be as popular as ever."

"That too, was surprising—the few people we knew. I sold tickets and I don't think there was more than twenty people out of a hundred and forty that I knew. And I've been here all my life. People have moved in."

Baked bean and casserole suppers are a Downeast tradition. For a flat price—usually four or five dollars—you can sample several types of baked beans, casseroles, cole slaw, potato salad, brown bread, choice of homemade pies, tea, coffee, or Kool-Aid. What has always impressed me about bean suppers is not so much the hearty food—it is usually very good—but the way it is served. Unlike the South, where communal dinners such as this are always done buffet-style with people lining up and filling their own plates, the hallmark of the bean supper is service. Everyone is seated at long tables—like picnic tables—and at five o'clock sharp, the servers—always local women—begin bustling in and out of the kitchen with hot and cold food. And don't those women work! "What can I get you dear? Some more coffee?

Some beans? Some brown bread? What kind of pie would you like, dear? There's blueberry, strawberry, lemon, chocolate, and apple." And the people eat fast and furious—no lingering over coffee and dessert. That's just not done. They're out the door by five-thirty. Got to make room for the second wave!

"There was a good crowd," Mrs. Joy said. "There was a couple of tables set up a second time. That means a whole lot of extra work. Had plenty of food."

My wife, Linda, a native of Arkansas, wrote the following account of a Downeast bean supper.

> I'll never forget one bean supper I went to. It was a very hot day and only two or three women were serving a room full of tables loaded with people. I have a vivid memory of watching one woman racing around with small bowls of food, huffing and puffing, the sweat rolling down her flaming red cheeks— a sure sign of overexertion. It was almost painful to watch her. I was used to the long, leisurely buffets of the South where you went along the buffet table and didn't feel the need to rush. Sitting at the bean supper you would eye a small bowl being passed from the other end of your table and wonder if it would make it to your plate with anything in it. There was an element of high tension.

We have been advised by a neighbor who attends bean suppers regularly that the best ones are usually early in the season. It seems that the women get "burned out" on bean suppers and by the end of the summer you're apt to get a lot of tuna casseroles or similar bland dishes prepared in haste.

Mrs. Joy looked towards the front window and said, "This is my favorite chair to look over towards the store. And when the tide is right, you can see clammers stopping there to get gas." She was referring to the Gouldsboro Grocery, a country store just down the road. I said, "It used to be that you couldn't dig clams in the summer because that's when they reseed."

"You've heard the old story, haven't you? Not to eat the clams unless there's an "R" in the month. The older folks—you wouldn't get them to eat any clams in the summertime."

"The diggers have forgotten all about that now," I said. "And they're in trouble."

"You're right. Well, like so many other things, I guess. I remember the saying, but I don't think I paid much attention to it if I wanted clams. But the older people really did."

I asked Mrs. Joy if she used to extend credit to customers.

"Did we! We're still giving it. It's still out. Lost it."

"You still haven't collected it? Well, maybe you'll still get it."

"I forgot it long ago," Mrs. Joy laughed.

"Was that a problem—getting them to pay up?"

"With a few. And others, you could let them have all they'd want. It wouldn't be much. Things were so much cheaper then. It wasn't too bad if they needed credit in the winter for four months. And you knew all your customers. Now I don't know anyone. I imagine that's why they have to be so careful on checks now. I never had too much trouble. I don't know as I ever had a check bounce—yes, I had one bounce."

"That's all? In fifty-one years?"

"Only one."

"Did your store ever get broken into?"

"Many times. And my father was broken into many, many times. I remember one time—I lived over at this next house. (She motioned to a nearby house.) My father used to come over and have supper with us. And while he was over there, they broke in—beer and cigarettes. It was someone who knew him well enough. They knew his habits. He'd be gone about an hour. They came in the side window.

"But he did have a strange thing happen. A customer used to come in with a baby carriage. He had a habit of coming in, so he put his groceries and everything else in the carriage with the baby, and the groceries were underneath. What he had stolen was underneath the baby. The officers found it."

"So he probably had been doing that all along?"

"Yes, my father just thought he was coming in with the baby, you know. But this time it was broken into. Nice way to start raising a baby!"

Mrs. Joy grew up in a white Cape Cod house along the granite coast in Prospect Harbor. We talked about her childhood; how she became a teacher.

She said, "There was no high school in Gouldsboro, but if anyone wanted to go, the town would pay the tuition to go to any high school they wished."

"Where was the nearest high school back then?"

"Winter Harbor. There wasn't too many people who went to high school in those days. Back in the tens and fifteens (1910-1915) very few started. I think there were twenty-two in my class. That was a big class that started in 1915. And five of us went through to graduation in 1919.

"We had nine grades. I taught school for a while after I finished high school. Most of the folks were eighteen or nineteen when they graduated. And we had good pay in those days. I used to get fifteen dollars a week. And I paid five dollars a week for board. And what did I have left? Ten dollars. You had to stretch that ten dollars. But food and clothing didn't cost anything then. You could go and get a big grocery bag—full of groceries—for a dollar or a dollar and a half."

I left Temple's Store and took a turn down Chicken Mill Road, a mile long section of old Route 1. The state used to maintain a small picnic area on the tiny pond here, but when Route 1 was re-routed in the late 1960s, they just let the park return to bush. Nowadays, the Bartlett Maine Estate Winery lies up in the woods across from the old picnic area. They make fruit wines from local blueberries, apples, and the like, and they seem to be doing well. This is the "new" Maine, of course, another business started by people from away.

It was late afternoon and threatening rain. I had one more country store to visit in Hancock County, but decided to leave that for the very next morning. I returned to the camp and then it started to pour. But I took my afternoon run anyway, while the rain fell in great sheets and the wind whipped the deciduous trees so that all I saw were the undersides of their leaves. I ran through the village of West Gouldsboro, past Chan Noyes' old store and all the way up to the top of Beech Hill, where on a clear day, you can look across Frenchman's Bay to the glacier-scoured peak of Schoodic Mountain. On this day, I saw nothing.

I stood waist-deep in the pond that afternoon, the fifty-six degree air feeling much colder as the wind stirred up whitecaps across the water. I began to hoot and holler like a frantic loon, to wave my arms, and pretend I was playing the violin, the trombone, the trumpet, the piano. Linda appeared at a front window of the camp and I began making silly faces at her. There was smoke

coming out of the chimney and the camp looked warm and inviting through the rain-soaked woods.

It would have been a good day to sit around an old pot-bellied stove in a country store somewhere, listening to locals tell their stories. Except . . . I still hadn't found a country store—not one— that had an old pot-bellied stove. Maybe those days were gone forever.

# CHAPTER 12

## THE GOOSE WITH THE ARROW THROUGH IT: DICK'S DISCOUNT GROCERY, GOULDSBORO

**"I**n the mountains of rural Arkansas, my grandmother, then only sixteen, married my grandfather, who was much older. Together, they had seven children. My grandfather died from complications with diabetes when my father, one of the younger children, was only seven years old. My grandmother had to run the farm and raise her children alone.

"Some years later, there was a man in the community who wanted to marry her. So my grandmother asked her sons what she should do. With the exception of my father, who told her to do whatever she wanted to do, they all said, 'No, no one could replace our father.' My grandmother acquiesced to her sons' sentiments. In telling this story, my mother said, 'I never knew who the man was who proposed to her, but on thinking of all the available men in the community—not one could have shined her shoes!'"

My wife, Linda, told me this story after we had visited Dick's Discount Grocery on Route 1 in Gouldsboro. I'm not sure how we had gotten on the subject, but we had been talking to Janet Hankins, a store clerk, about marriage; about marriages breaking up; about the availability of marriage partners. Marriage is a risky venture in any environment these days, but rural women seem to have it especially hard. Couples still marry young; men still prefer younger women; older women who divorce, or simply miss their chance may never marry at all. One academic study made national headlines when it suggested that women over thirty-five have a better chance of being victims of a terrorist attack than finding a husband.

"If I get divorced, that's it, I'm not trying again," Janet Hankins said, that day at Dick's Grocery. "My brother, both brothers, matter of fact, they was married. One was divorced after six years. My other brother was married three years and they got divorced. I said, 'Forget it. I'm staying together.'"

"It's too much trouble," I said.

"Really. Go find somebody else. You know, break 'em in, all that stuff. No."

"It's not worth it," Linda added.

"I'd go on my own," Janet said. "You know, always find something to do that was different—people to be with. No. I tell him I can't get rid of him. He says the same about me. And with the little girl; I don't think that he'd ever leave. We get along so good. But it's hard for me 'cause I work out here (country store) during the day quite a bit, and then in the evening I help. And he works all day and in the evening he doesn't want to help. 'Cause he's worked all day. We try to switch around so everybody gets a little time off. It is time consuming."

"Is your husband from around here?"

"Yeah, he's from three miles that way. (She pointed west.) Yeah, we grew up together. That was a kind of odd occurrence. We used to play out here when we was four or five, then we got married. That's kind of neat. I didn't have to find out who he was or what he was. I think we kind of acquired each other. I think my mother even babysitted him a few times. So I said, 'That's pretty good.' Said, 'Good enough for you. Good enough for me.' We finally have a little one."

Janet was in her twenties. She was short, and had long, straight brown hair, and a friendly, unpretentious way about her. She was the sort of person that you immediately like. Janet had studied computers and bookkeeping for two years at a college in Florida, and she did all the paperwork for the country store. Her knack for conversation gave the store a pleasant ambiance customers came and went in a good mood. It was the sort of store where you didn't mind standing around and talking for a while.

"I try to read the paper first thing so I have something to pick up with somebody that comes in. Even if they come in a grumpy mood, you get them smiling before they go out. That's what we try to do."

"So you don't discourage people from hanging around and talking?"

"Oh, no. We've got a chair over there that quite a few people use. They're not the rowdy ones staying, but old-timers—they come in. Breaks up the day for us too. It's the place everybody comes with gossip. If we haven't heard it, I guess it hasn't happened."

"How did you like living in Florida?"

"I loved the beach! (laugh) I didn't like the people, though. It was like they set you in the middle of an island and people walked around you—is what you felt like. You said 'Hi' to them and they go, 'What do you want?' You know? Like up here in Maine, you help somebody out. They weren't like that down there. They wondered what a young person wanted—how much money—for doing this."

"A price for everything down there?"

"Yeah. And you just didn't fit in. They knew you was 'country' all the way. Like, 'Guess they don't fit in with us.'"

("They knew you was country," I liked that phrase; I ran it over in my head. How did they know they were country? Do country people look or sound different? What subtle mannerisms would have given them away?)

A customer came in, so I looked around. I was surprised at all I found—fishing supplies, hardware, magazines, movies for rent, and pocket knives. "We have a variety of things—more than a grocery-type store," Janet said. "We've got marine hardware. We've got a full line of fishing supplies. We're the only store around that has that quantity of fishing stuff. Nobody in Milbridge has it."

"How did you decide what to sell? Did you experiment?"

"We looked around at what people didn't have," Janet explained. "Mainly, you kind of listen around. People say, 'Well, you should have this.' And if you hear it enough, then you give it a try. We were skeptical of movies. Where everybody had them, you know. But people kept coming in. 'Geez, we don't have to go to such and such a place to get a movie now.' Well, if they want movies, we'll give them movies. And they've treated us good on that."

"So you're moving towards a real general store?"

"Well, we've always been that. Like we raised a garden and we had extra potatoes. We want to sell potatoes—bring potatoes right out here. And we sell fresh berries in the summer."

A customer said, "You know this little tiny store down here— Temple's Store? Well, Billy Temple, he used to have a meat wagon—horse and buggy. Have the whole cow hung up in there— big pieces. He'd have his butcher stuff right there. He sold so many pounds of it—cut it off, saw it off, whatever, package it— there you go—right at your house—horse and buggy!"

We talked about town politics, taxes, and the rising price of shore property. And, as was often the case at country stores, the conversation gravitated towards out-of-staters.

"There's an out-of-stater down at Gouldsboro Point with a two-hundred thousand dollar house and he has geese all over his front lawn," the customer said. "Why he'd have all those geese shit'n all over his lawn and gettin' on his shoes, I don't know? And bringing it into the house on your shoes. Geez! And the geese go over to the yard of the guy next door and mess up his yard. Geez! And it got to where whenever he saw them coming he'd let his dog out. The geese would come home without feathers."

Janet said, "One of those geese has an arrow right through it. Strangest thing I've ever seen. Someone said, 'Look, that one's got an arrow stuck in it!' Yeah, I thought it must have been one of those fake arrows. I didn't believe it 'til someone showed me, but you could grab hold of both ends of the arrow and pick the goose up. Someone shot it, and it went right through and stuck without hitting any of the vital organs. So they just left it there. It would probably kill it if they ever pulled it out. Geez, somebody needs to put that story in a book."*

---

*Dick's Discount Grocery was out-of-business by 1989.

# Part Two

## Steuben——Jonesboro
## Washington County

# CHAPTER 13

# CAT'S TAIL UP THROUGH THE GRASS: STEUBEN, THEN AND NOW

F
rom Dick's Grocery, at the intersection of Route 1 and the Gouldsboro Point Road, it is only a quarter of a mile to Washington County. I know for a fact that it's a quarter of a mile, because back in the 1960s, when I was in high school, it was painted on Route 1. "The Quarter Mile" was where locals used to drag race. That tells you how little traffic there was on Route 1 twenty years ago. The "Sunrise County," as Washington is called, is the eastern-most county in the United States. It is also Maine's poorest county, with twenty-five percent of its residents on food stamps in 1980.

A right turn on to old Route 1 took me across Whitten Parritt Stream and into Steuben, my home town. When I was growing up here in the 1960s, we kids used to spend summer days hanging around Roger Smith's Store—the yellow store mentioned on the first page of this book—and Peter Moore's Auto Body Shop, which was just up the street. This area was the commercial and social hub of Steuben (970 residents in 1980). Entertainment was provided by locals who specialized in "squealing tires," peeling out of Peter's, leaving patches of rubber. Theater! Later, when the excitement had died down, we'd get bottles of pop at Roger's, grab our fishing rods, and head over to Tunk Stream, where we'd catch eels and "sling them up on Route 1, so's we could watch the cars flatten 'em."

In the late 1960s, Moore's Auto Body Shop burned to the ground, even though the volunteer fire department was next door. Moore's was rebuilt on a new site across the  street, but burned again a few years later. Roger's Store changed hands in the early 1970s and it too was destroyed by fire. The new owners reopened the store in a portion of the fire house and it burned to the ground in 1976!

Both the fire house and Moore's Auto Body Shop were eventually rebuilt along new Route 1, while a modern, ranch-style bungalow now stands where Roger's Store had stood.

The old yellow general store—which had meant so much to me—its front windows adorned with Tetley Tea signs and local notices, had been the  community information center; the neighborhood gathering place.  Certainly the store's demise left a void, but more importantly, it had served as a nucleus, or core, to which all of the town's appendages—its widely scattered population— adhered.  Put another way: The village store, like a good school system, or perhaps a strong local government acted as a centripetal force that helped to fuse the townspeople's whims and differences into a community.

So I drove through the  village, past the road leading to the old town wharf where we used to swim; past "Dizzy Rock" on Tunk Stream, where we used to catch chubs; past the post office, village green, church, school, and Parish House; across Route 1 and on to the East Side Road.

Florence (Flossie) Vasquez is the oldest woman I know. She was born in 1891 and still remembers when they put the railroad through Unionville, five miles north of Steuben. Flossie lives in Steuben, in a tiny green trailer on the East Side Road. It is an old trailer, but neat and cozy inside. A porch room was added years ago, and it was here that her son, Bill, a correspondent for the *Bangor Daily News*, had set up his word processor. I went to see Flossie near the end of May, when the poplar trees in the woods behind her trailer were just sprouting their leaves, and the lilacs all around it were beginning to bloom.

I had never seen anyone so old before, and I was fascinated by Flossie's face, the way her skin had been creased by time. Despite her age, she remained alert and energetic. She was thin and still attractive, and I thought: How beautiful she must have been many years ago as a young woman.

Flossie was eager to talk, and for this I was most grateful, because few people—young or old—have her gift for conversation. I also knew that it was her nature to take an interest in what others were doing, and when I told her I was writing a book, Flossie said, "Well, you knew I would help you, didn't you?"

"Oh, yes."

"I know the older Steuben," Flossie began. "The people worked hard. They were good people. They helped each other. You know, I started school when I was four and a half up on the 'Island.' I walked two miles through the woods."

The Island that Flossie speaks of is not an island in the traditional sense. Rather, it is an inland island, on high ground, between two streams. It is up, in that you travel uphill along the East Side Road to reach it. Years ago, before the blueberry fields on the Island had grown up in second-growth brush, you could look down at Steuben village and see the church steeple on the green, and the bay beyond.

Years later, when her own grandchildren were in school, Flossie said she was asked to speak about her early schooling to students at Milbridge High School. "And the children asked me, 'Bears?' 'No, they won't hurt you. You don't go between a cub and her mother and you'll be all right. The old bear will wag its head and watch you.' 'Wildcats?' 'No.' 'Wolves?' 'No.' 'Did you see them?' 'Yes.' 'Deer?' 'Oh, they're harmless. They're beautiful things.' 'You weren't afraid?' 'No.' And there were no street lights. There was a lantern, an old barn lantern, hung out at the end of our driveway. There was only two houses up there. It was up there on the Island. My grandfather owned one and we had the other one."

"Now is that near Aunt Minnie's house?"

"Yes! That's the one! That's where I was born. That was a beautiful old house."

A few summers ago, Linda and I hiked up the East Side Road, crossed a stream at the end of a beaver heath, and fought our way through the thick alders—deer flies and mosquitoes fierce—to the Island.

"I know Aunt Minnie's house is around here somewhere," I kept saying, but there was no house. It had vanished. We couldn't even find the foundation.

"No, it went down," Flossie said. "It just went into cellar. (An old expression) There used to be a log  put across the stream, chiseled off so you could walk across, and we could come through Grampy's field. And Grammy would see us coming and she always made a raisin pudding and steamed it in a nice molasses sauce for us. And she said she could always see the cat's tail up through the grass ahead of us. And the school children in Milbridge couldn't believe that I went to school when I was four and a half. 'No buses?' 'No, you walked.' 'No school lunches?' 'No, you brought your lunch in a little tin five pound lard pail. Put it behind the stove to keep warm.' 'Wood fires?' 'Yes.' 'No electric lights?' 'No, kerosene lamps.' Why they were amazed that was how we started school when we came down here." (Down to Steuben from the Island)

"Why did they call that the Island?"

"Well, that was the Island because you've got the river (Tunk Stream) on that side, and you had a brook on this side, and there was a little jet of land and that was almost surrounded by water. And this (Steuben village) was the head of the bay. And they'd always say, 'Got to go down to the head of the bay.'"

"Coming downtown—into Steuben then?"

"That was coming to the head of the  bay, 'cause you see, we're at the head of Gouldsboro Bay here." (Nobody except the old people used these expressions anymore.  In the past, people's speech had been more in tune with the land and sea.)

"There must have been a lot of houses up on the East Side Road back then," I said. "I've seen the old foundations, the old wells, and the roses, lilacs, and apple trees that grow where the houses once stood."

"Oh, yes."

"What do you supposed happened to all those houses up there?"

"'But, you see, they burned. (What didn't burn in this town?) Cecil Smith had a beautiful old house there, but it went in cellar. And, have you been in to Number Seven?"

"Last summer."

"Don't go. It looks like Tobacco Road. It used to be such a pretty village."

Number Seven is the name that people in Steuben use for Township Seven. Number Seven is simply a paved road, three miles long, that ends at Whitten Parritt Stream. You turn off the Smithville Road and travel west, into the woods. It is not really part of Steuben, but residents of Number Seven attend Steuben Grammar School and get their mail from Steuben. Once there had been a mill, a school, and a substantial community at Number Seven, but like many tiny places in backwoods Maine, the village has deteriorated into a landscape of mostly old ruins.

"My grandfather owned the schoolhouse he built at Number Seven, and he kept it in perfect condition—always painted red, and it was clean. And as I told the school children over in Milbridge, 'There was a pail of water, and there was a dipper hung on the side, and we all drank out of the same dipper. We had a roll of towel; we could wash our faces and we all wiped on the same towel. And we didn't get cooties!'

"The old school burned. There's not a school house standing that I went to school in. The one down here (Steuben), they moved over somewhere and built the new one. The one  in Number Seven was torn down.

"There were sixteen beautiful homes at Number Seven. Well, there's the Isabel Davis house—it's still standing, and that Perry's, and two others, that's all. And now that fella has that junkyard there—where there used to be an old log cabin that Raym Dunbar owned. And her curtains were always starched and a soft lamplight was shining through. And sometimes we'd be going into Number Seven and Papa'd say, 'It looked so I'd ought to stop and go in— looked so comfortable.' They'd say, 'Why don't you come in?' And he'd say, 'Well, I have to get home, you know.' The houses looked so nice, and their yards, nice. You didn't climb their apple trees either. That was their taxes."

"What do you mean?"

"Oh, they'd say, 'Uncle Jack Tracy and Andrew Leighton will tell you about it if you climb those trees.' Those were their taxes. They sold those apples, you know. Someone came from Massachusetts and packed them, and they would send them. That was their tax money."

As a teenager, I had noticed the many apple trees growing wild around the bays and fields in Steuben. I used to pick several baskets of them each fall—all different varieties, many that I have never seen anywhere since—and my mother made apple sauce and pies. But nobody in Steuben sold them then. The apple trees—always needing pruning and spraying for worms—seemed like part of the town's forgotten past.

"They were hardworking people," Flossie continued. And all helping each other. And when we came down here from the Island, Ella Lewis was our first Sunday School teacher, for whom the Steuben Elementary School was named. And she was a dear person. She was a good Sunday School teacher and she played the organ in the church. We wouldn't think of missing Sunday School. And often we went to church with mother. Dad, often, he'd play his banjo, sing his favorite hymn, 'On a hill far away / Stands an old rugged cross/ Emblem of suffering and shame.' Dad loved that. They said when he went to Boston on board his boat—when he was in there to get loaded—he'd go to the old Seaman's Bethel and play his banjo, sing hymns, get the old seamen in. He loved to do that.

"And he was in the Steuben Dramatic Club. (This surprised me! Steuben once had a dramatic club! How this town had gone down!) Every time Dad came home from a trip they'd have a ministrel show. He'd play his banjo, sing old sea chanties. You know, the night I was born—they say the last day of March was the worst snowstorm we had all winter. And papa was in a ministrel show up to Uncle John Smith's Hall, where the Grange used to have suppers. And they said he wore himself out, running back and forth to see if I was born yet or not. It was the worst storm of the winter. I said, 'That would be me. I'd choose that kind of a day!'"

"Do you remember much about the old country stores in Steuben?"

"Oh, goodness, yes! In Noyes' Store—in the back of it—was a sign that said: OUR QUALITY IS HIGH. OUR PRICES ARE LOW."

Flossie told me that Noyes' Store had burned. And when I asked her where it had stood, I suddenly realized that she was talking about Roger's Store! The old store that I had always known as Roger Smith's Store had once been owned by Len

Noyes. Flossie remembered another sign: STOCK IS HIGH. PRICES ARE LOW. ASK FOR CREDIT AND OUT YOU GO!

"There was Len Whitten's Store. That was on the other side of Len Noyes' and that burned too. And there was Rob Dutton's, right across the street almost and that burned. (I guess Steuben was always famous for its fires!) And Dora Smith, over here where Irving Parritt had the store right afterwards—that used to be Jeanette Leighton's mother's store."

"Hod Haskell told me he had a store there in the 1940s," I said.

"Yes, and they always made and sold ice cream. There was no trying to crowd each other out. All those stores made a living."

Once there had been five general stores in the village of Steuben, Flossie explained, and now all of those were gone. There was now a new country store on Route 1 in Steuben, called Mathews', and there was Ray's Meat Market, on the Dyer's Bay Road, but the village—what we as kids had called "Downtown Steuben"—was without a store.

Flossie showed me some black and white photographs of the town at the turn of the century. A grist mill, a group of loggers (she knew them all by name), stately homes painted white, her mother, her grandmother, and then herself: The picture was taken in 1913 when she was twenty-two. Flossie's great grand-mother was born in Portugal. Flossie's husband's family had come from Spain, and I thought, how unusual; most Downeasters have British or Irish surnames.

"There's me with one of my little grandchildren. That's my Bill (son). There's two girls we worked with up Kennebago. That's me up to Union, Maine. I'd just had the flu and I was knitting. That's some girls I worked with. And that's Uncle Thomas's family in Spain. And this is a play I was in: "Rocking Chair Row." I was Mrs. Take-um Pills. We made six hundred dollars with that play. We bought a new heater and a gas range for the church parson-age. And that's Captain Curtis. We were on picnic over the weekend. Look at our bathing suits. They covered you up."

"I should say so."

"And there was no dope selling. There was no liquor. Oh, once in a while a boy would drink, but almost never. And we'd go to a dance and there was no drinking. And there was no police protection. You didn't need it.

"And you didn't have to be rich or poor. You were all the same. And it isn't what you do; it's the kind of person you are. And Dad (Louis, her husband) and I never got rich, but we never had any trouble."

Flossie told me a story about a black man whom some local fishermen had found after a shipwreck.

"There was a colored family lived up here. A boat coming in had gone ashore. They didn't know what his name was so they called him Ed Over. He had a wife who was part Indian and part colored. And they lived up in Joe Cleaves's old house that he had for the caretakers of his farm. And her curtains were always sparkling white. And her apron shiny; and she always had a hot bisquit or homemade sourdough bread; and cheese that she made herself for us kids when we'd go up there. And Ed—Mr. Over—would come along and they'd be selling clams. He'd dug them, shelled them out, and was selling them. Papa'd say, 'Well, come in Ed, and eat supper. Then you can finish shelling your clams.' We didn't say, 'You've got to eat in the barn, you're colored.' He was clean, had good table manners. And when he and his wife died, Aunt Hannah Shaw, that lived down there on the hill, brought up Blanche Over, one of his children. And Aunt Mary Dutton brought up the other one, Edie. And Aunt Hannah had a project each year to raise money and all of us kids went. We made a quilt top one year; knitted a pair of stockings. I might have got them on a doll, but they wouldn't fit anybody else. But she always had us do something that'd teach you. And you didn't say, 'I can't come, Blanche Over's colored.' They were Steuben, those old families. My Aunt Hannah Shaw, Aunt Mary Dutton, Ada Noyes; that was Steuben. They made Steuben caring and sharing. Well, they started the Sidewalk Society."

The Steuben Sidewalk Society was established in 1988 for the purpose of raising money to build boardwalks around the village green. In those days the streets were dirt and it was easy for women to collect dust and mud on their long dresses. The ladies raised the money to build the sidewalks by putting on summer fairs, a tradition that continues today. I attended the 1988 summer fair, which celebrated a "century of service" to the community. As always, the ladies served tea at small tables inside the Steuben Parish House and sold fancy work, quilts, baked goods, house plants, and white elephants (odds 'n ends). The fair was a huge success; it was elbow to elbow in the Parish House, especially at the baked goods table.*

The wooden sidewalks have long since disappeared. But upstairs in the Parish House is an elegant wood-panelled room where the Society has always met. On one wall is an oil painting of a boy fishing in a stream that my mother painted and donated to the Society when she was a member in the 1960s. There are other pictures hanging on the walls too—scenes from a Greek drama, memorabilia from the Victorian era. Even the furniture—wicker, of course—dates from that period. And the smell—a distinct odor of musty books and old wood—takes you back in time.

"And Jeanette Leighton taught school. And when we were in church—carol Sundays—Christmas carols—she taught us those. Aunt Hannah played the organ and Aunt Sarah helped us with our singing. And they did things for the children. You were all together. You didn't say, 'Well, your father cleans toilets,' and things like that. 'I can't associate with you.' You didn't say anything—you just went along with the crowd."

"So there were no class differences?"

"No, and there shouldn't be. No."

Flossie told me another story; this one about an Indian family that once lived in a log cabin in Number Seven.

"Yes suh. My grandmother was sick with sort of a debilitating illness and the Indians found out she was sick. And the older woman came in, looked her all over, and they went out in the woods. They came back with this little handful of herbs, put them on the stove and steeped them. And it wasn't any time before she was feeling better. Or they'd kill a deer when Grampy was sick;

---

*Membership in the Sidewalk Society had been declining over the years—lifelong members were simply dying off—and 1987 was the first year in the Society's history that the annual fair was not held. The centennial celebration seems to have breathed new life into the organization, however, as membership doubled to twenty in 1988. Perhaps another reason for the Society's rebirth is the enthusiasm of its current president, a young woman who moved here in the early 1970s. Like many of the newcomers, she has brought new ideas and energy to the organization. For example, the Society sponsored a historical play, written by a member, and put on by the Girl Scouts in April of 1988, and a large public dinner in May. Through its fund-raising activities the Society has contributed to the volunteer fire department (In Steuben, a very worthy cause!), the ambulance corps, the church, and school system.

bring some fish, bring a rabbit, for broth, you know. And, no, there was no class distinction. And it's too bad, because we cheated the Indians. They were here first. And we treated them badly. And my will is with the Indians."

"They deserve their share." I said.

"They sure do. Well, we've all got a right to earn a living. And these people that come in and buy up the shore property think they own everything."

"You have to be wealthy just to live on the shore now." I added.

"Who wants to be wealthy? I don't. All I want is enough to pay my bills, help my loved ones, and I want nothing more. And I'll share whatever I have. You can't buy your way to Heaven. And people who have a lot of money and think they can buy their way haven't got a toehold."

The conversation drifted along. We got into education and the public schools today. Flossie said, "They're not as good—no! And you know, Susan (great granddaughter) said they told her they didn't need to know their multiplication tables. Well, I said, 'Susan, I'd like to know when I go into a store and buy some groceries, how much it's going to cost. I'd want to be sure I had enough money to pay for it when I went out.'"

"Some of the country store owners tell me they can't find kids who can make change," I said. "And if the electronic cash register breaks down, they're finished, they don't know what to do."

"In my day they just took it out of the till—they counted it out. Now down to Len Noyes' (the old store), you bring him a load of wood; he'd give you credit for that load of wood. And that went toward what you were going to buy that winter. Or you bring in eggs or butter or vegetables—dried beans, things like that. And you could get food and exchange it for bills. No. You know these people on welfare. Bill (her son) wanted this man who is on welfare to do some work for him. He said, 'I can get more money being on the State than I can working for you.' I said, 'Yes, but you don't have as much self-respect as you would if you worked for yourself.' You know, I have no qualms about telling people what I think."

"Good for you! Somebody needs to tell them."

"Well, the unions have outlived their usefulness."

"How do you mean?"

"Well, I was in Doug's Shop 'N Save up to Ellsworth. They were on strike. They were selling that red and green lettuce—those big heads for fifty-nine cents. And I picked one up. And this girl, one of the strikers, she grabbed it right out of my hands. I grabbed it back and said, 'You get your dirty paws off of me!' She said, 'Well, they're selling that at below union price.' I said, 'No union owns me! Never will!' I went over and paid for it and put it in my bag and said, 'Don't you put your dirty paws on me again.'

"You know, my papa said, 'Nobody's going to own me.' God owned him. His soul belonged to God, but his body belonged to him. And his father would say, 'You're only as good as your word. And if your word isn't any good then you're no good.'"

"How do you like that big store?"

"I don't like the big stores. I'm used to the old country stores. And, you know, they don't wait on you today."

"Tuttle's is the only country store around where they still wait on you," I said.

"Yes, and I like to buy things over to Tuttle's. And Frances Tuttle is a dear person."

I asked Flossie if Steuben ever had an ice trade.

"No, they didn't sell much out of here. But they kept it so they could sell their frozen eels. When we first came down here they were still sending eels to Boston and New York. I'll tell you what, this river here (Tunk) used to be full of shad. They sold the shad roe and pickled mackerel, salt mackerel, salt fish—Oh, stacks of dried fish."

"There used to be a lot of flounder in the bay," I added.

"Well, we don't even get smelts now," Flossie said. "There weren't any over in Whitten Parritt Stream this spring."

"Jimmy Parkin and I used to always go down there and get smelts," I said.

"Yeah, wade right out there and net 'em. Well, I think spraying poison has a lot to do with it. If you asked these old woodsmen, or my grandfathers about the spruce budworm that came every year— it's like the locusts. And they said it would take care of itself if you'd leave the birds alone."

"What do you mean?"

"Well, you see, they're killing off the birds. And they wanted to kill off the sea gulls. They did up to Portland. And then the eel grass stopped growing. And the harbor was full of things the gulls used to eat, you see. And the gulls kept it cleaned up. They had to bring the gulls back."

Flossie was quite an environmentalist. She understood the food chain. She understood the interconnectedness of life on this planet. How ironic that she told me all these things on the eve of the summer that medical waste would come floating up on beaches all along the Atlantic, that drought and then record-breaking heat would have average people talking about the greenhouse effect and the destruction of the ozone layer. We were coming to the end of perhaps the most anti-environmental administration ever in Washington, and as the 1988 election campaign got underway, I began to wish our presidential hopefuls—any of them—had as good a grasp of ecology as this ninety-seven-year-old woman!

"But today—kill it! Get rid of it!"

"One thing leads to another," I said. "One thing feeds on another."

"Everything—every little animal on this earth, Jesus put here for a purpose. And one thing takes care of another. They got rid of the wolves. Now they're trying to get them back. And the coyotes—they tell about coyotes eating children. My uncle, he went out West. He was going to be a flashin'-dashin' cowboy. And he was afraid of cows and he didn't like horses too well, so he wasn't much of a success as a cowboy. And he came home, and he brought this little three-month-old coyote in his pocket. And Grampy Smith brought it up. It loved cold fried eggs. Back when I grew up, they'd put a big platter on the kitchen table with a slice of ham or bacon or just salt pork. And fried eggs—put up in the warming oven over the kitchen range. And we kids could take those fried eggs and eat them, all before noon. And what there was left, Grammie used to give to the coyote. And the cat wouldn't eat the cold fried eggs, but the coyote would. He lived with the cat, slept behind the stove, went to the barn each night. The cat would come when Grampy got home, and he'd pick her up in one hand and the milk pail in the other, and the coyote followed behind. And they'd go to the barn to milk. He'd give them a big pan of milk and they'd drink every bit of it. And the coyote didn't eat me.

"Grammy would say, 'I'm going to kill that coyote tomorrow.' He'd make, oh, the most unearthly noise at the moon. Oh, they make the worst noise. But she never killed it. It lived to be twelve years old. Just died a natural death. And it didn't eat anything but what we gave it. They'll pick a carcass clean before they'll kill again. The dogs that run wild kill more deer than the coyotes do. The dogs kill them and leave them. The coyotes kill to eat only. And a wolf doesn't hurt you. They'll come and watch you to the end of the woods and then they'll go back in. But you're in their territory."

I asked Flossie if she had ever traveled out of the state of Maine.

"Well, we went to Boston. Mama'd take us on the train. And I've been on the old Frank Jones out of Milbridge—old side-wheeler. Yeah, sure—fun. Papa'd be coming into Boston. And we'd go up and stay with my father's brother. And she'd take us and we'd go down on the boat, the old two-master, the old ship; the lumber boat, the one he was captain on. And we were up there (Boston) when the Portland (ship) went down. The City of Portland—we were almost on that boat. We planned to take it home. But we stayed over and came down on the train the next day."

An article in the April 17, 1989 issue of the *Bangor Daily News* stated that:

### Steamer Portland Wreck Found Off Massachusetts

BOSTON (AP) —Almost 91 years after disappearing without a trace, the Steamer Portland has been found on the bottom of the Atlantic off the Massachusetts coast, three oceanographers said.

"The find is particularly significant, not only because the Portland was one of the worst maritime disasters in the Northeast, but because it remained shrouded in mystery," said Paul Johnson of the Smithsonian Institution.

The ship had left Boston at 7 p.m. on the Saturday after Thanksgiving in 1898 enroute to Portland, Maine, with an estimated 160 passengers. The storm hit about three hours later. There were no survivors.

Before it ended, the storm claimed 456 lives and 141 vessels. Because of the missing sidewheeler, it came to be called the Portland storm. Bodies and flotsam from the ship washed ashore on Cape Cod.

Flossie was seven years old then.

"It wasn't your time," I said.

"Yeah, and for some unknown reason we weren't supposed to be drowned."

"I guess not."

"And those whose time hadn't come were saved."

\* \* \* \* \* \* \* \* \*

Almost three years after I interviewed Flossie, the following editorial appeared in the April 9, 1991 edition of *The Downeast Coastal Press:*

### FLOSSIE AND MARION

Few things can rival Spring for renewing one's faith in life, but even Spring, while first providing an unseasonably warm and sunny day last week, seemed to take a back seat to the radiance emanating from Florence "Flossie" Vasquez.

Family, friends and neighbors from all around gathered Thursday at the Henry D. Moore Parish House in Steuben to honor Flossie on the occasion of her 100th birthday, attained a few days earlier, and what a remarkable time it was. Sitting, smiling and rocking gently in a comfortable caneback chair in the meeting hall of that grand old building, not far from the refreshment table covered with trays of homemade desserts, Flossie greeted with enthusiasm all those who stopped by to extend to her their best. Young and old alike, she kissed and hugged and called them all by name, serving up great dollops of goodwill from her endless supply gathered over the past century.

As alert and healthy as ever, her mind razor-sharp, anyone lucky enough to attend could only be humbled in her presence. Aware of her age and seeing her physical agility and spirit (until now she has lived alone in her own home), one marveled at what appeared an apparition but yet what one knew to be an uncommon moving reality.

Selectman Handy Pinkham performed what little formality there was, presenting Flossie with a large custom made community greeting card, signed by a host of Steubenites who had stopped by the Town Office in the weeks leading up to the event. The homely document, once placed in her hands and accepted by Flossie with magnanimity and eagerness, suddenly became a gilded scroll.

It was a poignant moment when her longtime friend and neighbor, Marion Thurston, barely two years her junior, clad in a bright yellow two-piece suit worn specially for the occasion, entered the hall with the aid of a cane. (Marion is the holder of the Boston Post Cane in Steuben. Flossie, though the oldest resident of the community, had declined the honor which is presented to the town's most senior citizen, when offered to her a couple of years ago, saying typically, she felt "too young" to have it.)

When Marion's turn to pay her respects came and she extended her hand, Flossie grabbed her arm, drawing her to herself, sharing together the exchange of sentiments and the intimate moment. Flossie soon offered Marion an adjacent seat which Marion accepted, and where a moment before there had been one great light, there now were two. The simplest and noblest of gestures, it was a rare moment of astringent grace.

The news stories tell us that at about the same time all of this was occurring, on the other side of the world, at another reception and before a much vaster audience, former President Nixon and President Gorbachev were meeting and shaking hands. No doubt, important leaders such as these two men will have much to say, for good or ill, about Man's fate. But last week's reception in Steuben reminds us that it is not for the famous and mighty alone to determine such an eventuality.

Indeed, while such as Nixon and Gorbachev may have much to say about whether or not Man shall endure, we should not forget that ever so much more can be learned from Flossie and Marion to determine whether or not, in the words of Faulkner, Man, like Spring, is to prevail.

# CHAPTER 14

# SEA CUCUMBERS NEXT DOOR: MATHEWS' COUNTRY STORE, STEUBEN

From Flossie Vasquez I had learned about the old Steuben. I stopped at Mathews' Country Store on Route 1 to learn something about Steuben today. Once, the tall white building had been a garage. Then one side of it had been made into a fresh-seafood business. Now the large wooden structure contains three businesses: Mathews' Country Store, a pizza place, and a Japanese-owned sea cucumber processing factory. Strange bedfellows, I thought: pizza, sea cucumbers, steamed hot dogs and morning coffee; Downeasters and Japanese businessmen, under the same roof in this little town on the Maine coast. No one is an island today. Even this coast—3,500 miles long, with thousands of islands—is dependent on markets on the other side of the world. There's never been much steady work around here, but the Japanese have a yen for sea cucumber meat, and now Steuben has year-round employment.

According to an article I read in the July 26, 1988 issue of *The Downeast Coastal Press*, the sea cucumber plant employs thirty-five to forty local people. The meat, described as "crunchy and ocean-like, and resembling the taste of squid," is considered a delicacy—in greater demand than lobster—in Japan. California, once the sea cucumber capital of the United States, is said to be nearly fished out. So the rising demand in Japan, coupled with the increasing value of the Japanese currency, have prompted the Japanese to look to Maine as a new source of sea cucumbers.

The work is not pleasant. You cut off the head, slit open the sea cucumber, remove the innards, and scrape out the meat—for five dollars an hour. Then you expect to get sea cucumber dermatitis, a skin disease, characterized by rashes, and caused by toxins in the fish. Understandably, employee turnover has been high.

In keeping with my theme of country stores, I stayed clear of the sea cucumber factory. I stuck to Mathews' Store, and asked the girl behind the counter if she could tell me the difference between a sea urchin and a sea cucumber. "The sea urchin is a little prickly thing," she explained. "The sea cucumber is all slimey."

I talked to the store clerk about the usual things: what they sold, business hours, clientele. I was trying to get a feel for Mathews' Store, to see if it was anything like Roger's Store, the Steuben Grocery, that I had known so many years before. But it was nothing like Roger's. Mathews' was the modern-style convenience store—walk-in coolers, a few groceries, snacks, cigarettes, gasoline, and a fast-food counter. Nothing much to describe; nothing really to write about. My writing here would have to depend on luck; on the characters I met, and on what they had to say. Gary, a middle-aged man with a Scots-Irish look about him—reddish blond hair and rugged features—was a native of Steuben. He had been out-of-state for a while, he said, but was back home to harvest his blueberry ground. I asked Gary if he had ever eaten a sea cucumber.

"No, I never did. Have you tried one, Arvin?" Gary asked a short, grizzled man who had just come into the store.

"Yeah, it's a toss up between a raw clam and a raw scallop. Sautes up just like lobster does—same color, everything."

Gary said, "I know they used to let people go in and look around, didn't they, Arvin?"

"Yeah, if you have a weak stomach don't bother doing it."

I wondered why the Japanese had chosen Steuben. Gary said it was because of all the draggers that came in here. Arvin explained that Steuben was only one of several sea urchin and sea cucumber factories the Japanese had established Downeast.

"Oh, sea urchins, well, Goddamn—got one in Lubec, one in Harrington, one in Stonington. Now those are sea urchins. But there's only two sea cucumber places—this one, and one down on Rogers' Point in Steuben." Arvin never smiled; he never showed the least bit of warmth. I couldn't tell if he was annoyed by our ignorance, or if this was just his usual business-like demeanor.

"Well, they have strange tastes in Japan," I said. "I know they like horse meat."

"They've got so many people," Gary said. "I can't imagine anybody beating them on sea cucumbers and sea urchins. And sea urchins, they don't hardly get anything out of them at all. Boy, they put some money out for them! It's a big market. I had a chance to go over (to Japan) and try some of that stuff when I was in Vietnam, but I never did."

"Well, I guess they eat some wicked stuff over there in Vietnam," I said. "They even eat dogs."

"Well, I'll tell you—it's good," Gary said.

"You've had dog meat?"

"Yeah."

"What does it taste like?"

"Well, it's good meat. I don't know how to explain it. It's not much different than—actually, it's better than venison—you know, deer meat. It's got a little tang taste to it. But I liked it. Of course, when I first ate it I didn't really know what I was eating. Over there, I was trading my C-rations for it.

"I've had snake and different things. Half the stuff I wouldn't believe it if somebody told me after I ate it. You see, I used to live with the village people anyway. That's why I got to eat a lot of the stuff. I was in a combined action group—the South Vietnamese people, the South Vietnamese Army, and the Marines."

"What year were you over there?"

"I was there in '67, '68, and '69."

"Right there in the Tet Offensive!" I said.

"It was quite an experience, that's for sure," Gary added.

"Snake meat, huh?"

"You'd be surprised. They can put together so much stuff—the right spices—that really, it was good. I went to a lot of places where they invited us in—like for Thanksgiving—for special occasions. I enjoyed going into those places. They're awful hospitable and everything. It was really something."

"Have you ever had any desire to go back for a visit?"

"Uh, I'd like to go back to see what the land looks like. But I don't really want to go back to see strangers. They were nice, but I wouldn't even know where to go. The people that I'd see—they move around. If a storm comes in and blows their house down, they'll build some place else or migrate around. You'd never find them. Well, it's been since '69."

Gary had been able to come to terms with his Vietnam experience, but it had taken a long time. He had been interviewed ten or fifteen years earlier, he said, by a professor at the University of Maine. The professor was writing a book. He had promised Gary a copy. The book never came.

"Maybe he never finished it," I said.

"Yeah, I don't know what ever became of him. I'd like to see what he had to say about me. It bothered me a lot to talk about it until lately. I never really wanted to talk about it. Except for that time. He said he wanted to see how Americans felt—about being in the war. I told him everything I could. I think I had my stories mixed up a little—you know—because it was a job for me to get it out."

Gary had gone from Steuben to boot camp, to California, to Vietnam. He had planned on spending four years over there. "I didn't think I'd like state-side duty because of all the petty stuff—the spit-shined boots and all that. I wanted to be more or less in charge of myself."

I tried to imagine what it had been like for him—to leave this small Downeast village as a teenager, to join the Marines, to be thrust into combat in the Tet Offensive. I couldn't even imagine it! What courage he must have possessed! In comparison, my own experience seemed so insignificant.

I had gotten a lottery number in the three-hundreds and had gone off to college. For me it was a matter of luck. And how much different it might have been if I were three or four years older—Gary's age—and subject to the draft. Then what would I have done? By 1969, when I graduated from high school, the war had already become an unpopular cause. Nobody talked about winning it anymore. It had become pointless. Still, it pains me to look back and realize . . . that while most of my generation hardly noticed the war was going on, a small minority—like Gary—were fighting for their lives!

Might the outcome have been different? I wondered how Gary felt after all these years.

"Well, I don't know. In a different land like that—I don't see how. You may win today, but tomorrow it would be back the way it was."

"Why didn't we invade North Vietnam?"

"Yeah. Even invading those countries—we're on the other side of the world. How can you ever control it? You might be able to control it for a while, but eventually it would go back to the way it was. It was a matter of time. It was a lost cause. It was a lost cause before we ever started. It was all political anyway.

"What really gets me was about Westmoreland—when he said that what troops we had there—we were doing such a good job that we really didn't need to send in more people because we had it under control. And there we was—nowhere near under control. We were outnumbered almost ten to one. It's pretty bad when people have to lie and cost young people's lives."

\* \* \* \* \* \* \*

A woman named Ann, whom I had known for several years, came into the store. She had worked in South Portland for eight months, she said, then had shingled and stained a house in Connecticut. Ann is an independent woman. She's cut pulpwood, done carpentry, dug worms, raked blueberries, driven a truck, and managed a blueberry lease. She has long blond hair, is medium height and build, and in her mid-thirties. Ann doesn't wear make-up; her long wavy hair is unstyled; she dresses for hard work. She's as rugged as most men, and lives in a camp in the woods with few modern conveniences. I asked her what she was doing now.

"Right now I'm cleaning chimneys and painting."

"Self-employed."

"Well, everything's a trade-off. Look at how much money you can make in Connecticut. But who wants to live in Connecticut? But I guess it's what you get used to. What you like. It becomes ingrained in you. I've got to have lots of trees. And it's got to be wild. Something about a tamed forest that it doesn't do the same thing for me."

"I want to ask you—while I have you here—how you feel about the way the Downeast area is changing?"

"It's good and it's bad, you know."

"You see both sides," I said. "I only see the negative side. I'm a no-growth person."

"So am I. I'd rather have it stay just the way it was twenty years ago. It's already too far gone. But it's also people who have to have a living. And people who want to live here have to do something. And it's a tragedy because the natural resources industries are shakey. They're hurting. You know, traditional jobs are vanishing. And they're becoming—like—they're scoffed at. Like—'Oh, you cut wood.' Or—'You dig clams.'"

"Do you think they're being put down?"

"Yeah, because a lot of the people who move here do. They have that attitude. Like—'You're a clam digger.' There's a certain connotation of it not being good enough. The old traditional ways are not—they're on their way out. And it's like, 'We've got to get some industry. You have to get progress. You've got to have things where people can really make a living—not just do these things they've always done. They've got to be able to make a living like we (outsiders) do—like southern New Englanders do.'"

"Have that many people come in that those attitudes are quite pervasive now?"

"Well, it's insidious. You don't realize that an attitude has changed until it's halfway gone. You're already going to places and you realize the people aren't from around here."

Ann paused for a moment, and then she said to me, "If these people had, like you, gone into Maine people's homes, and known people and realized what the real character is. I mean, you're inundated in it; you're saturated in it. So you feel it. And I do too. To me, it's the major life.

"But there's also this other attitude that's flowing in. And it's a lot more. Meaning, it's a benefit because carpenters and clam diggers can go out and build a garage for somebody. Or they can paint a house for somebody who has the money to pay them. And so they benefit and say, 'Hey, I don't mind a few out-of-staters; if they spend their money here; if they've got their money here and they hire me.' And do better—I've seen people who have done all the traditional things, doing better because of that. But there's also that, like, underlying thing." (Ann was referring back to that attitude towards people who do the traditional jobs.)

"Do you think the area could eventually lose its identity? Is that what you're saying? What a Downeaster is—could that disappear?"

"It could," Ann said.

"Sometimes when I'm talking to elderly people, I get a sense that I'm actually chronicling an era that has past—or is disappearing right in front of our eyes. And I've got to get it down before it's completely gone. I'm getting the sense that I'm seeing the last of something here that is so precious."

"It's giving me chills," Ann said.

"What do you think of this next door—this Japanese corporation processing sea cucumbers?"

"Well, it's just exploiting another resource. What are they paying the people, five dollars an hour? Relatively, that's good. And it's steady work."

"To the Japanese, that's chicken feed," I said.

"Even the people who think they're not getting used are getting used. And that's what's insidious about it. Even the people who think, 'Oh, they're nice folks. They're a nice couple from New Jersey.' Until they start realizing that they don't understand the way people like to live—want to live."

"Yeah, I see what you mean. They want to bring a part of New Jersey with them."

"Not everyone wants to be rich," Ann explained. "I don't want to be rich. I want to live the way I live—FREE. (Here was that idea of freedom again. I had heard it many times now; from several people in eastern Maine, so that the idea of freedom—of not wanting or needing to be wealthy, or even well-off—is, in my opinion, one of the dominant character traits of the Downeaster. Independent—or as Gary had said, not wanting to put up with the petty stuff, the spit-shined boots—hardworking, honest, perhaps frugal—in that you don't waste money on things you don't need, and you get your money's worth out of things you've got, and free—to work when and for whom you please: These are the dominant traits of the Downeaster.) And be happy, you know. And not have that, 'I have to make fifty-thousand this year, and next year, and next year.' And have this obsession—this economic obsession to have to make that much money.

"When you see the breakdowns of the counties and what the average income is; Washington County is the lowest, it, and Aroostook. And you read the Portland paper and it's 'We've got to do something about this. We've got to turn around this cycle of economic depression.'"

I had been reading about the "Two-Maine Concept," where economists were comparing southern, especially southern coastal Maine, where unemployment was very low and where people were enjoying unprecedented prosperity, with inland, northern, and eastern Maine, where unemployment was still ten to twelve percent and per capita incomes were among the lowest in the United States.

"But it's always been that way," I said.

Ann agreed, but then she added, "About five years ago, the average annual income in Washington County was like forty-two hundred. Now it's sixteen thousand something. And that's not an accurate reflection. The people who were here five years ago are probably still making forty-two hundred. It's the people who are coming in and bringing money with them who are driving up the average.

"But environment—we've got one of the best. They don't even put that into the equation. And what about life? What about if you go around and interview all these people and find out if they're happy? Find out if they're bummed out because they're only making seven, eight, or ten thousand a year."

"People I've talked to seem happy," I said.

"And how do they do it? And why do they do it?"

"They've got their own wood supply, their own vegetable garden."

"Right. And they don't have to drive in traffic for forty-five minutes to get four and a half miles. (This woman made a lot of sense to me!) So what, if everything's far away. You can get there! And they're hating everybody else around them, you know. It's needless."

"How do you feel about the proposed shopping mall in Ellsworth?"

"I think it's disgusting! And that's the frightening thing though. The attitude is that people who live in that world—they're driving down those roads and they're on that treadmill and it's just money,

money, money, get money, spend money, buy money. Go to the malls—spend. I just don't think they're thinking about what happens to the water."

"Or the air."

"Or even notice it. They're just thinking about how to get to work—today. And complaining about the traffic and complaining about their jobs, but not really realizing . . . you know, we were down in Connecticut for a week. And when I got home I felt like I'd been smoking cigarettes—you know, just breathing the air. And I think when somebody comes from an environment like this and goes to one like that . . . it is noticeable. It is . . . traumatic. You really do see a brown cloud over the city. People who live there don't."

# CHAPTER 15

## LOOKING FOR A COUNTRY STORE : PIGEON HILL ROAD, STEUBEN

Once there had been a country store on Pigeon Hill, a lobster fishing village on the Petit Manan Peninsula in Steuben. No one could tell me when this was or when it had closed or where it had stood. I went to Pigeon Hill one July day for a diversion, and to see if I could find the old store building. I turned south off Route 1 at the Rusty Anchor Restaurant and began a series of undulations along a paved swath through a mixed forest of evergreen and deciduous trees with a few fields here and there. The fields, like most of the open fields Downeast, seemed to be disappearing in second-growth bush. I had seen old photographs of Steuben at the turn of the century and much of the land that is now woods, the land going down to the bays and estuaries, was then mowing field.

Along the way, the original wooden houses seemed to be obscured by mobile homes, many adorned with butterflies, caricatures of fat women's behinds, carved birds and bears and dogs. There were lobster boats and skiffs, surrounded by traps, nets, buoys, and rope. And around many of the trailers were cars, buses, old skipjacks, skidders, snowmobiles, vans, trucks, all-terrain vehicles, and household junk. The green summer foliage did its best to cover much of the blight, and I wondered how it looked in November when the trees were bare, but the snow still hadn't come.

At one point I saw an old man working on his woodpile. The firewood stood between his white frame house and a mobile home. Perhaps the trailer belonged to a son or relative as is the custom here. Parents will sell off a piece of land to their children who then put in a mobile home. The elderly man looked "Old Yankee." He wore the khaki work uniform that local men always wore, and once could be purchased at any country store. He was thin, wiry-looking, clean shaven, and wore suspenders and a hat. His neatly stacked woodpile, his immaculate old house, even his personal appearance, seemed to suggest a work ethic two or three generations removed from the rundown look of the area.

I drove south, and as the road curved nearer the salt water, there was a marked contrast in the appearance of the dwellings. I had come to the "other" Maine—not the Maine where people struggle year-round just to scratch a living, but the "seasonal" Maine of sailboats and well-kept seaside cottages. I passed newly cut dirt roads going down to the water, a lobster pound, a bed and breakfast place, waterfront cottages, lobster boats, and then across the bay, I saw the unspoiled coast of Bois Bupert Island. An old farm house and a few camps were visible across the water. The island once had a school and a sizeable population, but now it is a wildlife refuge.

I did not see a store building, but the wildlife refuge, which not only included the island, but the remaining five miles of the Petit Manan Peninsula, beckoned me on. It was a sparkling clear morning, so I decided to park my car and hike two miles northwest to Birch Point. The point itself is a small peninsula that extends northward into Dyer's Bay, so that Pigeon Hill Road, from where I had just come, is to the east across the water, while Dyer's Bay Peninsula lies to the west.

It might have been the crispness of the air, but to my surprise, the woods were free of deer flies and mosquitoes. And what lovely woods they were! The old logging road became a tunnel through second-growth stands of birch, beech, maple, spruce, fir, and cedar. The scent of balsam, the springiness of sphagnum moss under foot, the sound of the thrush, and the aroma of the salt air—hot in the open, but still chilly in the woods—assured me of a memorable journey. The logging road—at one point I came upon the rusted chassis of a skipjack—had dropped steadily into deep woods, then began a long, muddy, slippery ascent, and finally, the brilliant green, grass-covered mud of low tide was visible through the forest. I emerged from the woods on the grassy shore of a narrow inlet, perhaps a quarter mile in width, and without any sign of humanity ever having been here.

Another climb—perhaps ten or fifteen minutes—and I came to a fork. Either direction would take me to water. I went east, then heard voices in the distance. One, two, and then, two more clam diggers appeared across the flats. They worked at distances of perhaps a hundred yards from each other, but not so far as to impede communication. Their brief exchanges echoed across the mudflats. Shirtless, backs bent, legs spread far apart and anchored in the soft muck of the channel—one hand in the mud pulling clams, the other hand dragging the clam roller—from a distance the diggers resembled models of prehistoric humans in a natural history museum.

I made my way through the rockweed to within talking distance of one of the men. He was blond, and young; I'd guess early twenties—a good age for this back-breaking work—and he complained about the no-see-ums.

"Ain't they wicked in this channel," he said.

"You need to get some baby oil. They'll light down on it and die." I had never tried it, but a friend who dug worms for a living told me he used baby oil. It seemed like a good suggestion to make—he'd be more inclined to talk if he thought I knew something about clamming. But he didn't reply.

"No hoe? A hoe's no good there?" I tried to get a conversation started.

"No, it works best just pullin' 'em here in this soft mud," he said. I now noticed he was wearing rubber gloves. So this was what the country store proprietors meant when they said that clammers would wear out a pair of gloves each tide. I had assumed they were referring to cloth or leather gloves to keep diggers' hands from blistering on their hoe handles.

"I guess I just don't know enough to get a regular job," he said. I wasn't sure what had prompted him to say that, but his self-demeaning manner made me uncomfortable. He obviously took me for an outsider, as I was carrying a camera. And what was I doing down here asking all these questions anyway? Why wasn't I out earning a living like everyone else? I mentioned the freedom he had.

"Yeah, the hours are good," he said. We talked for a while about the price per bushel, competition from other areas of the eastern seaboard, and the growing number of diggers. He seemed intelligent, and knowledgeable about worldly matters. He might have been successful at any number of things, but for now, at least, he chose the freedom of clamming. And for a man his age, it wasn't a bad choice. He would earn about a hundred and fifty dollars for about three hours work that day.

I left the digger on the flats, and on my way out the Pigeon Hill Road, I noticed a small gray house with a steep roof. At one time a barn might have been attached, as the building seemed to stand in such a way as to appear lonely. But, then my judgment may have been impaired by a certain memory I had of the place. I had been inside that house before. It was more than twenty years ago, yet I had haunting memories of the whole affair.

The house, which now appeared empty, had been the home of a girl I had known in high school. We never really had a date; we never really got to know one another. But I remember the house and its setting, because one spring evening, some friends and I— on the spur of the moment—had visited this girl and some of her friends there. The group of us walked down a dirt road to the bay that night; and while nothing intimate ever took place, it was the only occasion I ever had to be with this girl outside the structured atmosphere of school. And the early spring night—chilly, with the shrill sound of frogs peeping, and the dark image of woods, rocks, and the bay—had seemed terribly exciting, even "romantic" at the time.

She was a year older than I, and rode my school bus. She had an attractive, but not pretty face: even teeth, close together; short, straight, dark brown hair and eyes. She was thin; perhaps medium height, and athletic. But I was drawn more by her charm and sense of humor than by her looks: her eyes seemed always to have a devious twinkle, that I, a shy, somewhat reserved teenager, never really understood. What had it all meant, if anything?

Eric Hartman stands behind the counter at the Lamoine General Store.

Bob Card and Allan Lockyer at Card's Tideway Market.

Richard and Robert West at the Sunrise General Merchandise.

Allen Tuttle was one of the friendliest and kindest country storekeepers in eastern Maine.

Young's Store is a Downeast landmark.

Amos Kelley and Lucille Null at Young's Store

Leitha Temple Joy ran Temple's Store in Gouldsboro for 51 years.

Clam hoe and roller in Gouldsboro.

Flossie Vasquez and Linda Lockyer talk about the "old" Steuben.

An old store in Wyman.

The Cherryfield-Narraguagus Historical Society is housed in a former country store building.

A bear hunter in an old store in Cherryfield.

The old A.G. Godfrey Store building in Addison.

Everyone's a winner at Cirone's Trading Post in South Addison.

Allan Lockyer and nephew, Dave, at the "camp" in 1968.

Stan Tomasik at the Indian River General Store.

Warren Peabody at Alley's Bay Grocery on Beals Island.

"Uncle" Archie Alley and Linda Lockyer at Alley's Bay Grocery.

She and her girlfriends seemed to delight in teasing me. There was nothing malicious about their teasing, but it made me uncomfortable. I was different from the other boys on the school bus. I was not a native of the area and I was unschooled in the local social scene. But I was also polite—proper—in a middle class sort of way, and I guess, fair game. In some ways these girls from way Downeast seemed older and much more worldly than I, while in other ways, they seemed terribly provincial. Having lived in suburban New Jersey until age fifteen, I had never known any country girls. But I never paid her girlfriends much attention—I have since forgotten their names and faces—and I think this girl sensed that. It was as if I always looked right past the others and into her eyes.

Shortly before her graduation I gave her an oil painting of a stream in autumn foliage. I must have cared a great deal for her to have gone to such trouble. And it must have been awkward for me. It was also my best work at a time in my life when art was of special importance to me. I was serious about painting and planned to major in fine arts when I went to college. I'm not sure it was a very good painting, but she liked it—her gratitude was genuine. She seemed sincerely flattered—and was probably amused—that I had gone to such trouble to please her. It made me wonder if anyone else ever had.

I went to the high school graduation that year, and there I discovered the reality behind her playful exterior. He was a local man, much older than she. It was commonplace here: Men married women who were often several years younger than themselves. Girls are said to mature earlier than boys, and I heard men talk of "young stuff," and "robbing the cradle." Indeed, local men, well into their twenties, used to lurk around the school yards, watching and waiting. This man looked like a fisherman. And while I didn't realize it at the time, his light features, his ruddy, outdoorsy appearance, his quiet demeanor: this man might have been a Downeast version of me, only several years older.

The message was so vividly clear. He never spoke. I nodded to him, shook hands with her, and wished her the best. I never saw her again. She had been "spoken for."

But that wasn't quite the end. That summer I received a letter. She was living with a relative and working in a shoe factory in southern Maine. There was no mention of the man who was with her at graduation, but I just assumed she was earning money for marriage. I remember her handwriting: not the round ovals of little girls' or teachers' pets, but a clean, steady, flowing script, which has since led me to believe she was a strong and competent young woman, probably capable of doing almost anything. Yet the tone of the letter was irritatingly familiar. "How are things in the big town of Steuben?" Then something like: "But you make your own fun, right?" It was her old upbeat manner. She wrote about working in the factory, but I can't recall any details, and then hoped that I would write. It was obvious she wasn't telling me everything. I assumed she was lonely, and again, I wondered what it all meant. Was she just being friendly, or was she leading me on? Hadn't that "scene" at graduation meant what I thought it had meant? And finally, near the end of the letter, she wrote, "I wish I could have gotten to know you better." So final! And at that time in my life; so sad. I was sixteen then, and while I had many interests, and plans for the future, the experience had really shaken me. It must have, or else it wouldn't have stayed with me all these years.

It happened more than twenty years ago—before the Woodstock Music Festival, before Watergate, before Women's Liberation, before the "Me Generation." And as bright and energetic as she seemed, I feel certain she could have made it through college. Yet, I doubt the idea had entered her mind. Her girlfriends were not going, and she did not take the "college course" in high school, which was more an indication that one's family circumstances would not enable one to attend college, than an accurate measure of one's academic potential. But didn't they have guidance counselors or teachers at that high school who knew about loans and work study, who would encourage kids to go on to college? There was a rigid social structure in the high school, and to this day, I'm not sure if it was based on economics, class, or both.

I read recently that Maine is fiftieth in the nation in sending its kids to college. Why? I do not know, and one simply does not ask certain questions or intrude into other people's lives. I suspect that many potential first generation college students get little encouragement from home. It is not that people in rural Maine are anti-intellectual; rather, I think it is the old Yankee idea that it is frivolous to spend money on something you don't really need. And I also think that while rural people want what is best for their children, they really don't want them to leave home either. Home. It is not that people in rural Maine are anti-intellectual; rather, I think it is the old Yankee idea that it is frivolous to spend money on something you don't really need. And I also think that while rural people want what is best for their children, they really don't want them to leave home either.

Psychologists refer to this idea as the "hamlet syndrome"—that is hamlet as in village—where you fall in love with the girl next door, or else you end up marrying your high school sweetheart. Even John McKernan, the Governor of Maine, is said to have been a victim of it. A former basketball player (high school basketball is to Maine what high school football is to Texas), he married a cheerleader and was divorced several years later. The hamlet syndrome is said to be the bane of rural America—an affliction that stunts intellectual growth and has a retarding effect on small communities.

But I'm not convinced the hamlet syndrome is such a bad thing. On the contrary, it is the glue that holds small communities together, making rural places rural, enabling them to retain their unique character and provinciality, rather than becoming homogenized into metropolitan America.

All I know is that the girl who once lived in the gray house had been spoken for. And it was probably for the best. I did answer her letter that summer, but never heard from her again. And as I headed Downeast towards the next country store, I wondered how her life had gone.

# CHAPTER 16

## FINDING AN OLD COUNTRY STORE: WYMAN ROAD, MILBRIDGE

I have a photograph taken in 1964 of my parents standing with their backs to a gigantic granite boulder at McClellen Park in Milbridge. They're both smiling and bundled up against the chill. From the picture—taken two years before my father died—it looks as though the day might have been foggy or overcast. I have a vague recollection of snapping that picture. It was taken with a Brownie Fiesta camera that I got for my thirteenth birthday. That summer, I took numerous black and white photographs of our vacation in Maine. And there are also many pictures taken by my father of me, holding up fish that I had caught. There's the pickerel I caught at Scammon Pond. It was exactly fourteen and one half inches. There are several photos of me—a skinny, freckle-faced boy with a crewcut, wearing a flannel shirt and bluejeans, the end of my too-long leather belt curling outward—beaming, as I held up stringers of harbor pollack I had caught at Schoodic Point. Everything we did, and everywhere we went that summer is documented in my photo album—even the tiny green frog that I kept in an old tin kettle in the closet. There's a close-up of the poor creature on the front lawn of our house in Steuben.    So it was natural that I would have taken a picture of my parents at McClellen Park, a place they liked almost as much as Schoodic Point in Acadia National Park. But unlike Acadia, McClellen was—and still is—relatively undeveloped—just a rough gravel road leading in, and then the rock-bound coast, with several islands off to the east in Narragaugus Bay.

"I've never been down that road," Linda said one day, on our way to Milbridge. We were driving into town on Route 1 and passed the Wyman Road, which veers off to the right just beyond the Eastern Maine Crafts Co-op. I turned the car around at Strout's Hardware and said, "You want to take a ride down?" I hadn't been down the Wyman Road since my father died in 1966.

The old sardine factory was the first thing that caught my eye—that, and the United Methodist Church. It was as if I had forgotten about this road all these years. I'm really not sure why I had never taken my wife down here, but even this trip, I didn't tell her about McClellen Park being near the end. I thought I would just surprise her.

We passed several old frame houses. One Cape Cod house had a sign in front that read: PUCKERBRUSH FARM. The Wyman Road has a different look and feel to it than other roads Downeast. The high density of houses and mobile homes made me feel like a stranger in an unfamiliar ghetto. There's a Third World tumble down quality to the landscape here—and by that I don't mean poverty; rather, a chaotic mixture of humble trailers, nicely maintained frame houses, and lovely seaside dwellings, side by side. And there are lots and lots of wooden lawn ornaments.

I should think the Wyman Road would be a good place to live if you wanted to learn something about the people of eastern Maine. And as I grappled with various ideas and images—my mind occasionally drifting back to old memories I had of the road as a thirteen-year-old—I decided that the Wyman Road was more "native" than most roads going out to the points. Oh, there are plenty of summer people and transplants here too, but the landscape has a definite native quality—you know you're Downeast.

At one point, I said to Linda, "Look, there's a survivor—a big old elm tree. And over on the left here—look at the houses, mobile homes, and abandoned cars—all clustered together."

"It looks like those walk-in freezers," Linda said.

"Yeah, walk-in freezers, restaurants use them," I said.

I rattled off a list of things I saw: "A little yellow frame house, a mobile home, a girl on a bicycle, lobster traps, lawn ornaments—a deer, cow, pig, moose." Then I zeroed in on the vegetation: "Firewood, silver maple, an old apple orchard." And then I said, "Oh, look at all those lobster traps; there's a basketball backboard, and a lobster boat. This is quite a steep hill. Oh look, there must be seven or eight full-length aprons on that clothesline."

I was intrigued by the Wyman Road. It went by too quickly in a car—even in second gear—and it made me think this narrow lane was better suited for a horse and wagon. We passed another house trailer, a skipjack rusting in the weeds, the Berwick Boys Camp, a lobster boat named the "Bobby Jean", then Linda said, "Look at all the mattresses!" Someone had left several old mattresses outside. But what can you do with old mattresses? You're not supposed to sell them. Maybe they were airing them out. And there was more stuff here: some big dogs, a tipped over washing machine, an old snowmobile, an all-terrain vehicle, a fish shack, some lobster boats, a woodpile. I spotted an old blue car, more lobster traps, buoys, a long line of clothes drying. Indeed, the Wyman Road had a "lived-in" look. I liked it. All this junk made it seem homey.

I was staring out towards the bay, past an old house with imitation brick siding, and a barn attached, when Linda said, "Look at that—they have STORE painted on the front of that little building. It's a tiny, one-room store."

"There was a store on the Wyman Road many years ago," I said. "Maybe this is it. It just says STORE, and someone's written BEAL BOYS across the front. But you can still make out the word STORE. It's a gabled-front building. It has a door in the middle and one window to the right. And it looks like it was painted white at one time, but most of it has faded and worn away."

"It says TOBACCO and CANDY in a cross," Linda added."The A is where they intersect."

"Somebody has tied the door shut with a piece of rope," I said. "And there's bright green and yellow paint dabbed on it. We need to come back and take a picture of this relic—wild roses are blooming all around it."

"And Joe Pie Weed."

"And rock outcroppings. It sits almost . . . right on the road. And lobster traps right beside it . . . it would make a terrific picture with the bay in the background and the wharf and boats off in the distance. And across the road in a large white church. The sign reads: WYMAN VESTRY and they have a building fund-drive going. It says they've raised thirty-one hundred dollars so far. The church rests on a granite foundation. So this is Wyman—it's a little settlement, and that tiny building must have been the old Wyman Store."

Indeed, Linda and I had discovered, by accident, the center of Wyman, a little community—part of Milbridge—that, like Egypt, Maine, only appears on the most detailed maps. And like Egypt, Wyman seems to have deteriorated over the years. But if you stop, like we did, and look carefully at the landscape, it is easy to imagine this little community as it had been many years ago. I could visualize schooners coming into the wharf and leaving supplies to be carried up to this little store building across from the church. It was all still here—one only had to use one's imagination.

From there, we drove out to McClellen Park; and except for some litter here and there, it didn't seem much different from what I remembered. The big rock stood out; although it didn't seem as gigantic as the photograph made it look, or as I had remembered it. And while the picture of my parents—bundled up against the ocean's chill and smiling like two adolescents on vacation—had preserved for me a pleasant image, the sheer delight on Linda's face when she first set eyes on that magnificent coastline, more than made up for twenty-five years of memory lapse.

# CHAPTER 17

## DIGGERS' DEPOT: MILLET'S MARKET, MILBRIDGE

How to get started? It was a problem I faced every time I entered a country store. At some stores I went inside and for one reason or another—and it didn't necessarily mean the owner was unwilling to talk, or wasn't good at conversation; some days I just wasn't up to the task of drawing "material" out of a proprietor—I looked around, bought a bottle of pop or a newspaper, and came out without an interview. It's a travel book, I told myself, not a dissertation. There was no one I had to interview; no store I had to stop at. I would let the narrative take its course.

I had trouble keeping the conversation flowing at Millet's Market on Main Street in Milbridge, and after I had left, I wondered if I had gotten anything worth writing about. And it wasn't that Mr. Millet was hard to talk to; he wasn't. It was probably just the morning; the way customers came and went and sort of Balkanized the conversation. Still, I transcribed the tape just the same, and when I had finished, I decided that in spite of the fragmented nature of the dialogue—and there were many other stores where it had gone this way—it was still important. After all, it would give the journey continuity; and, it would give the reader a feel for Milbridge, a town of about one thousand people that advertises itself as the "shopping center of western Washington County."

The streets were torn up. They were putting in new sewers. A new, brick two-story Union Trust Bank building was nearing completion on Main Street. Driving in from the west you pass Strout's Hardware, Sawyer's Garage, Alpine Travel, then the Milbridge Associated Grocer—around here everyone always called it Bob Whitten's Store. It had been Frankenstein's in the 1960s— a very local version of a five and dime—a department store with precious little of this or that. Eventually, they added a laundromat out back, then auto parts in a room on one side, then furniture, then a little of both, and finally, they changed it to the Milbridge AG, a superette. In the grocery business, a store becomes a superette when it grosses more than one million, but less than two million dollars a year. Gross sales of over two million dollars a year make it a supermarket, like Gay's Shop and Save, which is just up the street, next to the Union Trust, and across from the Milbridge Theater, the only movie house between Ellsworth and Machias. The theater is brown; I remember when it was called the Colonial Theater; they played Bingo before each movie, and it was cheap. It's still a bargain, but just don't go on a Friday night—lots of crazy kids!

Behind the theater is a relatively new senior citizens' apartment complex that looks strangely out of place in this coastal town of old white Cape Cod and colonial houses. There's another laundromat, a redemption center, a restaurant, a gas station, a nursing home (almost new), Leighton's Department Store (ancient, and for sale), Millet's Market, Nichols' Barber Shop, the Sea Witch (gifts, crafts), Kennedy's Drug Store, another bank, then the Red Barn Restaurant. Cross the bridge over the Narragaugus River on Route 1A and you've seen Milbridge.

"Here comes one of those Wiscasset criminals right now," Mr. Millet said. I was in Millet's Market, a popular beer depot for clam and worm diggers.

"Are you talking about Wiscasset?" The elderly man—I learned that he had come to Milbridge from Wiscasset, Maine in 1931— had a way of drawing out each syllable so that Wiscasset came out

WHIZ-CAZ-ZET.  I had also heard it pronounced WIS-casset, but really wasn't sure of the correct pronunciation.  All I knew about Wiscasset was that it had two old rotting four masted barques in its harbor; the Maine Yankee, the state's only nuclear power plant; and large worming flats, after which a worm hoe, the "Wiscasset Chopper" had been named.

"We were talking about all the diggers that used to go to Wiscasset," I said.

"Geez, they go all over now," the man from Wiscasset said.

"A man whose been here as long as you have—he's become a millionaire," Millet said.  "Ain't that right?"

A customer had just come in.  He said to the man from Wiscasset, "The richest man in Milbridge, right there."

"How about lending me a little?" the man from Wiscasset said.

"Lend you a little!" the customer said.  "Geez!  He pays four cents a worm and he gets twenty-five cents a piece for them."  It was obviously an exaggeration, as the diggers were currently getting ten cents a piece for bloodworms.  Evidently, the man from Wiscasset was a worm buyer.  All these men seemed to like each other, however, as they joked back and forth.

"Look what I've got to put up with," the man from Wiscasset said.  "I'm moving out of town."

"Don't do us any favors, will ya'?" the customer said, as the man from Wiscasset paid for his newspaper and left.

It was in Milbridge many years ago that I got to know wormers.  It takes a certain type of person to be a worm digger.  I once heard that said about marathon runners.  The phrase grabbed me; I ran a marathon; I ran another.  Twenty years later, I still run marathons.  I also thought I wanted to be a wormer.  I tried it, but it wasn't me.  Wormers are rugged; they're tough; I'm not sure how many of them could run twenty-six miles, but they can turn over mud and find worms.  I think it helps to be slightly bowlegged and close to the mud.  It also helps to have bulging biceps and a strong back.  And like marathon runners, wormers come in all shapes and sizes, but to be a good wormer you have to want to dig worms.

I got to know some local diggers by playing baseball on the Milbridge town team during the 1960s.  Most of the men on the team were wormers, and while I'm not certain they were representative of diggers as a whole, they helped fix an image in my head of what wormers could be like. They talked a lot about how many worms they had dug. They talked a lot about women. I liked listening to them. I particularly remember the 1967 season, as the highlight was a trip to Bangor to play the Bangor Merchants "under the lights."

I rode with four other men—all several years older than I—in a large old car—a Lincoln or something like it. The driver, a big man in his late thirties, had insisted we roll down all the windows so as to "look classy" when we approached Bangor. All the way up to Bangor, the conversation had been mostly about who was—or who wasn't—"doing it" with whom. And there was an argument about whether a certain team member was or wasn't. The poor guy and his woman didn't stand a chance. He was "a queer" if he wasn't, and his girlfriend had "no morals," if he was. It went back and forth like that for a while, and then the driver began to assert his seniority; his bravado. But when he got around to discussing the "whores" in New York City, I began, inwardly, to doubt the accuracy of his stories; the breadth of his experience. He never mentioned any particular street or part of the city. It was just New York City, period, and I wondered if he had ever been to Times Square or 42nd Street.

"Geez, you fellas ought to go up with me sometime," the driver said. "Haven't they got the women up there to New York City!"

One of the men in the car mentioned the many women Downeast—down in Calais who "would," but the driver said, "Oh, no. No. They're all dirty down there. I wouldn't touch one of those women down there." It always interested me, that among wormers, at least, conditions were always worse the farther Downeast one went. The high school baseball and basketball teams were "no good down there"; the women were "fat" or "dirty" or "had no morals", and it was "the end of the world down there."

"Geez, haven't they got some women up there to New York City," the driver started again. He began to direct his remarks towards the youngest of the men, the catcher, who had just completed his freshman year of college. He paid no attention to me, a high school junior. It was obvious my presence was of no significance. The catcher was a short, chunky kid—a good build for catchers or wormers—close to the mud.

"What about you?" the driver started in on the catcher. "You want to go up to New York City with me and try out some of those women? How about it? You'll go with me, won't you?" He laughed along with the other two men as if it were an inside joke.

"Geez, I dunno. Uh, I don't want to catch the clap," the catcher replied. Pretty smart answer, I thought. I had wondered how he was going to get himself out of this embarrassing mess when the driver snapped back: "Oh, come on, you ain't gonna catch nothin'." It went like that the rest of the way to Bangor, with the driver taking the lead, the other two men going along with his tales, and the catcher trying to save face. They eventually got down to the microgeography of the subject. And here again, the driver asserted his leadership; his experience. "Well, you fellas can use the back seat of a car if you want, but I like to do mine on a good comfortable bed. Well, there, by Jesus! I guess prob'ly we'll show those Bangor Merchants how it's done!"

The Bangor Merchants made us look like the dubs we were. This virile group of worm diggers might have been able to dig a thousand worms a tide, and handle New York City's wildest women, but we couldn't seem to find a white baseball under those lights. Fly balls were lost, ground balls booted, first base overthrown, and one batter after another popped out, grounded out, or struck out.

The driver, especially, had a bad night. Each time he struck out, he would swing real hard, then cuss real loud, so as to give the impression that he was just having an off day. And the men on the bench would say to one another, "Geez, if he ever connects, if he EVER connects—you might as well kiss that beauty good-bye." But I don't ever recall the driver connecting; not this game, not all season.

We stopped at a take-out restaurant in Brewer after the game. "Geez, wasn't that some awful?" the driver lamented. "Didn't we play like a bunch of dubs!" The other men echoed his sentiments. But the driver, always upbeat, always the leader, took charge again. "Let's get us some beer!" the driver said. Oh no, I thought. Here we go.

"Yes sa', let's get us some beer," the other men echoed.

But the catcher was in trouble again. "Geez, if the old man smells that beer on me, I'll be in for it!"

"Oh, come on, your old man ain't gonna smell nothin'," the driver snapped back. The catcher went silent, the driver ate and drank, belched and drank some more, and the conversation grew more explicit.

"Geez, wouldn't I like to have one here right now!" the drive exclaimed. "I'd put the ol' peg right to 'er, wouldn't you? Wouldn't you like to have one of those New York City women right here now?" he taunted the catcher.

"Yeah, right," the catcher mumbled.

"Yeah, you wouldn't know what to do with it if you had it," the driver taunted him. "Geez, didn't we play like a bunch of dubs!"

Eventually, the subject changed to raking blueberries. It was August, after all, and we were heading back to Washington County. The catcher, it seemed, had spent the past week up on the blueberry barrens, but decided that he could make more money digging worms. "Geez, I don't like it up on those barrens," he began. "And that sun's so hot. There's no shade anywhere. The first thing I do when I get there in the morning is squat down in one of those gullies and take a piss."

"Geez, you mean to tell me you've got to squat like a girl?" the driver taunted him again. "You fellas hear that? He's got to squat like a girl! He's got to squat like a girl! Geez, isn't he some peculiar. Geez!"

When we got within a few miles of Washington County, the conversation returned to worming. It was as if the great adventure—the night out in the big city of Bangor—had ended. The talk of sexual adventure subsided; the realities of work returned.

"Well sa', how many worms you gonna get tomorrow?" the driver asked the catcher.

"Geez, I dunno, maybe six or seven hundred," the catcher replied.

"Six or seven hundred!" the driver said. "Why, when I was your age, I never got less than a thousand, still don't. Geez, aren't you a useless dub! You can't dig worms, you don't chase women, you won't even drink a beer!"

The catcher didn't say a word. Neither did I. Except to order a cheeseburger, fries, and a Coke at the take-out, I never said a word the whole trip.

And as I stood there in Millet's Market, I wondered how many of the old wormers were still out there on the flats. I knew one digger who had gone from worms to clams, and in so doing he had elevated clam digging to a "profession," or at least that's what he called it. But suddenly, in his middle thirties, he retired from that profession, and went into sales. Sort of like old ballplayers, or aging lifeguards, these diggers; they want to hang on to those "glory days" for as long as possible. "Maybe I've got a couple more seasons in this old body?" "I'd like to play one more season." "I'd like to dig one more year." "Maybe if I had another day's rest between games." "Maybe if I had a little more rest between tides— no more double tides though." And for some diggers, it goes like that for two or three more decades. "I haven't been all week." "Just as soon as this weather breaks." "Just as soon as we get that spring tide." "I like to go in the summertime, when the days are longer and the tides are bigger, and I can get out there and get some decent clams." "Well, actually, I don't dig too many clams these days—my back's had it."

Mr. Millet had run the store since 1948. His father owned the three story Victorian building with the mansard roof back then when it had been a restaurant. "They played pool upstairs," Millet said. "My father had a store along side Gay's Store. He had that one, then moved his stuff up here—early '50s, I think. I've been here ever since."

Millet's Market is a relic. It might have been a general store years ago, but now he sells mostly soda pop, cigarettes, beer, newspapers, and some clam digging gloves. I once asked an employee at Millet's how the store had survived all these years and she said, "beer." Millet's is a popular beer depot for working men in the area. Indeed, a cabinetmaker from Steuben once told me, "When you're all dirty, you just don't feel right going into Gay's supermarket with all those women. So you stop at Millet's."

I asked Millet if he knew when Gay's supermarket came in.

"1960, I think. Carroll and his brother, Lawrence, and Frank Gay—they worked it."

"I guess they really put a squeeze on the country stores," I said.

"Yeah, because there was six of them in town." Millet described where each store had been. Several of the buildings were gone now; at least two others had become crafts shops, and this one was the only structure still used as a store.

"I guess it's too late to worry about it now," Millet laughed. And that was all he had to say about country stores. He stopped talking; so I said, "I see you've got these wrinkles. Do you sell a lot of them?"

"Sell pretty good, ayuh. Sell pretty good when you can get 'em. Sold twenty-four (they were in half pint containers) last night. Sell twenty-something every other night. I don't know why, myself. I don't like them. I don't like any shellfish. I don't really like lobster. I don't like clams. But I like about every fish that swims."

Millet talked fast, and in spurts. It was hard, sometimes, to pick up on what he had said, but when you got it, it was usually very funny. He had a quick wit. I asked him what he liked about his business.

"Well, it keeps you in out of the slime. Oh, I don't know, it's just a habit now, I guess. Christ, you get used to it."

"Do you plan to be in the store several more years?"

"Oh, I might if I live that long. If the store don't burn down. Some of them kinds of things happen." Millet said he was almost old enough to start drawing social security. He smiled in a shy way, and with his crewcut and light features, he seemed almost boyish at times. I asked him what he thought about the land developers and the way the area was growing.

"Well, it's like everywhere—I guess it's good up to a certain point."

"Do you think it's driving up the price of land so that Maine people can't afford houses?"

"Well, in southern Maine I know it has. Down here I guess shore property—I remember when you could buy it for little or nothing. Course you can't do it anymore. Of course a lot of people keep moving in here. A lot of people. I mean you see camps and all kinds of things sticking out of the woods. You see names in the paper and you don't know who they are."

I wondered what it was like to have lived so long in one small town that you recognized every name in the newspaper. And how unsettling it must have seemed; to have known such stability, only to see it dramatically change in one's later years. Millet wasn't the first Downeaster I had heard mention unfamiliar names in the newspaper. The local newspapers are read religiously, especially the court news and the obituaries. Still, I don't think it was the appearance of the unfamiliar names that disturbed people so much as the fact that these new names were often the names attached to deeds of land. Years ago, Downeasters might have been cash poor, but they were land rich—not that the land had had much of a cash value back then; it didn't—in that the land was unspoiled, abundant, and bountiful, and it belonged to them!

"People come in and cash a check," Millet said. "You see the name on the check. A lot of people come."

It was change, especially the accelerating pace of change, that was on my mind when I drove the winding stretch of Route 1 between Milbridge and Cherryfield. There were still several mowing fields along the highway here; even a working farm, a relic from another era. Once there were many farms Downeast, but like old country stores, they too have vanished.

# CHAPTER 8

## ONCE THERE WERE FIFTEEN COUNTRY STORES: CHERRYFIELD-NARRAGUAGUS HISTORICAL SOCIETY

I n 1900, there were fifteen country stores in Cherryfield, an old logging and blueberrying town on the Narraguagus River, six miles north of Milbridge. Many of the old store buildings still stand as relics of an era past. One has been refurbished and painted a navy blue. The sign on its facade reads: KNAPP-SAKS (gifts, crafts). A derelict old store in the center of town is now a used clothing business called the Recycle Shop. Across the river, a sign on another old store advertises windjammer cruises—a modern function, in a nostalgic sense, for an antiquated building.

I had an appointment with Marjery Brown, a pleasant, middle-aged woman who is the president of the Cherryfield-Narraguagus Historical Society—itself housed in a former country store building. I hoped that Marjery could tell me something about the town's past, as well as explain why only one of the fifteen country stores operating in 1900 was still in business.

"People moved away," Marjery began. "At the turn of the century there were close to two-thousand people living in Cherryfield (1980 population-983), working mostly in lumbering. Some in blueberries, but lumber was king."

"They weren't building ships here then?"

"No, they had stopped building ships by then, I think. During the 1800s, they built quite a few ships just down here below the bridge."

"I understand the water level was higher then?"

"Yes."

"How could that be?"

"Because, well, the river banks used to be two or three feet further out into the river—more than they are now. They just washed down and they filled the river up with silt. They used to be able to bring some schooners right up to where the bridge is."

"They never dredged back in those days?"

"Not that I know of. The ice usually did a pretty good job of scouring it out. They had the banks cribbed up with logs so that they weren't washing in all the time. And as they no longer used them, the cribbing came to pieces. Nobody kept it up."

"If you look at old maps and old pictures, they show how much land there was out into the river that's no longer there."

"So the river is wider now, but it's shallower?"

"Yeah. Of course, that's what Narraguagus means—wide and shallow. It's an Indian name."

"I would think, if they were doing a lot of logging upcountry, the removal of trees would have caused some erosion that would have added a lot of silt to the river."

"Then, all of the bark and stuff from the mills was thrown into the river. That contributed to it. It would wash down a certain distance and then just hang up, I suppose."

I said, "Joanne Willey (secretary of the historical society) told me they used to jump off the back of the Nash Building (store building on the other side of the river) and swim."

"Yeah."

"I've been over here at high tide and it just doesn't seem possible that ships could have ever come up this far."

"A lady down the road here who is in her eighties said, 'Oh, I wish they'd dredge that river out so it was like the way it was when I was a girl.'

"The lumbering gave out soon after the turn of the century. They cut trees like there was no tomorrow. And the spruce budworm struck sometime around 1912, I think, and that finished it. Tomorrow was here. There was nothing more to do. So anyone who had a family to raise—they had to move away. I understand the undertaker—in the early 1920s—moved away because there weren't enough old people in town to die off to keep him in business."

Indeed, Cherryfield's population of 1,859 in 1900 declined to 905 by 1950, and finally bottomed out at 771 in 1970. It had rebounded to 983 in 1980, and I would guess it has grown somewhat since then. "I've seen a big change just in the last fifteen years," Marjery said.

"Now I would imagine there are more old people than people of any other age," I added.

"Fifteen years ago, they figured that sixty-five percent of the people in Cherryfield were retirement age. Since then, it's changed, because we've had an influx of younger people from all over the place who want to get away from the rat race—and moved in and went back to living off the land. It took a few years to weed out those who weren't serious about doing it, but we have quite a few people who have stayed here. They keep to themselves pretty well. They're quiet. They're substantial citizens, so-to-speak.

"The people who move here—we have two kinds that come in: those that come to get away from what they left; and those that discover they want what they left behind and want to change the town. They want a pub on every corner—that kind of thing.

"Of course, the land developers are beginning to strike. You'd be surprised the people who will pay twenty-nine thousand dollars for a forty acre lot they've never seen. 'Ten minutes from Bar Harbor,' one of their brochures says."

"More like two hours," I said.

"From where they wanted to put one subdivision in, you would have to drive all the way through and come out in Deblois, and out around this way. And they don't bother to tell them, that in the wintertime you can't get into it except on snowmobiles or snowshoes. They tried to keep the road open to build it that first winter, and finally after we had two or three snowstorms that drift—Oh, from the blueberry barrens, they drift terrible, ten-foot drifts up there—they finally pulled their equipment out and gave it up.

"Like that fellow that called the first selectman in Deblois. First selectwoman, I should say. He was trying to get in touch with the Deblois Public Works Department. Well, she laughed and laughed and laughed. She said, 'Well, I guess you've got the nearest thing to it there is. I'm the selectman up here. We don't have any Public Works Department.' He wanted water and electricity to the lot that he'd bought. 'There's no public water,' she said. 'There will be no electricity to your piece of land.' She told him how many miles it was. She said, 'We just got electricity up here in Deblois something like fifteen years ago.'"

"There's only about fifty-some-odd people there," I said.

"Yeah, same way with telephone service. She said, 'We just got phone service here recently, and they're not going to run it down in there unless you have a small fortune to pay to have it done.' She said, 'We can't even guarantee you fire protection down there. We have a local volunteer fire department, but we can't guarantee you fire protection down in there.' Well, he was pretty upset. He said, 'Do you think I've been taken?' She said, 'Well, in my opinion you have been.' He said, 'Do you suppose I could get my money out of the land?' She said, 'You could if you didn't try to sell it up around here. But nobody up around here is going to pay twenty-nine thousand for it!' He had bought it sight unseen! And he was trying to make arrangements to have all these things hooked up."

Marjery told me that Mathews' Store, a mile north of Cherryfield center, is the only store out of the fifteen country stores operating in 1900 that is still in business. And it still prospers, despite the fact that Route 1 now passes a mile south. I wondered why they had opened the store a mile uptown in the first place. Marjery explained that the blueberry factory had moved uptown in the early 1900s when the railroad first came through. Mathews opened their store near the railroad and the factory, but over the years the town's economic center gradually shifted southward. Put another way, Mathews' site has remained unchanged, but its situation—its relative location—has changed.

When lumber was king, the center of Cherryfield had been as far upstream as schooners could travel. When the railroad came through, however, the town shifted north, to be closer to the depot. It wasn't just a freight line either; Marjery told me that Joanne Willey's grandfather, president of the Union Trust Company, used to commute to and from Ellsworth each day, back in the 1930s. But as the railroad's importance waned, and the automobile became the dominant mode of transport, the town gradually shifted back downstream to be along new Route 1.

Mathews' Store may seem old to us today, but it only dates from the railroad era. Unfortunately, most of the town's oldest buildings have disappeared. Only a handful have survived, and it was these that Marjery told me about. She began with the old store building that now houses the historical society. "It was built in 1865 by Francis Patten, and he ran a boot manufactory on the top floor. He made shoes and boots. At that time, the first floor was Patten's Meat Market. But over the years there have been various things; including a telegraph office, a barber shop, law offices, a pool room, a jeweler's shop, and dry goods store.

"In the 1960s, the old store was owned by Carlton Willey, the Major League baseball player. And his father ran it for him for quite a few years. And when his father got so that he didn't want to run the store anymore, Carl sold it to his uncle, Kenneth. Then Ken ran it for a couple of years and went out of business and the building just stood here."

The bank gave the old store building to the historical society in 1976. Because it had always been used as a store, and because the historical society could prove when it had been built, they were able to get it on the National Register of Historic Places. Out of 109 country stores in operation between Ellsworth and Machias in 1900, here was one store building that had been brought back from the dead.

"Is it my imagination, or does this old store building lean, you know, tilt to one side?"

"The sills and floor stringers had rotted out about half way up. So we jacked it up, replaced all those, and it still—if you look at it—it's crooked. Although part of it is the paint. The paint makes it look that way."

The store building that now housed the Recycle Shop was older still. It had belonged to Jeremiah O. Nicholas (What a great name!) in the 1830s.

"It was a general store, and they handled corn and oats, and groceries and general hardware," Marjery explained. "It was built on the bank so that they brought things up the river and unloaded through this opening in the back of the building. They could come right up under the building and unload there."

Unlike the old store building that housed the historical society, this structure had been altered—its doorway had been changed in order to accommodate another business—and could never be placed on the historic register.

"We have our segment of the town that has been trying for years to have that condemned and torn down because it's an eyesore," Marjery said. "I'd hate to see these old buildings torn down."

Across the street from the historical society was the Knights of Pythias, it too housed in a former country store. The sign on the building read 1904, but Marjery said the store showed in a picture they had of the town in 1853. It had once been a company store owned by the Campbells, a family that had been in Cherryfield since 1790. She pronounced it "Cam-bell," and not "Camp-bell" as many Downeasters do. It was an elegant old building in the gable-front style, with large front doors, and large paned windows.

Out of the fifteen country stores operating in Cherryfield in 1900, perhaps ten of the old store buildings were still standing. Not bad, I thought. It was an historic river town with many beautiful old homes dating from as far back as the 1700s. There were New England Colonials, Georgian, and Victorian houses— most built by the old lumbering families. I didn't ask Marjery who lived in these stately homes today. I think I knew.

# CHAPTER 19

## BLUEBERRY RAKERS' DEPOT:
## C.H. MATHEWS, CHERRYFIELD

"I noticed you have 1891 on the front of the store."

"That's true," Bruce Mathews said. "We researched that. My grandfather and great uncle were the starters. I wish I had some more written information on this store. It must be one of the oldest along the coast."

Indeed, C.H. Mathews Store, at the intersection of old Route 1 and Route 191, in uptown Cherryfield, is the only survivor of fifteen country stores that served Cherryfield in 1900. And when you enter the old store, with its steel ceiling, and large white frame house attached, it is easy to imagine what it was like here in 1891. Nothing much has changed. It smells like an old store; the wooden floors creak; and except for the modern cash registers and Associated Grocers' prices pasted on the windows, Mathews has a nineteenth century ambiance.

"I know a lot of people go to Ellsworth," Bruce said. "How are you going to compete with that?" Bruce was in his late thirties. He was medium height and build with thinning hair. He had worked in radio—a job he truly loved—in several places in Maine, but came home to manage the family business when his father, now seventy, had gotten too old to run it.

"Have you tried to do anything different the last couple of years to stay more competitive?"

"Well, I've got some ideas, and Associated Grocers, who feeds a lot of these small stores, has got some small ideas. But just competitive pricing, I would say, and fast-food service, is the key.

"I think the number one thing I want to be—this is my goal, my father's goal too—is to be the top food store in Cherryfield. We were the last ones to take on beer. There were five stores at the time, in the fifties and sixties—five food stores conglomerated around Main Street, Cherryfield. And we survived—number one. First store to go cash. In the older days you would charge. That was a big step for him (Bruce's father) for those days. And that was a key move because we're the only survivor of those five stores."

"You don't give credit to anybody?"

"No way. You cannot. You have to buy more groceries. We have two deliveries a week that amount to over three thousand dollars. So as fast as you take it in, you put it right back into buying groceries that they're going to take out the next week. And that was the big move for the fifties. It was daring. We lost some customers 'cause they didn't trust us—er—we felt that they got the feeling that we weren't trusting them anymore. But that was not the point. We were looking ahead to the future in those days. So there we were, the only cash store with the lowest prices around; and the only way we could offer the lowest prices was to get cash. And as long as we got it in cash we could take in sixty-seven cents for an item instead of eighty-five. Cash was much better than credit. But that was the key move in the fifties.

"Now we're to the point that bigger volume stores like Shop 'N Save and Red and White on both sides of us can lick us on variety easily. And the key to variety, I feel, is the population of your town. We can only grow as fast as our environment."

"Yeah, I noticed there has been some development around. How do you feel about that?"

"Well, I feel that our competitor down the road (the Maine Grocer, a franchised convenience store) has benefited from it. And he is what he sells. He's a fast-food man. He specializes in coffee, hot dogs, take-out service, and that's what we have to do—

somehow incorporate the quick take-out service, which is a big mark-up if handled properly.

"We want food shoppers here in the aisles. And we'll carry as large a variety as we can afford. So our goal is, within a year, to add forty feet to the store. A lot of it will be frozen food refrigerators because this is where it is today—that and microwavable foods.

"There's only one time of the year you make a lot of money and that's blueberry season. And the more customers you fit in here, the more money you take. It's like any business in this county—get it in July and August or forget it."

"Yes, it is amazing that you've been able to survive about a mile off the main drag."

"I would say it's the blueberry factories—the two factories—they're our key. And off to the lakes and beaches and ponds up on the ridge. But we still have a lot more to do. I'd like more fast-food services here—coffee, steamed hot dogs. I definitely think that's coming. And possibly a small-time bakery. We've got store plans that call for a buildup in almost every department. And the layout calls for great improvements—straight walls down the side—no juts. You see, this business was built around the house. (This is what I found so appealing: this massive white farmhouse, surrounded by large old maple trees, attached to a three story gable-front country store building. What a relic! What a gem! And how pretty it must look in the fall when the maples turn a brilliant orange and glints of light filter through to the river below! I wondered if Bruce realized what he had here.) Well, you didn't worry about customers in those days. You could go upstairs and shop—the second floor. There was a third floor too, in those days. You see where honesty has gone? You could trust people to go upstairs and shop and not worry about what was stolen in those days."

Bruce had many ideas and plans for the future; still, I couldn't help but wonder why the store hadn't changed—in decades. He also talked about speed, accuracy, "our forte," and an ability to use figures. He wanted me to know that he was on top of his business.

"The way I believe in serving customers is to give them the best food for the lowest amount of money. That's the best I can do. Say, 'Thank you, hope you come back again.' And at the same time I want to be accurate; I want to be right when things are rung out. 'Cause I want their trust; they'll come back here if they trust me."

Sort of the L.L. Bean mentality, I thought. Sell them a good sturdy flannel shirt or a pair of rubber soled hunting shoes at a fair price and the customer keeps coming back. L.L. Bean finally caught on. Indeed, after all those decades and passing fads and trends, the nation finally came around to seeing it their way. Perhaps the same would hold true for Mathews'. In an age when nearly everything was franchised, here was Mathews' Store; it hadn't changed in seventy years!

There are two-hundred thousand acres of blueberry barrens in Washington County. The county alone produces over ninety percent of the nation's wild blueberry crop. Cherryfield is known as the "Blueberry Capital of the World."

Because of the rockiness of eastern Maine's glaciated land-scape, machines may never completely replace the hand blueberry picker. And, since most of the blueberry fields Downeast are rocky, Bruce Mathews has the glaciers of the Ice Ages to thank for the labor intensiveness of Washington County's blueberry harvest. If this were wheat, or sunflower, or soybean country, there would be no need for hand pickers—rakers, as they are called, because these are low bush berries and you "rake" them with a short-handled, forty or fifty tine rake. Several thousand people descend on the blueberry barrens every summer. The sun is hot; they labor long and hard; they work up huge appetites and powerful thirsts. A country store owner couldn't ask for more!

The past two summers, Linda and I have raked blueberries for a young minister in Steuben. He's in his early thirties and works as though he had a mandate from the Lord to rake berries. He cuts his own firewood for his parsonage; he maintains his church and grounds; he performs all his duties with enthusiasm; and, he drives an old car. The young minister and his wife live humbly—old Yankee frugality to me; good Christianity to them.

I like raking blueberries. You get paid for what you rake—about three dollars a half bushel box. I've never considered myself a "serious" raker, however, because ever since I first started raking, back in high school, I've always raked in Steuben. "It's not like the barrens," I've always been told. "I'm just trying to get my back broken-in and then I'm going up the barrens where I can make some real money." That's what a guy from Bangor told me a couple of summers ago in Steuben. He had just bought a new Harley Davidson motorcycle. It had cost him thousands of dollars. He raked with us for a few days—until his back was broken-in—and then he departed for greener, or should I say, blue-er fields. The BARRENS—the name itself has always carried with it a sort of mystique—is a vast open landscape of granitic rubble and magnificent blueberries north of Cherryfield. Oh, what money one could make on the barrens! It is a blueberry rakers' paradise. I had heard stories of people raking a hundred boxes a day. "I wish blueberry season would last all year," the man with the motorcycle had told me that day when he departed for the barrens.

All that I knew of the barrens, I had got second-hand; much of it from Josh, a friend who had lived in Cherryfield, on and off, for several years. Josh is a leaseholder (crew leader), and when I found him, he was living on board a forty-six foot sailboat that he had obtained in a trade for his former residence, an old school house. It was what he had always wanted—a sailboat and the freedom to come and go as he pleased. He had just spent two years working in Boston.

"So you just sailed the boat down, and Monday you start blueberrying?"

"Yeah, blueberry fever," Josh joked. "Like Joan McMurray would say, 'There's gold on that ground. All you got to do is bend over and scoop it up.' Blueberry fever. You know, I thought I'd make a fortune. I was going to take like cheap plain glasses with clear lenses, and I was going to paint little blue dots on them, and call them 'bumper crop glasses.' Oh, they'd love it—"Wow!"" Josh mimicked a blueberry raker in the fields and said, "'Are they thick or what?'"

Josh was always a comedian. We were classmates in high school, and had gone to the same college in Arkansas our freshman year. "What's the name of that college you're going to down there?" Josh had asked me a few weeks before graduation. "Oh, I thought I'd go there too." We went to New Orleans on my motorcycle that

Thanksgiving and to Mexico that winter. But Josh left college after that freshman year and went on to other things. Sometimes I didn't see him for years at a time. He became one of those Downeast characters you always heard about, second-hand, but couldn't quite keep up with. "Oh, Josh's gone off to such and such." "Oh, he's now living with so and so over to such and such." It has been like that for years. Josh knows more people, especially women, and has had more addresses, than anyone I've ever known. A nice looking man with thick wavy brown hair and mischievous brown eyes: Josh has done more living the past two decades than most people do in a lifetime. He defines himself through his lifestyle. Indeed, whatever lifestyle he embraces at a particular time he does so with such energy and enthusiasm that it becomes his identity. So after several weeks at sea, it was as if his boat had become his idea of himself. And now that blueberry season was fast approaching, I assumed he would embrace that with similar enthusiasm. I also wondered what sorts of characters raked berries for Josh. he told me about one of his rakers, an organist for a rock band.

"And he is a scream," Josh began. "He's a character—one of a kind. He's got this van that has VAN FOR RENT: FOURTEEN SWEDISH FIREPLACES: THREE JACUZZIS. He has this fox-colored thing. The van is like falling apart. But he is a character. And I wouldn't care if he raked a box a day, just to have him out there—just for the laughs.

"Well, he's cruising around in this van and he drinks rum. And he's got this canoe and is living out on Schoodic Lake. And we had this group of punk rockers from Ohio that raked on different crews, basically—the 'Ohio Gang.' And I had a few of them with purple stripes down the side of their heads and Mohawks, and, you know, it was kind of the deal like—if you had some of the Ohio Gang, some of them were good and some of them came with them, because the ones from the year before said, 'If you go blueberrying, you'll make big money.' Well, I wound up with a bunch of the new ones that were kind of a fizzle. They didn't do shit.

"Well, anyway, the Ohio Gang had this camp on Schoodic Lake, and this guy in the van, he was up at the other end of the lake, and he had a canoe. Well, he had this kid with him from Beals Island who was a clam digger and he was the classic Downeast hick. He hadn't gone too far and he hadn't seen too much. And he was probably seventeen years old or so. And he wound up with this guy and said, 'Well, let's go canoeing.' So they put the canoe in and they started paddling around the lake. And it got dark and they see this campfire. 'Cause this guy in the van, he raked for me, and he knew some of the Ohio Gang. He said, 'We were paddling along and we see this campfire. I said, 'Let's go in there and check it out. Looks like a party going on.'

"He said they pulled in there—'Sure enough, I couldn't believe it. It was the Ohio Gang. They were around a big campfire; had all these instruments like wooden mallets, tambourines; all home-made instruments. And they was pounding and having this big jam session. And they were all naked—the whole bunch! There must have been forty of them—women, children, the whole bunch!'

"He said, 'This kid from Beals, his eyes were about that big around (Josh help up his hands, and opened his thumbs and index fingers to the size of tennis balls.). And it was like a big jungle beat going on.' He said, 'That kid just stood there, didn't say a word. And they're all blown out of it on drugs. It's just like going back to the pygmies.' He said, 'What a scream!' 'Cause this guy, he jumped right in. He was ready to party. Geez, I can just picture him around that circle with that campfire and everybody naked and that kid from Beals Island with his hip boots on, looking at them. 'What's this?'"

"Wow, some characters on the barrens," I said.

"I mean, I've seen guys down there—two of them—who were living underneath an old camper top."

"You mean just the shell, but no truck underneath?"

"Yeah, somebody had thrown away a cap. It wasn't a camper; it was one of those old caps. They had found that on the barrens, all stove to hell, that somebody had thrown off, and they were living under it. Why they thought they had the Hilton. 'Cause when it rained—they didn't have it jacked up—they just had it right on the ground, right on the rocks, and had their sleeping bags under it."

"Is there something about blueberry raking that draws out this element?"

"Yes—there's freedom there." (Here was that idea of freedom again: Freedom to rake or sit on your pail; freedom to make as much or as little money as you want. There is some freedom in blueberry raking, but are you truly free if you have to earn enough money to live on for any length of time? I'm not so sure the serious raker is any more free than the serious clam or worm digger. With clamming, worming, or blueberry raking, you're free as long as the season lasts; as long as your body holds up and you've got the energy and drive to keep on working.)

"Freedom?"

"Yeah. And I'd say that everybody there is real independent."

"What do you suppose those guys that come from as far away as Ohio do the rest of the year?"

"Lots of them follow the circuit. They go apple picking. I've got one raker, he'll go, 'Well, this year I'm going to do it.' And the first paycheck (Josh clapped his hands.)—GONE. You know, he's out of it. Gonna buy a piece of land; gonna get this; gonna get it all together."

"The American dream."

"Last year he did do good. You know, I encourage him. I like my beer and drink, you know. I have a party for them every year.

"I went up to Cape Breton to see the Indians."

"Mic Mac Indians?"

"Yeah."

"So they come down from Cape Breton every summer?"

"Yeah. I insult them when I call them, 'Are you white?' That was the thing I'd say, 'You're a white man, aren't you?' 'Oh, man,' he'd say. 'Low blow! Don't call me white man.' Or I'd get six of them sitting on their buckets and I'd say, 'Do you have a powwow permit?' I said, 'Five Indians in one group—that's all we allow. Six of you become a powwow. It's against the rules.'" Josh was laughing as he reflected back on this story and I got the feeling he was anxious to be reunited with his Indian crew. I got the impression there was a mutual respect between the crew and leaseholder—that Josh was fun to work for; that the Indians were fun to be with.

"They live on a reservation up there?"

"Yeah. I went up there. They really didn't expect me to show up, and it kind of threw them off guard, you know—that I actually made the trip up there and looked them up."

"To see how they were doing?"

"Yeah. I have good luck with most of them."

"This is good money for them, too, I guess?"

"Yeah, most of them use it for their kids' school clothes. At least the ones who rake for me do. You get a little competition. It's the same old ballgame—you get one big patch (thick patch of berries—good raking!) and they're all stalling, waiting. They see that patch coming and they're all sitting on their buckets, and it doesn't matter if they're (the rakers) white, black, green, or blue. I play it real hard. I ran down one time and a bunch of Indians were waiting for a patch and I didn't twine it. (string it off)* I stopped twining so there was no strips.  So they sat on their buckets and they waited and waited and all of a sudden there's no more strips left. And they said, 'No more strips!' And I said, 'Oh yeah, waiting for a strip?'  And I'd twine them about eighteen inches wide."

"Eighteen inches?" (Strips are usually about twenty feet wide.)

"Just about the width of their rake. They just stood there with their mouths' open.  I said, 'You've come up against the wrong dude.'  (I got the impression that josh thoroughly enjoyed this game.) Basically, my job is to keep the rakers from screwing each other."

"Were there any fights?"

"Not my crew. I work real hard at making it fair. I don't rake both sides of the road and say, 'Pick whatever side you want to rake.'  I rake one side all the way down to where I end my machines and I shut them off and bring them right up and start on the other side. And one guy goes, 'Geez, I've got to walk all the way back?' I said, 'Yeah, that's it.' I've seen it where they've raked both sides of the road at once.  And good berries on one side, while on the other side, it just keeps going down to where no one will rake the stuff.  And the ones raking the bad side will be

---

*Crew leaders divide the fields into long strips. Each raker is given a strip to rake. Only when they have finished that strip do they move on to another.

bitching about the ones that are raking the other side. So, I ended it. I got my little system down. I set all my machines out. I twine both sides all the way down. And then I say, 'This side.' And they rake all the way down to the last machine. It's all one side, and when we swap, we all swap together. And I've got a nice quiet crew. 'You don't like it? Go somewhere else.'

"It wears me down. It's hard. You are everything to most of these people. I've had people beg me for jobs and then rake for an hour. It's like, 'Wow, man! I didn't know it was this hard!' You try to say, 'Hey, hang in there. You're going to make it.' I've heard of blueberry rakers making three hundred bucks a day."

"Yeah, I don't work that hard at it," I said. "I do well to average fifteen or sixteen boxes a day. Of course, you can't compare the small fields in Steuben with their rocks, ferns, and puckerbushes, to the barrens."

One July evening, a few weeks before the start of the August blueberry harvest, Josh, Linda, and I squeezed into the cab of his pickup truck and went trundling over the rutted dirt roads of the barrens. It was like we had left Maine altogether and landed on a high plateau like central Mexico, or maybe East Africa during the rainy season when everything is lush. The barrens are vast; the scale is grander than anywhere else in Maine, save the ocean. Trillions of little round blueberries against green, orange, and finally, as they ripen, red leaves—as far as the eye can see. When we came back down from the barrens into the thick Maine woods below, I felt as though we had just come home from a trip to some exotic place!

"I'd rather have someone who raked sixteen boxes a day," Josh said.

"And rake them clean."

"Reasonably clean. I'm not asking for perfection. But a guy that shows up every day and rakes his sixteen boxes is better than the guy who shows up and rakes forty, butchers them, butchers his strips, butchers his boxes, bitches and complains. The Indians— you never hear a peep out of them. But if you put a half white and half Indian crew, then the Indians are saying, 'The white guys are doing this.' And the white guys are saying, 'The Indians are doing this.' And I'm saying, 'Bullshit. You're all a bunch of assholes!

And I'm here to tell you you're not going to screw each other no matter what color you are. And if you're going to sit on the bucket and wait for the strip, you ain't getting it.'"

Josh and I had gone to college together that first year in Arkansas and then he had come back to Maine. There was something about the coast—the islands or the water—that held him. He had worked—and had been first mate—on boats up and down the East Coast. He had been all around the Caribbean and the rimland of Central and South America—places that I, a geographer, had only read about in books. Josh had always been free. He also stayed on top of the trends—social and economic—and I could rely on him to tell me the latest. Like—"What ever happened to the back-to-the-land movement? Has that peaked? Have all those people given up and gone back to whatever they were doing before?"

"I feel like what you see left of that is still supplying blueberry raking in Cherryfield. Like Mary (I assumed that Mary was one of Josh's many women over the years.) came up with me from Kittery and she said, 'Well, now I know where all the hippies went.' I think what it comes down to is—a lot of people realize that life is a struggle. Like—living in your camp isn't a struggle for you in the summer." (Josh was drawing an analogy between blueberry raking and Linda and I living here in our camp with no electricity, plumbing, or telephone. Both were examples of short-term human struggle. At the same time, both the blueberry raker and the rustic camp dweller are grabbing at freedom—a freedom that you know is going to end soon enough.)

I said, "No, this isn't too much of a struggle in the summer, but it would be year-round."

"This is a good change. This is probably a very good humbling experience. It keeps you in touch with who you are."

"And the people we know here. This is home base."

"And that's important."

"Well, what are you going to do when you finish with your blueberry lease this year?"

"I don't know. There's two things I'm sure of right now. One, is I have a boat. Two, is that I'm going blueberrying. You know what's funny? I've been working on the Boston Fish Pier, for, let's say, close to two years. And I've never pictured myself there—even while I'm working. They'd say, 'Josh? He's down at the Boston Pier.' 'No, he's not. He'd never do that.' And the neat part, though; in that little community there's some nice people. I had friends there. I got four jobs offered me. Come on down and make me a full partner. I've got friends there, and there are nice people. It's just all the garbage around it. Here I'm working on the pier; I'm working on a boat there; I can't park there. And the dog's not allowed on the dock."

"That's no good," I said. "If the place isn't fit for a dog, it isn't fit for me."

"I said, 'I've got some friends here, but you people can keep this'. They said, 'You're going back to Maine?' 'Yeah,' I said. 'The dog will be able to shit where she wants. I can park my car where I work. I don't have to have a permit.' I said, 'You've got to have a permit to scratch your ass around here!' It's all coming to that—it is. But I feel something about those islands out there."

So Josh had quit has job in Boston; he had turned down four job offers, and he had sailed his boat out into the Gulf of Maine, past the islands, and all the way Downeast. He was home again; and for a month or so, while he harvested his blueberries, he was once again a free man. "Free at last, free at last!"

# CHAPTER 20

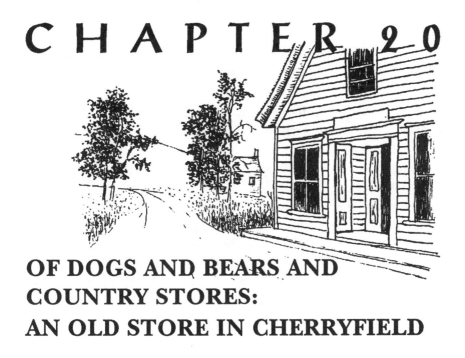

## OF DOGS AND BEARS AND COUNTRY STORES: AN OLD STORE IN CHERRYFIELD

My friend, Josh, told me a story about an old store in Cherryfield. "They had a dog," Josh said. "What the hell was that dog's name? They had this dog. And you'd come in, and that dog had certain customers it knew. It would come over and put its paw on your foot if you were eating a candy bar. And as you ate that candy bar, and it kept going down, the dog's weight would start going down. And by the time you were done with that candy bar, that dog would be on one paw—balancing.

"Yeah, you'd be eating, and that dog would come over and put its paw on your foot. He'd put his paw there real gentle, and if you didn't pay any attention, slowly the weight would go on. So eventually, you'd go, 'Geez, Christ! That dog's standing on its paw or what?' And the thing was as big as a fifty gallon drum!"

"Was it a Lab?"

"No, no. It was just this mongrel. Molly—that's what her name was. People would come in and say, 'Hello Molly.' And the dog knew who she was going to beg off of. Yeah, you'd be standing there eating that cake or that candy or ice cream—she loved ice cream.

"Well, you talk about country stores and how everybody used to set stuff down (buy it on credit—put it on the slip). Just like up at Young's Store. I don't know if they still do that."

"Sure they do," I said.

"Now that's the mark of a true country store."

"Yes, a real country store," I agreed.

"Well, you come in. 'Can I set it down 'til times get better?'"

"And sometimes they'll come in to Young's and pay off a dollar or two," I added.

"So Molly there—they had that dog trained. They'd take a candy bar and unwrap it, and they'd throw it right on her paw. Or they'd take a piece of bologna—inch thick—throw it on the floor and say, 'Molly, that's bought on credit.' And that dog wouldn't touch it. That's the way they trained her. Anything bought on credit, she wouldn't eat it. And you'd sit there, and Molly would look at that bologna, and she'd look at it. And you'd say, 'Well, Molly, that's paid for.'"

"And then she'd inhale it?"

"Yep."

"Are you telling me a story?"

"I'm telling you the honest-to-God truth."

The old store was a relic of the era when Route 1 passed through uptown Cherryfield on its way to Harrington. But Route 1 had been rerouted many years ago, and now the old store stood a mile north of the center of town, so that only a handful of locals, and people heading up to the blueberry barrens, ever passed this way. The old store was obsolete. But it still looked and smelled like a country store. It had an old potbellied stove, and old wooden counter, wooden posts, and wooden floors that slanted to one side and creaked and groaned when you walked over them. They sold boots, stove pipes, camping supplies, kerosene, nails, and green work clothes. And, of course, they let people set things down. I once asked the owner about it, and he had said, "I have given out credit. It is the worst thing anyone can do. People will run up a slip and then leave town, or they will take their cash and go to a supermarket and want you to carry them for the rest of the month when their money runs out. They can tell you the biggest lie, and have a smile on their face at the same time."

The old store went out of business in 1985. It's surprising it survived that long. Indeed, if it hadn't been for the annual blueberry harvest, the old store might have closed years ago. It's too bad blueberry season couldn't last a bit longer. In August of 1984, I wrote in my notebook:

> It's blueberry season and the old store is actually doing some business. I watched two young men get out of an old car and enter the old store about eleven in the morning. Their blue-stained clothing indicated they were blueberry rakers. One man had hair down to his shoulders; the other man had long hair too, and no shirt. In a few minutes, they emerged from the store with two six-packs of beer and a box of chocolate doughnuts. They drove a quarter mile or so, then hit the brakes. They put the car in reverse, then squealed the tires back to the old store. The shirtless man got out of the car, went into the store, and came out a minute later with a pack of cigarettes. He got back in the car and they burned rubber all the way out of town.

It was raining buckets the last time I was in the old store. A cat slept soundly on the wooden counter, oblivious to the pattering of raindrops on the window; and to the man in front of it talking— about traps and snares and hunting bears. He was a big man; large hands, his shirt-sleeves rolled up, exposing his massive fore-arms. The big man wore green work clothes and a baseball cap; he had a plug of tobacco in his cheek, and a smug half-smile as he held up the head of a bear he'd shot. And he had an audience— a following. Two local men—early twenties—stood there silently, puffing on cigarettes and taking in every detail, as the big man drew a sketch of a snare he used to trap bears.

"They stay down in the low wet areas where it's cooler," he explained. "When they put the bee hives on the barrens so's the bees can pollinate—that's when the bears come out. They can smell the hives just like you and I can smell food. The smell is what brings them up to high ground. The bears don't want the honey; it's the young bees they eat—for protein. I don't get any money for shooting them, but it's good clean fun."

The number of bears along the Maine coast is said to be increas-ing. One theory suggests that clearcutting of the forests in northern

Maine is destroying their habitat and driving the bears southward. The number of bear sightings is up; the bears are becoming a nuisance, and a subject of controversy. There have been reports of bears breaking into camps. In Birch Harbor, a bear attacked a horse. And in Gouldsboro, a story was going around concerning a woman—a camp owner from out-of-state—who, when filling out a handgun permit, let slip, "I don't worry about people breaking in, but I do worry about the bears." Finally, there was the story about the elderly woman who put food out for the bears each night. It was evident that Downeasters had mixed feelings about bears.

And bear stories are always newsworthy in eastern Maine. On May 14, 1988, the *Bangor Daily News* ran an article by Rick Hewitt entitled: "3 bear cubs rescued after mother shot." Accompanying Hewitt's report was a picture of a wildlife biologist holding two of the three small bear cubs captured in Sullivan after their mother had been illegally shot. The article explained that the hunting season for bear usually runs from September through November. If apprehended, the killer could be fined as much as one thousand dollars. Meanwhile, the five month old cubs would be taken to a rehabilitation center in northern Maine. And by mid-August when the bears had grown to about fifty pounds each, they would be released in the wild.

Three orphaned bear cubs had been rescued. It was a heart-warming story. And, if it is true that you really can judge a society by the way it treats its animals, then Downeast Maine is in pretty good shape. In South Carolina, I once had to call the police and report a case of animal abuse. I then watched through my back fence as the policeman ordered the man on the other side to remove the chain that had gouged a deep bloody gash in his dog's neck. I also hoped he'd order the man to feed the dog—the pitiful creature's ribs were sticking out—that I had been trying to feed over my back fence for several weeks. And worse: The dog had no house. I finally tossed over a large cardboard box for the whimpering animal to crawl under on rainy nights.

The South Carolina county where we live has no humane society, and there are dead dogs and cats on the highways all the time. And in South Carolina, I seldom see dogs as passengers in automobiles. It's as if the fastidious Southerners do not want dog hair in their air-conditioned cars. How different from eastern Maine, where one only has to go as far as Doug's Shop 'N Save in Ellsworth to find a huge parking lot overflowing with cars and trucks containing dogs of every imaginable breed. Go on a Saturday and it's like dogs' day out. Indeed, Downeasters seem to like to drive their dogs nearly everywhere.

In some respects, Downeast Maine is a society much like Great Britain, which has a high degree of tolerance for eccentric people, especially animal lovers. After all, Barbara Woodhouse, Britain's celebrated dog trainer, allowed her dogs to sleep on her bed. Still, despite those Downeasters who will do most anything to save an animal, there are others who will shoot a bear for sport. But are the bears really a nuisance? Do they really pose a danger? I have my doubts.

I was running down the dirt road to our camp two years ago when I saw what I thought was a large dog coming towards me. It was late afternoon, with the breeze blowing hard in my direction, when the dog—getting closer now—was suddenly transformed into a bear! I had never seen one in the wild before, yet there it was, still ambling towards me with two tiny cubs trailing behind. Fifty yards might have separated us when the mother bear stopped, looked, then turned into the woods. One cub followed its mother; the other cub climbed a pine tree, and I turned and jogged back up to Route 1.

Another day—coming from the other direction now—my dog, Hallie, and I encountered a yearling in almost the same spot. Hallie's ears went back. I froze in my tracks. The black bear perked up, then bounded into the pines. On several other occasions, I've smelled them in the woods, seen the alders move, and heard and "felt" their presence.

Finally, I was running along Route 1 one summer day, when from a distance, a large hairy creature sprinted across the highway in front of a line of traffic. Was it the "Wild Man" I had heard about in Sullivan? A car had pulled off to the side of the road after the creature had passed, and when I reached the car, the driver said, "They usually travel in pairs. I thought I'd wait here a minute and see if another bear comes out." I didn't linger. From a distance the bear had been but a hairy image. And had the car not stopped, I might have wondered if I had just been hallucinating— the image conjured up from fatigue on the run.  I wasn't sure what I had seen, only that I could never have outrun it!

# CHAPTER 21

## FREE COW MANURE: FRESH DAILY
## ANDERSON'S GENERAL STORE,
## HARRINGTON

I was in Anderson's General Store on Route 1 in Harrington, an establishment more famous for its free cow manure than for anything else, when a woman named Gloria began telling me how much the town had changed. I knew something of Harrington. I had a job here during the summer of 1973, and had fond memories of this lovely Downeast village. But Gloria said, "Harrington has gotten crowded. It's not like it used to be."

"Oh?"

"I would have been satisfied here, but we've got all kinds of problems coming in now that we didn't have before."

"Like what?"

"Like drugs. I don't want our kids exposed to that. Some of them come in here (store). There's a girl with an earring in her nose—which is her right. But don't come around here reeking of pot."

"Are these locals?"

"Oh, no. These are out-of-staters."

But that wasn't all. Gloria was concerned about the land developers, the Canadian oil companies, and the Japanese seafood processors. These outsiders were taking over. She said, "I think the developers are pricing the local people out. These clammers and wormers—they're being priced right out of the housing market, and that's wrong. These people have worked hard all their lives."

As we talked, an old man entered the store and picked up a newspaper. He didn't speak much English. And the few words he spoke, he uttered with a Spanish accent. When he left the store, Gloria said, "The Panamanians have been in Harrington buying land. He's a retired Panamanian diplomat. I don't know how much land he has, but it's a lot of property."

"I understand one of the developers has a large tract of land in Harrington now."

"Well, Tom Selleck's limousine pulled up here one day," Gloria said. "I wasn't in here, but I heard about it from one of the girls who works here. He didn't come in the store. His bodyguard came in with this 'let's kill somebody' attitude and asked for some wine, and they didn't have it."

"But Selleck was sitting in the car?"

"Well, they assume he was. It was this big white limousine with all this dark glass. There was a chauffeur in front, and this guy was his bodyguard. He had a big old—."

"He had a gun?"

"Oh yeah, a great big thing."

"The kind with a shoulder strap?"

"Oh yeah. He came in the store and scared her to death. And he asked for some French wine, and they just don't carry that. So she said, 'Well, we have free cow manure.' And he was offended. He got very upset. He said he wasn't able to find this wine in Ellsworth. I don't know why he thought he could get it down here. Scared her to death to see a gun on somebody!"

Anderson's General Store has become famous in recent years for giving away free cow manure. Tourists who have stopped and read the, FREE COW MANURE FOR STORE CUSTOMERS: FRESH DAILY sign, have taken this bit of local color back home, where newspapers in such diverse places as Baton Rouge, Louisiana and Jacksonville, Florida have written about it. It has been a story on both Maine and national network news broadcasts, while locally, people from as far away as Jonesport often drive over for the manure.

Getting back to the subject of developers, Gloria said, "You should see what they've done. They just went in there and bull-dozed down here on Pineo Point."

"Are they building a subdivision?"

"I've heard up to twenty-five houses," Gloria explained.

"Are they two-acre lots?"

"I don't know."

"They probably want eighty-thousand a piece," I said. (That was a figure I frequently heard Downeast. Of course, eighty-thousand dollars is cheap for a saltwater lot in central or southern Maine these days.)

"Probably, and can you see a clammer—this guy who just bought cigarettes—trying to afford that? (A grizzled, middle-aged man, who looked as though he had led a hard life, had just left the store with a package of Marlboros.) He's out there clamming and he doesn't have a pension plan to retire on."

"And he's not young," I said.

"No, he's not young. And these clammers starting out—they can't afford that."

While we were on the subject of work, I said, "There's something I've been wondering. Young people Downeast—especially men—seem to prefer manual labor. Is that a misconception?" (When I had gotten my first college teaching job, a high school friend who had worked many years in an auto body shop said to me, "Well, I guess that's better than nothing." He didn't take me seriously. In his mind, what I did for a living wasn't real work. Real men work with their hands. "It has carried over from the days when Maine was a frontier," another friend once told me. "Life was always hard here. It was a tough winter. Everyone was measured by how hard they worked.")

"I don't know what it's going to take to change that," Gloria said. "I know they've got some good teachers up here at the high school. Quality teachers. I've got a friend who teaches up there and he runs into the same problem. There are some talented kids around here too."

Gloria mentioned a local boy who worked for one of the blue-berry processors. It was seasonal work. The wages were low. "And he was perfect college material," she said. "But he wouldn't go to college."

"But I love these people," Gloria continued. "Last spring, Bob Anderson (the owner of the store) hurt himself. And he had no problem. People came every day and took care of the cows for him. And they never charged him."

I knew something of the Harrington that Gloria talked about. It was the old Harrington—the little Downeast village, with its friendly, hardworking folk—that had made such an impression on Gloria, and on me. I had a job in Harrington during the summer of 1973, building a grass tennis court for a summer resident from out-of-state.

There were no land developers, Japanese businessmen, or retired Panamanian diplomats here in 1973, but the man from out-of-state—he was more of an occasional weekend visitor than an actual summer resident—and his associate, Don, who was my real boss, were, perhaps, the beginning of the "new" Harrington that Gloria had described. The out-of-staters served us beer (Michelob, or "Mister Mil" (Miller) as Don called it) on the job. They also served us lunch—the best grade of salami—all we could eat. A local teenager—his parents were the winter caretakers of the house—hung around all day while we worked. He stood at the ready—at your service—to satisfy our whims and needs. He'd bring us a beer, or a bottle of pop; and, if you asked him, he'd gladly jump on his bike, peddle over to the general store, and fetch us some fresh fruit. Bing cherries were our favorite. The out-of-staters treated us very well—royally, you might say. We worked hard, and we were much cheaper than the union labor they were accustomed to, so when the salami ran out, they gave us a lunch allowance and sent us two miles down the road to a little eatery (gone now) called the Pilot House.

I would arrive about eight in the morning. Inside, the large colonial house resonated with the sounds of Tommy Dorsey. Don, the engineer, a balding, middle-aged man, would make us breakfast, and talk about his passion—swing music. "Oh, those Big Band days were something else," he'd say. "You guys don't know what you missed." He was a pleasant man, and he enjoyed our company. At last, my friend, Aidan, and I would saunter out into the summer morning—the sun high now and hot—and begin our work, digging postholes, grading the land with steel rakes, and laying the rolls of sod.

The biggest task was setting the heavy wooden posts that would support the fence around the court. I had taken geology courses in college, and I was certain the posts would eventually lean. "We're on the floodplain," I'd tell Don, the engineer. "We shouldn't be building down here." Indeed, the property sloped down to the estuary of the bay, and as we dug, the holes filled with water. So Aidan and I would lie on our stomachs, reach down, and bail out the water. But Don didn't seem to worry. I guess he had gotten used to working for a wealthy man; and, if the owner wanted a grass tennis court—regardless of the short time it might last—then so be it. Such a contrast from the frugal Downeasters I was used to working for.

The heat came early that summer. And soon there were four of us straining in the sun. The new guys had come all the way from Cutler. "We heard it was all the beer you could drink," one of them said. How rapidly information spreads in small societies. A stocky Downeaster named Greg showed up next. And all that week as we strained and sweated in the early summer heat, Greg kept saying, "Geez, just as soon as I get my paycheck, I'm gonna get me some of that Colt .45 Malt Liquor. Geez, hasn't that stuff got a kick to it!" Greg was about twenty. He looked thirty-five. He lived from day to day. And on Monday there were four of us again.

That summer, I got to feel the rhythm of the town. The big house—with its swimming pool soon to be completed, and the tennis court under construction—was in downtown Harrington. And from that tennis court, Aidan and I and the guys from Cutler, could observe the town, and the town could observe us. We were something new in Harrington—a topic of conversation. People stopped to talk; or drove by slowly, just to look. Once, a big, bearded man in a Volvo 544 sedan (the old roundback model that was popular with hippies, back-to-the-landers, and anti-nuke types) pulled up. Aidan knew him and said he was a log diver. He would dive, Aidan said, with scuba tanks to the bottom of rivers and haul up huge logs that had gotten snagged.

"And he makes a living at that?" I asked.

"Well, you know, it's his thing, man," Aidan explained. We were the center of the universe that summer, and all of Harrington's "stars" revolved around us.

The Big Man from out-of-state—who we rarely saw—knew all the workmen's names, and this surprised me. Aidan said he was the president of a railroad, but still, he seemed to pride himself in keeping on top of each and every detail of our little operation. The railroad may have been his vocation, but I got the idea that this place had become his avocation. And near the end of the summer, after he had seen us work, he offered Aidan a job out-of-state. Aidan was a few years older than I. He was married and had two small children. Aidan was intelligent—one of those gifted people who starts college but then decides it's all "Mickey Mouse."

But Aidan was also a good listener who could follow details, and a good worker, one of the best I've ever seen. "It's hard to find good workmen these days," the Big Man had said to Aidan. "I want you to take some steaks home to your family and think about my offer." It had been a good offer, but I don't think Aidan ever thought of himself as a workman. He just happened to have a job building a tennis court that summer. Of course, Aidan turned down the offer. He still lives Downeast and seems as happy as a clam!

The Big Man from out-of-state never offered me a job, but then he knew I wasn't available. He once asked me, "What are your future plans, Allan?" The tone of the question was like: "Young man, just what are your intentions with my daughter?" And I said, "Oh, I go to college—down in Arkansas." And he said, "Good. stay there." That's all he had said. He only spoke to me one other time, and then it was to say, "Allan, you're wasting my labor. We can move that dirt with the backhoe." He then directed me to another job, one that could not be done by machine. He was a no-nonsense corporate man—the type of executive that Van Heflin portrayed in the 1950s movie, *Patterns*—the organization man concerned ultimately with the "bottom line".

And what did this big city executive think of the people Downeast? I got the impression he liked Downeasters; but I also felt they frustrated him. One morning, he told Aidan and me, "You know, the people in southern Maine are much more industrious than people around here. They're more disciplined. They're more interested in getting ahead." And as I reflect back on what he said, I'm reminded of what Barbara Vittum had said earlier in my journey: "The other thing I noticed about people from away—they come here to escape, and when they get here, almost right after they get their house built, almost the first thing they do—they want to change it like to where they came from."

Back in the present-day country store, I began talking to Bob Anderson, the owner. "This is a very hard business," he began. "I haven't had a day off in six years. I haven't had a vacation in six years and I'm tired and frustrated. And you can't get help. Nobody wants to work, especially in Washington County. The welfare system is a way of life here. And welfare pays them more than I can pay them."

"Do you think it's because they can make more money clamming or worming?"

"No. I had a heck of a girl in here last winter. She worked all winter, and as soon as the good weather came in the spring, she left. I said, 'Why?' And she said, 'Well, I don't want to work anymore. I get more than enough money on my welfare payments.' And she said, 'I was just in here all winter 'cause I was lonesome and wanted to talk to people.' And the next thing I know, she wanted to come back because she was a little short on money. And, she quit again after about a month. And I said, 'What's the problem this time?' She said, 'No problem. I just got pregnant again. My welfare is going to double, and my food stamps and everything is going to double. I have more money than I can possibly need now.' She said, 'Why work? I've got two children.'"

Bob had been a high school physical education teacher for many years, then a dairy farmer, before buying the store in Harrington. He had lived in several states. I asked him if he had ever thought of going back to teaching, here in Maine.

"No. I got enough of teaching. I loved the kids, but I can't put up with the garbage (hassles), the administrators, the parents. From what I can see in education today—and everybody's condemning education—it's just babysitting. They don't want to teach the kids anything. They don't want to help the kids. And every superintendent that I ever got into trouble with said, 'Anderson, cut it out. You're making waves. Roll with the tide.' I said, 'I don't want to roll with the tide. I want to help these kids.' Nobody gives a damn anymore. It's just babysit them; get them through the year. And don't make any trouble. And it's an awful injustice to the kids.

"I'll never forget my first teaching job. I was teaching physical education in high school. I had high school girls—I can't believe it today—who didn't know anything about menstruation. So I got a Walt Disney cartoon, "The Story of Menstruation," and showed it to my freshmen girls. Some of the people in town wanted me arrested because I was a lewd man! No sex education! And this was in progressive New York State. And it was suggested to me that I better not come back the following year.

"But the thing that got me involved in this—I delivered a baby in the girls' lavatory to a high school senior that year. And in talking to her, she didn't know what was going on. She knew about sex, but she didn't know about birth control and children. I said, I've got to do something for these kids. And I knew it was going to be controversial, but I didn't think it was going to cost me my job."

But that had happened years ago—back in 1957—and times had changed. Or had they?

"They have a hell of a lot of girls pregnant at Narraguagus High School. And somebody needs to be teaching them something. I'm selling condoms. And people come in here—they're (condoms) right behind you—and they're giving me hell. I've had preachers come and tell me I was going to hell—that I was the most sinful person in the world. I said, 'You can condemn me all you want, but if it's going to help one kid stay away from AIDS, I'll sell them. I'll give them away, if I can afford to.'"

"Is there AIDS Downeast now?"

"Well, that's it. And the minister said to me, 'Well, there's no AIDS in Washington County.' I said, 'I'll tell you what I'll do. I'll donate a thousand dollars to your church if you will give me a thousand dollars if I can prove there's AIDS in Washington County.' He said, 'I can't do that. That's sinful. That's gambling.' I said, 'No, you're wrong and you don't have the guts to admit it.' I said, 'You go down to the Machias Hospital, talk to the Head Surgeon down there, 'cause he comes in here every day and we talk. And there is AIDS right here.'"

I could work up a powerful appetite in one of these old-time country stores—or a terrific headache. And as much as I enjoyed talking to Bob Anderson, I decided it was time to saunter over to Mom's Restaurant across the street and have lunch. And it was just like coming in from the barn—you know, all old-time Maine farmhouses were connected to their barns—and into Mom's kitchen. There was a playpen, and a baby, and a couple of young women talking "kids". I sat at a booth by the window and sort of felt like I didn't belong in that family.

# CHAPTER 22

# TOWN MARKET TURNING OVER: COLUMBIA FALLS

B y accident, I arrived at the Town Market in several years ago, on the very day that a Downeaster was turning over the keys to a newcomer from out-of-state. The Downeaster had seemed like just a kid; he might have been twenty-five or thirty years old. The Town Market had been handed down to him by his father, but he was still young and restless, not ready to be tied down. He showed me the tide clock on the wall and said, "Most of my customers are from about age fourteen to thirty-five—mainly fishermen, clammers, and wormers. They start coming in the store a couple hours before going out (on the mudflats) and get drunk on beer, and come in again after the tide to buy more beer. I sell a thousand dollars worth of beer a day! Clams are selling right now for forty-eight dollars a bushel. They were up to fifty-four dollars. They make a lot more money in a day than you'll ever make."

The Downeaster was a feisty little guy who didn't mind telling you about his store. His mood was upbeat—euphoria, I assumed, from having just unloaded an albatross. But I felt sorry for the newcomer. Everything he said made me feel a little sad. He was so friendly and optimistic; he had so many plans. The newcomer was about thirty. His pretty, young wife was pregnant with their first child, and he was all excited about that. They had been living in the South, but did not want to raise their children there. "Too many drugs." "Of course." It was obvious they were looking for something—that probably didn't exist anymore—and I had my doubts they would find it here. The newcomer had a college degree, but had "grown tired of writing reports." And like so many others who come here from away, they wanted to take charge of their lives . . . by having their own country store. They would live in the apartment above the store, go cross country skiing in the winter, hiking in the summer, and raise their family amid the serenity of "unspoiled" Washington County.

I returned a year later to find the front of the store bumped out and shingled in cedar—all this to make room for a small laundromat for the local diggers. And I thought: You get a couple of clammers going and they can talk an out-of-stater into anything. No Historic Register for this old store building; rather, a radical change in function. Inside, the single large room had been partitioned, and I could hear that all-too-familiar and mind-numbing sound of a video arcade. And I thought: You get a couple of kids from Downeast Maine started and they can talk an out-of-stater into anything. The newcomers had built a game room with a pool table and video games on one side, while on the other side where the groceries and beverages were, a small television was turned on, and there was the newcomer's wife entertaining the baby on the counter. I didn't like what they had done to the historic old store. The noise from the game room and the television soon got on my nerves. And the sadness that I had felt the previous year—then in anticipation of reality setting in for these nice folks; now because the "improvements" they had made seemed only to suggest desperation—suddenly returned.

But the game room had done very well, the newcomer explained. It paid the utilities and gave the local kids something to do. "There's nothing in this town for kids," the newcomer's wife said. The out-of-staters meant well. They were nice folks who wanted to make Columbia Falls a better community. And I noticed that they had a nice way with their customers—not just a "Thank you, come back again," but a genuine concern for the well-being of the townspeople—which made me think they were well-liked in the community.

But if there was anything that could put me in a prickly mood, it was outsiders imposing their suburban values on a rural community. We had always found plenty to do when I was a teenager in Steuben. We fished, we hunted, we went out on the bay in leaky wooden boats. We went swimming in the summer, and ice skating and ice fishing in the winter. We went exploring, we built things out of wood, we played sports at School; we did all the neat things that kids playing video games ought to be doing, like experiencing the wonders of life itself, rather than staring into a machine.

I soon learned, however, that the changes the newcomers had made in the store were only superficial. Indeed, proprietors may change certain things, but in a culture as steadfast as that of Washington County, it is the customers who ultimately determine the character of the store. And like the young Downeaster, the newcomers found that their business still revolved around the tide clock on the wall. "About two and a half hours before low tide the store is jumping," the newcomer said. "We're really a convenience store. We sell items which turn over fast, and some boots and gloves, items the clammers need. I thought about adding wine, but decided it wouldn't sell around here. They want beer in quarts during the summer, especially during blueberry season, and cans in the winter. They'll come in and buy a case of quarts."

A few years later, the newcomers were gone. They had sold the Town Market to another couple from out-of-state, who had renovated the store's interior, and turned it into a small eatery which included pizza, deli sandwiches, and hot dogs. The old store seemed to be doing well.

The Town Market had been Columbia Falls' first gas station, back in the days of the Model A Ford. The old store stands in the village center, on old Route 1, across the street from the historic Ruggles House—now open for tours—and adjacent to the elementary school. Over the years, the Town Market has had many owners, one who even lowered the foundation a couple of feet to make it easier to climb the stairs to the front door. The higher foundation had allowed a deeper cellar for storing grain. Once there had been shipyards, gristmills, and three blueberry factories in Columbia Falls. That was back in the nineteenth century when the town's population peaked at nearly seven hundred. The 1980 census counted five hundred and fifty, but the town is said to be growing once again. And the Town Market, made over numerous times by Downeasters and then out-of-staters, has seen it all. If only stores could talk!

# CHAPTER 23

## THE OLD A.G. GODFREY STORE
## IN ADDISON

An article in the October 21, 1983 issue of the *Maine Times* began with the following paradox: "Addison is growing; But the town is disappearing." Indeed, Addison's population had jumped from 773 in 1970 to 1,133 in 1980, but the village had fallen into obsolescence. The general store stood empty, the small supermarket boarded, while four of the town's nine elegant homes along Front Street were vacant. The *Maine Times* reporter had interviewed one of the town's selectmen who said, "Addison is almost like two completely separate worlds. Up here in North Addison, it's Washington County. Down in South Addison it's like southern Maine, where land is sold by the lot and you own a yacht, not a boat."

It was the same pattern I had seen throughout eastern Maine: trailers and poverty inland and away from the shore; affluence and out-of-staters near the water's edge. Much of South Addison's growth is at Cape Split, a fashionable summer and retirement colony, nine miles south of the town of Addison. Young people are also moving into the environs of Addison—which also includes Indian River—as they are in other towns in eastern Maine, to live closer to nature and to escape the hectic pace further south. Some, described in the *Maine Times* article as "short-timers," don't last, while others "scratch along as best they can." The *Maine Times* story ended with this comment from the selectman.

"The reason I believe in this area, I've watched the migration north and east, mostly from Boston. It's still coming. It'll take a while to get here, but I'll be ready for them when they come. If I can make a living and be happy who cares, that's all you need and I've got that here."

And what of the old Addison general store? The *Maine Times* article even had a picture of it—a classic two-story, rectangular building with a gable front. There was nothing remarkable about the old store, only that it seemed to tilt to one side. It looked like many old store buildings I had seen. Old country store buildings are easy to identify as they exhibit a uniformity of design. Like this one, they are simply long rectangular structures with gable fronts. Old store buildings are examples of folk architectures, originally built of posts and beams, later with sawed lumber. Years ago, townspeople would get together and raise entire walls—like a barnraising.

I went to Addison to look at its abandoned general store, to photograph it, to peak in its windows, and to see if anybody could tell me something about it. I had also heard there was once again a country store in South Addison, nine miles on, and wondered what it was like.

At the Four Corners Shopping Center in Columbia I turned south off Route 1 and drove slowly as the road meandered around a tidal inlet. The countryside still looked wild here, just the green meadows with thick spruce and tamarack woods beyond. Small dwellings began to appear: an old train depot converted into a house, a mobile home with a well in its yard. The well cover had plastic butterflies on it. A sign in front of a house read: W.K. GENERAL CONTRACTORS—NEW HOMES, CARPENTRY, GARAGE EDITIONS, BLOWN INSULATION. Sometimes it seemed like nearly everyone in Washington County was some sort of carpenter or builder. It was what people turned to when the clam flats petered out, or when all else failed. I had been advised to learn a trade myself. Downeasters had told me: "A college education is nice, but if you want to make it around here you need to get with a carpenter or an electrician and learn a trade."

I passed a house for sale, more butterflies, a bird house on a tall pole, and then a big cabin cruiser boat, also for sale. Suddenly I was in downtown Addison among the big stately white homes along Front Street. Some were in the colonial style with five windows across the second story, and four windows across the lower story with the front door in the middle. One house had an eagle over the front door, an anchor in the yard, a small boat and a woodpile in back. I came to the Mayhew Library, the Addison Volunteer Fire Department, and then the Captain's Den and Groceries—the old general store building. Apparently, someone had tried to operate it since the *Maine Times* report, but the store was empty once again.

Beyond was a long estuary and then the bay. Several small lobster boats were anchored in the channel. Directly across the street from the general store, Brown's Yankee Grocer and Meat Market was still boarded up. A big abandoned boat rested next to it in the empty parking lot. Nobody was around. It was July of 1988 and Addison appeared to me exactly like the town described in the *Maine Times* article of five years before.

On foot now, I noticed a sign on the old general store that read: BEWARE. ATTACK DOG LIVES HERE. The sign had a picture of a little puppy gnawing at a bone. Such a forlorn looking place. In the July haze, downtown Addison might have been an illusion, maybe a ghost town.

But there was life down the street. Voices echoed in the morning fog. A small garage across from the Lodge Hall had taken on some of the general store's functions. It sold candy, soda, and auto parts, and served as an official inspection station. Inside, a mechanic told me to go into the Lodge Hall and ask for Lawrence "Bill" Crowley. "He's one of our town fathers. He'll tell you all about that old store. He used to own it."

Bill Crowley was a soft spoken Downeaster, probably in his seventies. We went from a cramped office out into the darkened Lodge Hall and sat across from one another at a long folding table. The hall still contained decorations, perhaps leftover from a Fourth of July dance. It had all happened so quickly—the drive into town, the cursory examination of the abandoned store buildings, the encounter at the garage, and now, suddenly, an impromptu interview with one of the town fathers in a darkened meeting hall. But this was how it had gone all summer. Some of my best conversations were chance encounters with people along the way. Bill left what he was doing and gave me an hour of his time.

"Was that old general store in your family?"

"No. It belonged to A.G. Godfrey. It was the A.G. Godfrey Store. It was more or less a department store. They had groceries on one side and clothing on the other side. He sold it to Jerry Brothers. Jerry only had it for three years and then I bought it from him in '49 and I was there 'til 1980. And then I sold it to a fella from Rhode Island. He's resold it to someone from Cape Cod, I think. I don't know what he's going to do with it."

"Why did you get out of it?"

"Too old. Too old to be in there fifteen hours a day." Assuming Bill was now in his seventies, and he got out of the store in 1980, he would have spent some of the most productive years of his life, say age thirty-five to age sixty-five behind the counter. It's all what you want in life, I guess. It sounded like prison to me, but then I remembered what Frances Tuttle had said: "There's no better life for a young couple." I didn't ask Bill if he was married.

"Was the Four Corners supermarket going when you had the store?"

"It was just getting started. Times have changed. It would be a struggle."

There was now a large Red and White supermarket three miles north of Addison at the Four Corners Shopping Center on Route 1 in Columbia. I assumed its establishment in 1980 was largely responsible for the demise of Brown's Yankee Grocer in Addison. Four Corners—the shopping complex, which was said to be owned by an out-of-stater, included a gas station, fast-food take-out, clothing, and furniture stores, in addition to the supermarket—advertised on radio and in the local newspapers as "the place where Washington County shops." Four Corners was a bustling place, giving one the impression that people living midway between Milbridge and Machias—in towns like Addison, Columbia, and Jonesport/Beals —did their grocery shopping here.

I asked Bill how old the A.G. Godfrey store building was.

"Oh, I'd say it's at least two-hundred years old, probably. It needs a foundation put under one side of it. I've done a little work on this side, but the other side is just set on posts. There's no basement under it, but it's stood there well."

Bill used to make home deliveries. He also kept the store open seven days a week. There was no potbellied stove, and no one played checkers when Bill had it, but he remembered a time when they did. "They did back when Godfrey owned it. They had a room out back. They used to go talk over town meetings and they played cards. It was more or less a department store. When I first bought it they had some old suits and derby hats. I took all that stuff to the dump, but I should have kept it. And stiff collars— shirts with those stiff collars. And in those days they didn't have transportation—on one side of the store there used to be a hitching post and people would come with horses. That was before I had it. They'd come and tie up their horses there."

"It looks like you could have brought a schooner in there (bay) behind the store. Did they bring the store goods in by boat?"

Bill couldn't remember that far back. He knew they used to bring coal ships into the town wharf, but his store goods came by freight train to Columbia. He remembered when cigarettes were ten cents a pack, then twenty-five.

"Everybody said they weren't going to smoke anymore. But they still kept buying them anyway." Bill remembered when bread was ten cents a loaf, "but most everybody still baked their own." He'd seen flour go from wooden barrels, to hundred pound sacks, to twenty-five, to five, and finally, to Bisquick.

"Did you carry people on credit?"

"Too much. If I had what people owed me now, I could go to Florida and stay."

Back in '49 there had still been a sardine factory in town. It went out of business and finally burned, Bill said. And in South Addison, in the Basin, there had been granite quarries. But they had also closed. So what was left?

"Clams, they're getting depleted. They used to be able to dig five to ten bushels. Now they're lucky to get a bushel. When I first owned the store—thirty-five cents a bushel for them."

"I noticed quite a few lobster boats anchored in the channel."

"Yeah. They go just shedder time (when the lobsters are shedding)—July and August. Probably they'll be all through by October."

"So they're not really making a living at it?"

"It's part-time. But down to South Addison—they go down there. They go later (in the fall), but they don't go the winter season same as they used to. They probably go from March until December. And they get ready the rest of the winter for another year."

"What do these people here in Addison do the rest of the year?"

"There's a lot of them that goes clamming and worming, and lobstering a little bit. Might work in the woods cutting and take time to go blueberrying in blueberry season, and go brushing (for Christmas wreaths) in November."

"Did you find that the store slowed down quite a bit in the winter?"

"Spring seemed to be when you'd have a hard time. At that time they used to have to register their cars the first of March. And then came April and they had to pay their income tax and that would be a harder time than any other time. Winter wasn't too bad. But when you'd get to the spring of the year you'd think it would get better, but it wouldn't. Not 'til about June—you'd struggle around here."

"Is the town growing again—people moving in?"

"Yeah. I'd say it's growing a little, especially with property selling. Unreasonable prices. It's pushing our town evaluation right up."

Addison's evaluation was similar to Milbridge's, Bill said. Yet, when you look at what each town has to offer, there is no comparison. Milbridge has stores, restaurants, a motel and movie theater, but Addison has nothing.

"Islands are selling. We had one that sold for $387,000 not too long ago."

"Out-of-stater?"

"Out-of-state. Down the Cape—Cape Split—we had one acre of shore property sell for eighty thousand dollars. We've been valuing it for ten thousand an acre, so that threw that out. People that live there and lived there all their lives on a small income, they can't afford to live there anymore. What's going to happen, we don't know. This is my last year as an assessor. It's just too much of a hassle. Getting too old to bother with it anymore."

"Is there still an old store building down in South Addison?"

"No. There used to be Cirone's General Store down there, and that was built over into a house, and now his grandson, Kenny Cirone, has built a new store down there just beyond the Grange Hall. His grandfather was blind and run a local store down there, and done well for being a blind man."

"Blind?"

"Blind man, ayuh."

"And he was still able to run the business?"

"That's right. Everybody was more or less honest with him. He had a row. He'd put one dollar bills just one row. He didn't have a cash register."

"So he just did it by feel, I guess, by touch?"

"Ayuh. He was a little . . . short, Italian, and he used to go 'round and play a violin—Cirone's Orchestra."

# CHAPTER 24

# EVERYONE'S A WINNER: CIRONE'S TRADING POST, SOUTH ADDISON

T he road to South Addison crossed the Pleasant River and wound its way between green fields and old farmsteads that dropped down to the bay. Many of these were weathered gray nineteenth century Capes like the house I was gazing at when this book almost ended. It was a close call. The approaching vehicle seemed to come from nowhere. I veered right and took a deep breath.

It was a landscape that took me back in time; to when photographs were still black and white; cars just black; few people had cars, and most folks still used horses. It was a soft, mist-coated landscape—like an impressionist painting—and it made me reflect back on the A.G. Godfrey Store that Bill Crowley had described. And it was easy to imagine horse-drawn carriages trundling along this narrow land—unpaved then—over the windswept hills and down to the store in the village below.

The landscape here seemed distant from what was happening to the coast of Maine, tricking you into believing that change hadn't got this far, and perhaps never would. And oh, how I wished that were true. It was not; but, as I drove that narrow winding road, past those old weathered farmhouses with their gray shingled barns tumbling down, I saw the Maine coast as if seeing it for the first time—and what I saw gave me goose bumps.

There wasn't much in South Addison but Cirone's Trading Post. I didn't care to go to Cape Split—even if the once potholed road was paved now—and look at what the out-of-staters and summer rusticators had created, so I went inside the one-story plywood building and read: UNATTENDED CHILDREN WILL BE SOLD AS SLAVES. There was much to read in Cirone's Trading Post. The inside walls were lined with hand-lettered signs congratulating people who had won money in the state lottery. CONGRATULATIONS RUTH BURGESS, and then the amount of prize money was listed. CONGRATULATIONS JULIAN INGERSOLL, CRAIG CIRONE SR., RUTH BURGESS, again. It was impressive; the entire inside of the store building—except for the ceiling—was plastered with the names of winners, and I thought: Everybody's a winner at Cirone's Trading Post.

I had never bought a scratch-off (still haven't), and I had never bought a Megabucks lottery ticket. Gambling had never interested me, and after seeing all the Megabucks machines and watching people in store after store buying the dollar-a-piece scratch-offs, I began to realize there was something here to write about. Only I hadn't expected to find such evidence of it here in South Addison, especially after driving those lovely miles along that rolling road. But it had come to an abrupt end, and I was suddenly jolted back to the harsh reality of contemporary America, with its lottery-crazed population. And I thought: What is it like HERE in the winter? In due time. I first asked Ken Cirone about his grandfather, who had run a general store in South Addison years ago.

"He was totally blind. He could make change faster than I can. He could tell time. He had a pocket watch with raised Roman numerals on it. He could tell you almost to the minute what time it was."

Ken Cirone had retired from a state job and had always thought it would be nice to have a store back home. It was something he had always wanted to do, so he did it. And his trading post filled a niche, because the nearest store—Four Corners Shopping Center—was twenty-five miles round-trip. His store had been open only two years, and now it was for sale.

"Well, I had a heart attack. That slowed things down. Rather than build on and make it bigger and get more involved, I just figured we'd sell it. I'm not even supposed to be working here now. You say, 'I'll go in for two hours.' I plan two hours in the morning and two hours in the afternoon, but then you have to grind hamburger. You've got to unload the truck, you've got to— We close at six. Ordinarily, we should be open at six in the morning to catch the fishermen—six 'til nine—we should be."

I wondered if there were even enough people in South Addison to support a store. Surely, there weren't more than a hundred. Ken wasn't sure what the population was, but it was more than a hundred—perhaps three or four hundred. South Addison covered a lot of area, he said; it included Cape Split, Moose Neck, Merritt Point (peninsulas), and then it also included an area they called the Basin—a winding road around Wohoa Bay, between South Addison and Indian River. There was Reynolds Bay and West River, and there were islands offshore named Goose and Crowley—a lot of coastline here, with houses tucked away in the woods, on coves and points—like Bare Point. This country was all new to me; our camp in West Gouldsboro, only thirty-six miles from here, seemed to be in an altogether different part of the state. I was deep in Washington County, farther away from Bangor or Portland—in psychic distance, that is—than New York is from Los Angeles. Psychic distance is not distance in miles; rather, it is the cultural distance, or difference between places. Cultural distance is harder to overcome than geographic distance. It is harder for a rural person to move to a big city, or vice versa, than it is for an urbanite to move from city to city. If the psychic distance is too great the move may not occur at all; or worse, the migration may fail. Plenty of urbanites have moved to places like South Addison only to find they miss some of what they left behind. For a while they may struggle; they may even try to change their new home to something more like the place they came from. But sometimes the cultural distance is simply too great; the cultural barriers prove more resistant than expected, and the newcomers leave.

But our world is getting smaller; psychic distance is said to be lessening. In New England, especially, the back-to-the-land movement brought down many of the barriers, and moving to the suburbs is no longer the "in" thing. Quite the contrary, more and more people, especially middle class baby-boomers raised in suburbia, are rejecting that environment and seem to want to move the other way—to the country, particularly if it is coastal (another national trend—people are moving from the heartland—the Middle West and Great Plains—to the coastal areas), like Cape Split, where Ken Cirone lived. "Oh, there's some people who have lived there for years," he said. "Pretty nice little place. There's some out-of-staters who just come in the summertime, and there's some that moved here the last couple of years."

It didn't seem to bother Ken Cirone a bit that people had moved in. He seemed to like people. He was himself a likable guy. So I asked him about all the names of lottery winners on the store walls. I said, "You must sell a lot of tickets."

"It's the cards—the rub-offs."

"Scratch-offs?"

"Yeah, we have some people who buy a lot of them. In a little over a year we sold 61,200 tickets."

"Sixty-one thousand! I had no idea!"

"There are a lot of gamblers down here."

"Have you ever totaled up how many winners you've had?"

"Yeah, right there on the blackboard. I don't know if it's quite up to date. When we started we had one hundred dollar winners. Now they don't. But we had three up over the door. That's where we started. Then we went to the right; then we started back this way." And it wasn't long—a year and a half—before they had the whole store plastered with the names of winners.

"You have four, five-hundred dollar winners; seventy-four, fifty-dollar winners, I see."

"Probably seventy-six, fifty-dollar winners now," Ken said.

"What does that time notice say? 'One lucky lady—Ruth Burgess—twenty-one, fifty-dollar tickets; two, five hundred dollar tickets.' Do these people come in every day and scratch them off?"

"She buys a lot of tickets. Down here in the wintertime—people don't have too much money, but they'll buy those before they'll buy food—some of them."

"What do they do in the winter?"

"Starve—they dig clams all winter. Oh yeah, it's incredible. We talked with the lottery people the other day and they agreed we sold a lot of tickets for a store this size. And most of them that buy them live in this area. I've got an uncle who sometimes buys fifty. Everybody's a gambler."

"Does anybody down here feel differently about it? You know, on Beals they don't even sell beer."

"Oh, there's a few religious people that live close by here. They didn't like it very much when I put the beer sign up. Beer is one of my biggest sellers. I get eight cents selling those tickets. There's four hundred tickets in a book, so I get thirty-two dollars for each book I sell. There have been days when we've sold two books."

Ken's son had helped him build the store. His daughter and sister helped him run it. His wife worked five days for the state, then helped him in the store on weekends. It was too much for her, he said.

Like most Downeast country stores, Cirone's trade revolved around the clammers and fishermen. "You watch the time when the tide is for clamming—they come in and have coffee and their doughnuts. And after the tide they'll come in and have their lunch—grab a six-pack of beer and relax the rest of the day—whatever. Yeah, lobster fishermen and clam diggers—seasonal work around here mostly. And blueberry season—they rake blueberries. Then they go back to clamming or worming. There's a lot of worm diggers too. Life's different down in here."

Indeed, we were fifty-four miles from Ellsworth, seventy-eight from Bangor, and you could "feel" the distance. A big, burly fisherman came in. Ken said, "We get a lot of fishermen in here. He's got hungry. And probably this afternoon he'll want a beer to wash it down."

"Probably be back on the return trip," the fisherman said.

"Did you get your engine in yet?" Ken asked.

"No, that's what I'm going to check right now. See if I can afford a beer this afternoon."

"How many times a day do you stop in this store?" I asked the fisherman.

"It depends on how humid the day is," Ken joked.

"On a good day—four, or five, or six."

# CHAPTER 25

## INDIAN RIVER VARIETY

A t first glance it looked like a Dairy Delight or some sort of ice cream stand. The sign on the little red building read: INDIAN RIVER VARIETY. This was a new country store, or at least a business that wasn't here the last time I came this way. I was traveling south on Route 187, a few miles north of the village of Indian River, and I decided to stop.

I never knew quite what to expect when I entered these establishments for the first time. And given the high turnover of country stores, I always wondered why anyone ever bothered to open a new one. Surely these people knew what they were getting into: the long hours, the boredom, the government regulations, the fact that you're married to that store. Still, there never seemed to be a shortage of people willing to try their luck.

The Indian River Variety was crammed into one tiny room. Toys hung from the ceiling, lamps adorned the front windows, videos lined one wall. A doorway led to a larger, nearly empty room, where on the wall I read: NO VULGAR LANGUAGE OR OUT YOU GO! It had once been a game room, but the pool tables were gone. A lone customer sat eating a sandwich in the mostly empty hall.

"I run a tight ship," Charlene Gray, the proprietor said. "They had three fights down the road, in another game room, this winter. And it was all because of drinking and dope. He had a rough crowd and we have the good crowd. And we got canceled on our insurance. I felt worse for the kids than anything, and we weren't making any money on them. But at least they had a place to go. If it works we're going to put it back. The kids need it, but I don't want the foolishness. We have five kids and there was no place for them to go. And I mean they brought families and children."

Charlene was a pleasant, middle-aged woman, who lived by a firm set of principles. Ronald, her husband, had thick gray hair and the bluest eyes I've ever seen. I got the impression the Grays were straightforward, religious, and caring folks who liked to talk. They seemed well-suited for a country store.

"We've got a little bit of everything," Charlene said. "I've got so many things in here we can't display them properly. And people don't know what I've got. They come in and so much hits them. When we get a walk-in cooler, then we'll sell beer and wine. I'm not fond of that part of it, but that seems to be where the money is. It pulls people to you, and while they're here, their conscience tells them they've got to get something for the kids or their wife. Isn't that terrible? But this is what's happened."

Ronald told me he was brought up with a country store—that he didn't like standing in line at the supermarket. "I'm still country," he said. "I don't like the red lights either." He had driven a truck for many years, he said, and it was easy for me to imagine him at Dysart's Truck Stop in Bangor, eating a cheeseburger, his bulging wallet chained to his jeans, while country music played in the background.

"So far this building's been different things," Ronald explained. "My daughter ran a crafts shop in here, but that didn't pay. We was catering more to teenagers—milkshakes, hot fudge sundaes, hamburgers."

"So this was sort of a community recreation center?"

"Yep. I'm kinda disappointed the pool tables are gone. I'm hoping I'll have another building before fall, but that's a hard trick. To start with, it's over two-hundred dollars for a soil test."

Ronald went into a long discourse on septic systems. He had built and sold two houses, and it was evident he knew a great deal about construction. But I wanted to know more about the country store and its place in the community.

"Indian River is a split community," Ronald explained. "It's part Jonesport, part Addison. Addison's a group of communities. We have this section of Indian River and South Addison—that's called the Basin area. Then you've got the West Side, East Side, the Bridge, Addison village—a whole lot of little communities."

Ronald Gray had lived his entire life in Indian River. Charlene was born in Concord, New Hampshire, but grew up in Jonesboro, Maine. I asked them if they felt country stores had a bright future in eastern Maine. "They're always going to be here," Charlene said. "The sad part about little stores—at one time, when we were first married, they didn't have a supermarket down here. (Gay's Shop 'N Save Supermarkets opened in Milbridge and Machias in 1960.) We did all of our shopping at Volk's General Store (closed now). Then when hard times came you could get credit. And then you caught up. But you still patronized that same store. They don't do that anymore. When they need credit, they come to you for it. But after they've paid you, and they've got money, they go to the big city. But there are still people who need milk or bread."

I wasn't sure what Charlene meant by "big city;" she might have meant Ellsworth, which has several supermarkets. As early as 1960, there were four supermarkets in Ellsworth. And for residents of Hancock County, the weekly shopping trip to Ellsworth was probably commonplace by the 1950s. But Washington County was more remote; it had grown much more slowly, and as recently as 1960, Addison (which includes Indian River) still had four country stores. Then in the late 1970s, the C & M Supermarket opened on Route 1 in Columbia. And by 1983, all of Addison's country stores had closed. I asked Charlene if she still gave credit.

"To very few. I don't give it to very many because I've been stung just once. It wasn't much. Still, I know pretty much who will pay and who won't. Some checks I'll take, and some I won't because I know that person. You have to be careful, because if you aren't, you'll be ruined."

Like most country stores in the area, the Indian River Variety was patronized by clam and worm diggers. Charlene cashed their checks and made their lunches. And the local wormers were doing well, especially over in Harrington, which has a large shoreline. But there were also areas where the flats were dead—no clams, worms, nothing. "Why would that be?"

"Worm digging really turns it over," Ronald explained. "Especially sand worming, with those long hoes going deeper."

"The Wiscasset Chopper?" (I dropped that name to show that I wasn't totally ignorant about worming. But actually, I didn't know one hoe from another. And when Ronald explained the different hoes to me, I realized that the hoe I had borrowed and then struggled with on my one day of worming in 1968, was a sandworm hoe—the wrong kind for bloods. What if I had gotten the correct hoe? Might I have had a totally different—even an enjoyable—experience? Maybe I'd still be a worm digger. Ronald Gray made me realize I owe some kind soul a word of thanks for lending me a bogus hoe twenty years ago!)

"No, the Wiscasset Chopper is the little curved one for digging bloodworms. They're near the surface. So that hoe's been duplicated down here. They started out cutting up old baby carriages—the springs. They gave them that spring action. That's tempered steel. That's hard to duplicate with regular steel without a forge to heat the whole thing and then retemper it. They tried stainless steel on them, but then stainless steel will bend."

Bloodworming hoes are made in Harrington and Steuben, Ronald explained. And like the shorthandled blueberry rakes, worm hoes are a local specialty. "My father built the sandworm hoe for years, over here," Ronald said. "That takes three dung forks cut up."

"Three what?"

"Dung forks—spading forks. And they liked his hoes. They were smooth. There weren't any rough places. When he got done it was like a manufactured hoe."

Sometimes when I was in country stores talking about clamming or worming, the subject abruptly turned to drugs. It was as if there was a curious relationship between mud, money, and dope.

"We'll have diggers stop in here and buy a lot of candy," Ronald said. "They buy a lot of candy when they're smoking marijuana."

I had never heard of that before. Apparently, the drug causes a craving for chocolate.

"I won't even sell those papers," Charlene added. She was referring to the papers used to roll cigarettes.

"They're not rolling tobacco?"

"No. Not when they come in and buy a pack of cigarettes and ask for those. That's a dead giveaway. Well, isn't that ridiculous? But they don't think about it, see? I'll tell you what a lot of them are doing. They're buying a bottle or two of beer, and they have their drugs, and they sip a little bit of beer—so you've got the smell of beer—so you think they're loaded on that. But they're not, they're high on dope."

"Marijuana has been here quite a while now," Ronald said.

"But now they're into the coke—sniffing coke," Charlene added.

There were airstrips nearby where planes brought it in the night, the Grays said. Or else they just flew low and dropped it, several times a month. And there were many camp break-ins now too, and these the Grays attributed to the need for money to pay for drugs. The break-ins usually took place during the winter, when money was tight, and when the camp owner's weren't around.

I had always felt the stories about diggers and drugs were exaggerated. And I had known diggers who worked hard, saved their money, and remained "clean." The appeal of digging, I thought, was the freedom it allowed: no time clock, no bosses, no coat and tie, no special skills or education required. One only had to work hard to earn a good living.

Charlene said, "We always think of them as people that aren't very well educated that are on the flats making their money. But a lot of school teachers found they could make more money on the flats instead of teaching school. They gave up teaching to go on the flats."

I had also heard there were more young people digging now—that unlike earlier generations who left the area for jobs out-of-state, these kids were more apt to head for the mudflats. An administrator at the University of Maine at Machias told me that: "Young people around here don't think they need a college education. They think they can just go out and make a living digging clams or worms." Immediate gratification—It was most evident in the local landscape of all-terrain vehicles, fast cars and pick-up trucks, mobile homes, satellite dishes, and snowmobiles.

"Those three wheelers (all-terrain vehicles), they run all winter," Charlene said. "They go anywhere and everywhere. I don't like them. And you'd think living in a country area that you wouldn't have to put up with that. But let me tell you, they'll come and I'll bet there will be at least ten of them. There'll be a whole gang of them and they'll travel. And I've told them, if they'd stay on the road, nobody would complain. But when they go across and make their own path on your blueberry ground or your lawn, then, of course, you get aggravated. Well, it pounds things down and nothing will grow there. You look at it when you're driving along. You can tell where those three wheelers have been. And they buy those big four wheelers, and that spins it up worse than ever. They don't care—it's not their land they're tearing up."

Charlene's comments made me think that as more land passed from native to out-of-state ownership, the problems of land abuse and scarification were bound to get worse. Why should people who can't afford land care about land they can't afford? A couple of years ago, Linda and I went to look at some acreage for sale in Steuben. On our way there, we parked our car at the end of a dirt road where some wormers were camping in a small trailer. It was about ten in the morning and they were having a beer. When I asked the men if we were on the right road to reach the property for sale, one of the men smirked and said, "Oh yeah, an out-of-stater owns that. We go up there and help ourselves to brush (for wreaths) every November." I took the comment as a warning. I think he was implying, that regardless of who owned the land, he always had and always would, help himself to the brush. And I thought: Well, the guy has to make a living. And who can afford to buy the land and pay the taxes on it on a worm digger/brush cutter's wages anyway? It was beautiful land. And as we walked around it, I kept thinking about what the man had said. In his own mind, he probably thought of the land as his—he had probably grown up with that idea—to use or abuse as he saw fit.

I thought the same way about land when I was growing up in Steuben. I went hunting all over the place and never gave a moment's thought to who owned the land. It was just wilderness.

If drugs and crime were getting worse in Indian River, these problems were much more serious elsewhere. The Grays had a daughter living in Charleston, South Carolina, where her husband worked undercover as a drug enforcement officer in the Coast Guard. I imagined his job as one of high excitement, or at least that line of work conjured up images—and I had got this idea from watching Coast Guard commercials on television—of fast boats and major drug busts. He couldn't even wear his uniform, Charlene explained, for fear of being "wiped out." And there were nights when even his wife had no idea of his whereabouts; nevertheless, he didn't want a desk job. He was too young, too adventurous for that.

The Grays had driven down to South Carolina for Christmas, and their comments—those of Downeasters seeing the Deep South for the first time—were interesting to me since I was now a resident of South Carolina.

"I thought Washington County was a disaster area," Ronald said. "But this was terrible!"

"The poverty?"

"Yeah."

Charlene said, "Just driving through, looking at it—the roads we were on, the fields, everything—it's a real shame."

There are many similarities between eastern Maine and the coastal plain of South Carolina. There is the rural poverty of abandoned vehicles, dilapidated mobile homes, and wooden shacks; the poverty of people still struggling to draw a living from the land—the old, back-breaking way—in an age of high technology. In April, I drove the back roads of Marion County, South Carolina, where we live, and watched gangs of black laborers putting out tobacco plants. The field workers—their heads usually covered with hats or wrapped in bandannas to protect them from the relentless sun—are among the South's poorest people. Many are illiterate. Many still live in unpainted tenant shacks, with dirt yards, outhouses, and patches of collard or turnip greens. Sometimes I'd see a bony dog with pups (I often saw one dead on the highway), or an old man chopping firewood. Cane fishing poles were usually leaning against the porch, and in some places, the County had parked metal dumpsters in front of these shacks— as if to suggest that these people really didn't matter. And how humiliating it must be for the inhabitants of these dwellings to sit on their porches while cars and pickup trucks pull up and empty their refuse into the dumpsters out front. Take the dumpsters out of the image, and you might well be in a West African or Caribbean backwater. Such Third World poverty is harsh enough, but superimposed across a landscape of affluence, it becomes crueler still.

There was a small, timid boy who rode my school bus in Steuben, Maine years ago, that some kids called "Stink." Nobody wanted to sit near this less fortunate kid, who came from a home without running water. It was painful to watch the shame and terror in this little boy's eyes when his peers said, "Oh Stink, you sit right there and don't move." A friend recently told me that the boy they called Stink had died suddenly. "He was only about twenty-five," my friend said. "But the really sad thing was that a few years before he died, he was in the hospital in Bangor for a while, and when he got out, he had to hitchhike home. Nobody would even go up and get him."

In eastern Maine, and in the rural South, it is often those who work the hardest; those who labor in the fields, forests, mills, or mudflats, who have grown the poorest. How ironic, that in this Age of Information, when more than seventy-five percent of workers simply provide services, that the minority—those who actually grow, harvest, and make the goods the rest of us cannot seem to live without—are losing ground. Indeed, clammers and craftsmen, farmers and fishermen, loggers and miners: the proud people that two hundred years ago accounted for nine of every ten American workers, are now the people the rest of us marvel at through the windows of our air-conditioned cars and offices.

Charlene said, "I know where Pammy (daughter) is there's a lot of blacks and they are poor. They'll come in and clean your home for little or nothing."

A white man I know, who had grown up in South Carolina, told me that his family had always employed black people to clean their house and do their yardwork. He said that they would "clean the windows, and scrub and wipe that glass until it was absolutely spotless." But on one occasion, he had seen the inside of a black family's house, and there was so much dirt he would have been afraid to eat off their table. It had been a rude awakening—an eye opener; years later, he still carried that one image around in his head. And when I asked him how someone could be so meticulous when cleaning another person's house, yet so careless about their own, he went silent. He just stared into space as if he had never thought about it; perhaps it was too complex to explain to an outsider; or else he just accepted it as the way things were.

I wondered if the black people the man spoke of were just too exhausted from cleaning white people's houses to clean their own. And how much of his story was exaggeration, resurrected from his subconscious—the white Southerner's idea of how blacks lived? Finally, I wondered how much of a role history had played—generation after generation of aliens in a strange land, far removed from any place they could really lay claim to. Might being landless tenants or renters have caused them not to care anymore? Is this what happens when people lose title to their land, and subsequently, their destiny? "Where do you stay?" This was what my students had asked me when I taught at a predominantly black college in North Carolina several years ago. To "stay," rather than to "live," I assumed came from a cultural pattern of being tenants or renters, rather than landowners.

In eastern Maine, I had heard many generalizations about the deplorable conditions in which clam and worm diggers lived. Again, I wondered if perhaps the diggers weren't too exhausted from their labor on the mudflats to keep their homes in order. But I also knew a digger whose home was meticulous; his house, driveway, lawn, and garden; everything carefully painted, maintained, mowed, and tended. And I was told by a friend that the inside of the digger's house was so clean you could eat off the floor. Even the undersides of cabinets were kept spotless. So I assumed the same about blacks in the Carolinas; that each one was different, that people generalized too much about people they knew little about.

"We saw them (blacks) selling baskets along the way," Ronald said.

"They were beautiful," Charlene added. (The Grays were referring to the sweet grass baskets that black women in South Carolina are famous for making.) "We didn't stop to get any. We were in our little car out here—that little Ford. The car was full."

We talked about the historic homes, and I learned that the Grays had seen the areas of Charleston that tourists usually saw. They thought the Antebellum mansions were beautiful, but they were less taken with the area where their daughter lived. "There's no privacy," Charlene said. "They're so close. Places you'd think there would be no place for a home, they'd put one there."

The Grays' daughter lived in a community of cul-de-sacs—a safe community where strangers were not welcome, where a patrolman kept watch. I had seen several of these new communities in South Carolina. There was usually a nicely landscaped entrance, then an attractive sign—perhaps with the name of a former plantation—and finally, a broad, tree-lined roadway leading in. They had the look of exclusivity that I took to mean "upper middle class and white only."

"So they're in a good place," Charlene said. "I don't worry so much about the children. You know, you just can't help but wonder."

The two children, ages seven and nine, were coming back to Maine to spend the summer. Both of their parents worked, Charlene said, and it wasn't fair to leave the kids in a day care center all day. And then there was that dreadful heat. Charlene said, "The hard part is that there's no change in the seasons. That, I would miss terribly. I know the children mind it when they get here—how cold it is. And when they first went down there—Oh, they thought they'd die! Pammy said, 'Mom, you could never survive!' I said, 'No, I don't think I could.'"

# CHAPTER 26

## SEA SCOOTERS AND ROT GUT WINE: INDIAN RIVER GENERAL STORE

Driving into Indian River, I passed a Dairy Bar, a white Cape Cod house with a woodpile on its north side, a garden in back, and a pup tent set up. Another large woodpile appeared in the distance, then a gray shingled house with a barn attached. A sign in front of a mobile home read: CHANDLER'S CARPENTRY AND CABINET INSTALLING—FREE ESTIMATES. Another sign: ROCK MAPLE FARM—EGGS AND MILK was on my right. I saw a big furry black and white dog, another mobile home, this one with horses out back, and some junked cars. It looked like someone had recently pulled the engine out of a van on the right side of another mobile home. There was a tripod of three spruce poles with a chain hanging from it. And then I began to see more mobile homes, then more, until finally, it seemed like all I was seeing were house trailers of every conceivable vintage. Where would all these people live if it were not for mobile homes? And what was rural Maine going to look like when all these mobile homes were no longer fit for human habitation? Maine has a returnable bottle bill. Maybe what it needs is a bill for recycling old house trailers.

I came to a house with a satellite dish and a sign in front that read: EMERSON'S—CLIFTON AND MARY. A "Garfield the Cat" ornament was out front. From the top of a steep hill, I saw woods and bay and blueberry fields off in the distance. Then more mobile homes, shingled houses, numerous vehicles, a boat and trailer; I then passed a mobile home with its front door wide open, where three men sat inside—all bare to the waist—smoking cigarettes. I was finally coming into the village of Indian River, with its abandoned school building, abandoned church, abandoned country store, and abandoned old cars. I passed a little tiny house with another abandoned old car outside, some bicycles, more lawn ornaments, a blue Cape Cod house, a skiff turned upside down, firewood in mounds, and finally, an old weathered gray Cape Cod house that really caught my eye. It had eight windows on its gable end, and two windows on either side of the front door, and not a trace of paint anywhere—just dark gray clapboard. It was a very old house, but its ridge line was still straight. Beyond was another mobile home with a barn behind it, tumbling down. Most of the barns, like most of the old stores, were either falling, or had already fallen down. I saw a nice-looking vegetable garden beside a white Cape Cod house, while across the road, I could see—and hear—Indian River, itself tumbling into the bay. There was yet another mobile home, more woodpiles, some abandoned trucks; I slowed down, then pulled into Indian River General Store.

Stan's Place, as the Indian River General Store is known locally, is an unpretentious one-story wooden building, with a couple of gas pumps out front, a table, chairs, and pool table inside. Stan's is the local hangout in a Downeast community short on social and cultural amenities. In June of 1985, my wife, Linda, wrote the following description of Indian River General Store.

> The pool table was the first thing you saw when entering. It was closer to the counter than the few aisles of food and drinks. The room was smoky and a half dozen guys were playing pool. I felt uncomfortable. it was like entering a male inner sanctum.

It was much improved now. Stan had "added on", and the pool table was now at the end of the building, leaving room in front for a table and chairs.

Stan Tomasik, the proprietor, is probably in his forties. His face is mostly beard—red and ruddy, hair and beard turning gray—and although he's originally from Rochester, Massachusetts, Stan looks like a man whose most at home on the water or in the Maine woods. Indeed, Stan's appearance seems to fit the store and town, be it the 1980s or the 1890s. His long sleeve shirt always unbuttoned to the waist, exposing his hairy chest, Stan can talk non-stop for hours. I had heard, however, that he was thinking of selling out.

"Yeah, too many hours," Stan said. "I came here for fishing and hunting, right? And I haven't. It's basically seven days a week. I get half a Sunday off. It's three-thirty, four o'clock in the morning 'til, you know, nine o'clock at night."

"That's a long day."

"There's always someone knocking on the door. It depends on the tide. Everything goes by tides around here. You don't make enough money to hire somebody for eighty hours a week."

Stan was still living in the basement of the store. He had wanted to build or buy a house when he came here in 1984, he said, but running the business hadn't left him any time. He was also by himself. I stopped at this store many times between 1984 and 1989, and Stan was there every single time!

"I don't care what I do as long as I get a little time off." Stan said. "You're sort of pinned down—can't get away three or four days at a time. And there's not enough money in it; even if there was it can get to you after a while."

All around the inside of the store were antiques—an old ice saw, jugs, bottles, some hand tools. Stan said he liked to take motor trips, stopping a day or two at different places to "see the lifestyle." He said, "I like to collect junk, not necessarily antiques; junk, I call it, 'cause it's not high-grade stuff—cast iron skillets, old guns. I mean, what I can afford. I like to buy something and maybe resell it for a few dollars. Maybe not make a killing, but pay for the road expenses, the food. Not so much the lodging, but, you know, the gas."

Stan had my attention, but in the background, a group of local diggers sat around the table discussing the Boston Celtics. I wanted to gradually work my way over to their table and take in some of their conversation.

I brought up the subject of clamming. Even way down here in Indian River the clamming was said to be poor. "You can scratch a peck full," Stan said.

"What do you think? Too many diggers?"

"Part of it," Stan said. "It's dug out, I would say. More and more are getting into it. It's like lobstering. there's more and more guys in it and they're dragging the bottom of the ocean."

"Why do you think there are more clammers getting into it now?" I had finally worked the conversation around to something of interest to the men sitting at the table.

"I don't think that's the reason 'cause—it's just this long. To begin with, you can't dig twelve months a year." A dark-haired, stocky man in his late fifties had spoken up. In a strong, clear voice, the man said, "You shouldn't dig in the summertime anyway. Years ago, in the '30s and '40s, we couldn't dig clams in the summer—May, June, July, and August. (And I remembered the old rule that Leitha Joy had mentioned: Only dig clams when there's an "R" in the month.) Clams are like everything else—they go through a cycle."

"So the State wouldn't let you dig them in the summer?" I said.

"Oh, no," the stocky man replied. "We couldn't dig clams in the summer months. Then they started that fresh market in the '50s. Then the clams disappeared."

The stocky man's name was Colin. He had lived in the area most of his life. He was a rugged, good-looking man, with dark brown eyes and high cheek bones, and wavy dark brown hair combed back.

Stan said, "And they get a supplemental check from the State, okay? So they can do this, and a lot of it is paid by check or cash, and they supplement their income unrecorded. And there isn't too much else to do in the area, other than woodcutting, wreath-making, berry-picking. And some people will do a little work provided it's under the table money. Then when school's out a lot of high school kids will clam or worm, which puts a crimp on it. But I'd say it's the adults that's doing it. They're on some sort of agency, which they didn't have in the old days." (I assumed he meant the dole—welfare, foodstamps, aid to families with dependent children—government programs that didn't exist years ago.)

"Well, back then, I'll tell you what we had—sardine factories," Colin said. "If you made a living you worked for it. There were no freebies. Back in the '30s and '40s, even when I was bringing up my family, we couldn't dig clams in the summer, but all there was to depend on down in Jonesport was sardine factories."

"So you could always work there?" I asked.

"Oh, yeah, in the summer months. And then in the fall we started to go clamming. There was no big price, but still, we had clams. Because in the summer months when you dig clams you're hurting the flats. That's all there is to it. You're hurting them."

"You shouldn't dig them at all then?"

"No sir. That's when they're seeding. That's when that sperm is going floating around."

Stan added, "Even in the flats that are closed, there's always someone rummaging around when they shouldn't be. And then they'll be in at night with a headlight, clamming."

"They're digging double tides now in the summer," I added.

"Oh yeah," Collin said. "Well, I used to do that. But after the fresh market came in—all these trucks, and everybody buying clams in the summer."

"Yeah, seventy dollars a bushel last summer," I said.

"See, this is what happened," Colin explained. "Because you've got diggers now who say, 'Hey, you can't shut the flats off now because this is when we can make money.' But it's a lot easier to find something to get by in the summer than it is in the winter months. Between Jonesport and Beals, those two towns, there were over twelve hundred diggers at one time. But you couldn't dig summers. Then, most of those people went to the factory. They worked seasonal work. Some mowed lawns, some raked blueberries, and they got by until the first of September and then they started clamming again. See? Then, of course, lobster fishing started picking up, too. And some went lobster fishing—things like that. But now they have wrinkling—they can pick periwinkles. They can dig worms. Alright. They've got mussel dragging now. Lot of guys, lot of boys go out quahoging now in boats. Alright. But you've got all these other things now. They can still rake blueberries. Blueberry crops around here the last couple of years have been pretty good. There's different things they can do to fill in those three or four months."

We talked about natural cycles. First, clams, then rabbits, next, squirrels, and finally, rabbits again. Colin said, "Years ago, on Beals; of course, the older people, they used to set right on their back porch and shoot what rabbits they wanted. Never had to go in the woods and hunt them. No. And out here in this area—of course I've done a lot of hunting all around here, but I never went rabbit hunting. But I have a friend that did. And look—he'd go in, and look, in an hour's time you couldn't carry the rabbits that he could kill!"

"Is that right?"

"Ayuh, and see now, I don't remember if they ever had a limit years ago on rabbits. They did on sea scooters because I've gunned sea scooters."

"Sea what?"

"Sea scooters," Colin said. "Well, they're like a duck, a big bird. You take decoys and go out in a boat. They don't come into land. They're a sea scooter. They go up the coast. You set right in the boat and kill 'em, in the boat, you know. You're allowed seven. That's some sport! I've done that ever since I was eleven years old. Deer huntin' and that—I love it!"

"How is the deer herd around here?"

"The deer is coming back," Colin said. "But our woods is being taken; just look around, see. Really, they are—clear cut."

Stan said, "There's some development, and, like years before the snowmobile, the existing roads were there. It gave the animals a lot of protection. Now, anybody can go into the woods, whether there's a road or not, with these three and four wheelers (all-terrain vehicles). I guess they can hunt from them. But it's just the idea of the presence of motors in the woods. It changes the atmosphere. He (Colin) walks a lot. The motor vehicles—like, everyone's got them. That's opened everything up."

"When I go hunting I don't use a three-wheeler," Colin said. "I hunt right on foot or I have tree stands. You'd be surprised where those three wheelers will go. I couldn't drive there. I couldn't believe it 'til a few years back. When Bobby hauled that buck out for me one time, Stan. I couldn't believe where he could go with that thing. You go right through a swamp with them. I was sitting up there one afternoon when this guy comes through the swamp. Well, you know there's no deer going to be there!"

There was an article in the newspaper that very morning about a man in Athens, Maine who had been caught with the remains of thirteen deer. He was fined over fourteen thousand dollars and forced to relinquish his firearms for one year. He was poaching for a business and selling the hides.

"That guy should be banned for life," Stan said.

"If that happened in Canada they would confiscate everything he owned," Colin added. "They'd take everything. They'd take everything. They wouldn't fool around."

I wasn't sure where Athens was. Colin said, "Athens, Maine, ayuh, near Skowhegan. Yeah, you got all the thieves, crooks, and poachers all up that way. They're not down these parts. When Joe Emerson owned this store there was game around here. There was some game. In the '40s."

Stan said, "They said this was once the second-highest beer sales store in Maine. Salesman told me."

"Why do you suppose that was?" I asked.

Colin said, "Because all the Christian people from down to Jonesport and Beals came up here, you see."

"Oh, that's right, you can't sell beer on Beals."

"They never drink," Colin laughed. "Those people on Beals don't drink. No! You know they don't!"

"They say this store once sold four hundred cases of beer in one day, years ago," Stan added.

"I drank my share of it, but I didn't care who knew I drank," Colin said.

Stan said, "They'll buy beer and say, 'Put it in a bag to keep it cold.' And it's like sub-zero out there! Then there's some that say they're buying it for someone else."

Stan mentioned someone who always bought Old Duke. "It's a cheap, rot-gut wine," he said. "They told me he used to have a drinking problem."

"Drink! Well, I guess he'd drink," Colin said. "He was pretty open with his drinking. He didn't care who knew it. That's the way I was when I was drinking. I didn't care who knew it."

"Well, why do you suppose they won't sell beer on Beals?"

"Well, it's the people," Colin explained. "They run the town the way they want. Listen, they just can't have it. Do you realize how many churches there are between those two towns—Jonesport and Beals? Well, there's the Pentecostal Church, the Wesleyan Church down there. Then the Mormon Church and the Congregational Church—them four's in Jonesport. Then there's either three or four on Beals.

"I'll tell you what happened down there. You see, they don't have beer sales on Sunday. Once, they didn't even sell beer in Jonesport. They was a long time getting cold beverages in that town. Then in later years, younger people voted it in. Do you know that the church people and some others, they got together and they took it to the town meeting five other times, trying to get rid of it? And finally, the State said, 'No more!' Yeah, sure. Because the church people said, 'Bottles are going to be on the side of the road.' God, I remember when I grew up in that town and people drank then. They had beer sales years ago, back then, and there was no more bottles around the streets then! The thing is, they're taking their money out of town. But they're still doing it because they don't want you to know they drink."

Stan said, "You want to hear a real good story? Years back, I used to go to Belfast a lot. And I went to this Shop 'N Save—this big market—with my buddy's wife. She had to buy a few items, so I was sitting in the parking lot. I see this old car pull up and a woman gets out and goes into the market. And meanwhile, this fella gets out and lifts up his hood, right? And he picked up a little bag or something—that's what it looked like, right? And he looked around and (Stan went through the motions of drinking a bottle.). Put it back in the battery box on one side. Closed the hood, right? And this woman comes out, gets in the car, and they were on their way."

Stan took me to the back of the store and showed me some of the wines he sold: Old Duke, Cool Breeze—"The flavor is Passion fruit". He said, "They've got these wines now that are fourteen or fifteen percent alcohol, which is maximum. I've got some guys who buy it by the case and come back later in the day and buy another case—besides beer. They'll drink it warm or cold."

"That Old Duke, boy, he sells quite a bit of that," Colin said. "I've got a friend of mine that drinks it all the time. He drinks it just like you drink beer."

"Do you remember that red port wine they used to drink? That Red Fairview. Was that the name? My uncle, he drank so much of that—it made his circulation—it done something to the circulation. And he went to Togus, the army hospital, and he had to have his leg taken off. And later on he died."

"Is that right?"

"He was only sixty. He came back from the second World War—that's all he would drink.

"I'll tell ya, when we was younger fellows, there was an older fella who would get me to drive for him. He'd say, 'Take me by the Guzzle.' Do you know where the bootlegger was? Up that road there?"

"The Guzzle Road," I said. "Up the Guzzle—in Gouldsboro."

"Yeah, there's an old guy used to sell whiskey, or about anything you wanted. I'd drive a couple of them up 'cause you see, at that time, there was no such thing as Sunday sales around here. I know they would go in and he would meet them at the door. You'd never see him. When they came out they had what they wanted."

"When was that?"

"Back in the '40s. You see, there've been a lot of changes in these places now." Colin had graduated from high school in 1947 and had served in Korea. When he returned to Maine, he dug clams for a while, then went to work in Connecticut. But like most Downeasters, the pull of the ocean had been too strong. "I love to be near salt water," he said. "There's nothing like Maine." Colin's children were now grown up and married, and he had lost his wife the previous year. She had heart failure. Colin had suffered a heart attack himself seven years ago, then had to have open heart surgery. He was now fifty-seven and had survived four bypasses.

"You don't look fifty-seven."

"Oh, I take pretty good care of myself. When I quit drinking, everything straightened out. I used to smoke three packs of cigarettes a day too."

"What do you do in your spare time?"

"Oh, I keep busy. I walk, and when it's hunting season I have plenty to do."

"He's got a lady friend that keeps up with him in the woods now, right?" Stan said. "He's found his match. She can walk in the woods and he's getting tired. She does whatever he does and she enjoys it. And that makes a pretty good team. He doesn't realize it, he's got a good catch."

"Yeah, really, she enjoys it," Colin said. "She enjoys hunting. She likes to go in the boat. See, I go around the islands. Oh yeah, she goes right along."

"She's about your age then?"

"She's fifty-nine."

"Older woman."

"She's got me by a couple of years. Her birthday's in March. She's feisty as a cormorant. You can see why I'm trifling."

Stan talked about diving for old bottles at the bottom of harbors. Colin mentioned an old bottle he had found down on Head Harbor. We moved on to artifacts and arrowheads, then Colin said, "So you see, there had to be someone here before I was here."

# CHAPTER 27

# MILLIONAIRES AND GHOSTS:
# STEWART'S GROCERY, JONESPORT

These days, folks down in Jonesport take the Maine State Lottery seriously. I was in Stewart's Grocery, talking to Donald Stewart, the store's owner the past thirty-two years, when he said, "At this lottery machine two years ago, we sold a seven million dollar ticket. Those folks were twenty-seven years old. They still work. I didn't sell them the ticket personally, but I was here that night. Almost a year to the day, that same woman came in and won a thousand dollar ticket. You know, in a small town, everybody just thinks it's fixed. But then someone in their own community wins one. It happens."

"How do you feel about gambling?" I asked Donald.

"Hell, I play the horses. I don't care. I went up to Bangor yesterday and spent forty dollars on the horses."

"Well, you know, over on Beals they won't even sell liquor."

"They're still in the Dark Ages over there, but they drink half of what I sell."

Jonesport is a lobster fishing town with about fifteen hundred residents. It once had several sardine factories and at least seven country stores. Today, there's a small IGA supermarket, a tiny convenience store, and Stewart's Grocery, a one-story, red, wooden structure that contains a full line of groceries, housewares, snacks, beer, wine, and liquors. I asked Donald if Jonesport was growing.

"Oh sure, the town's growing. For many years it stayed about the same. You knew everybody in town. And then the last, maybe eight years or so, it's got so you know only half the people; the rest, you just see 'em. Or you saw them last year; so you say, 'They must have a cottage or something here.' They come here in the summer, buy a piece of land, put up a cottage, then use it for a couple of weeks. There's no industrial growth."

"Are any of the canning factories still operating?"

"No, the only thing that's goin' on now is down there to Look's— they're building a marina. There's no industry other than the ocean."

"How have you managed to survive in business all these years?"

"Hard work—fourteen hours a day. Always have been open seven days a week. We close half a day Christmas and half a day Thanksgiving. I have dinner, then I open up at four o'clock in the afternoon. That's Donald the third—grandson." A young boy suddenly appeared behind the counter as if he were a fixture in the store. "My son runs the little video rental store across the road. That's his. He works here part-time. But he keeps busy in the video. They do alright."

I mentioned the box full of dried fish on the front steps outside, and Donald said, "Oh yes, that's a staple. You can't buy it everywhere."

"Do people still come in to socialize?"

"Not as much as they used to. When we first started, we used to have a crowd that would hang around 'til closing time and tell stories, lies, one or the other."

"What do people in Jonesport do for a living other than lobster fishing?"

"People go brushing (to make Christmas wreaths). Blueberrying. They work whatever's going. We've had a good life here."

"What advice would you have for some young person wanting to start out in the country store business?"

"I'd tell them to go work for somebody else. Get their paycheck Friday night and say, 'The hell with it!' in plain English. They'd have no worries. And the rules and regulations—every time you turn around there's something new. They won't leave us alone long enough to make a living."

A man came to cash in a four dollar winning lottery ticket. I stood in the doorway while Donald waited on him. It was a warm, humid morning. A salesman mentioned how hot it would be in Bangor when he got home that night. It was hot everywhere this summer, even down here in Jonesport, where it's usually cool and foggy.

"I tried to get *Down East* Magazine and I tried to get *Yankee*, three years ago, February," Donald said. "My son's house burnt down. Of course, I'm on the Fire Department. And I tried to get both magazines to do a story on the place being haunted, but they wouldn't do it. What happened was, it was snowing; the house got on fire and we went down and put it out. But when we was investigating what had happened, an image of an old man come on the wall. The house had been re-done by a local carpenter— new sheet rock and paint and wallpaper. Everything was new in the room, so it wasn't something that was under some old paper or under something else.

"At the same time that we was all discussing this over, we had a telephone in the kitchen that was all burnt and melt down, and it started ringing. One of the firemen was a little jumpy, and he said he was going to leave out through the back door. A young fellow grabbed the phone up and answered it, but nobody was there. It was a little unusual to have all of these things happen, so I went down and cut the picture right out of the wall. I had a local boat builder build me a round frame, and we put the picture in it and I've got it up the house under glass.

"It's a picture that you've really got to look at to see. It's unbelievable. It's an image from the fire or the smoke or whatever. I'll get the picture for you if you want to look at it. You can make out a number of different things in it. But the old house was owned by a sea captain. And the sea captain was lost at sea, and a long story goes with him. Maybe the face in the picture is his. You can also make out a picture of a whale, and another of a baby's face. You wait a minute, I'll go get it."

Donald went across the street and came back in a few minutes carrying the picture. He stood it up on the floor of the store and we began to study it carefully. He said, "It's images through your mind. You can look at it and see different things in different places. This looks like maybe a horse's head. You can see an eye and a nostril."

I examined the image carefully from several different angles, but I failed to see the face of the old sea captain. I really wasn't sure I could see any of the images that Donald spoke of. "People can put so much into a picture when they look at it," Donald said. Perhaps that was so, because at the moment, I failed to see the images he spoke of.

"All of the people I've talked to say they wouldn't even keep the picture in the house," Donald explained. "I say, 'Why the hell not?' Right after I got it—I have smoke detectors in the house, and all of our smoke detectors went off at once one night. That's the only time it's ever happened! No fire, nothing, they just went off.

"My son was living in that house at the time. We'd just put a wood stove in it and they think it started around that. He had checked the stove, fixed it up, and left. His wife had gone up to her mother's up here. Took the three kids and went for the night."

"When did the old sea captain die?"

"Oh, you'd have to go back in history for that. Back in the late 1800s or early 1900s."

"But you think that's his face in the picture?"

"Oh, I can think anything. But the old sea captain lived there, and he did go on the high seas, and as far as we know, he was lost at sea. I believe they went to Florida or the South and they picked up a load of something. And there was a bad storm coming up, and his wife and adopted son went ashore and came up here in a stage coach. But his ship was wrecked. He never made it back."

"The twins that's in the Fire Department—they're twenty-seven years old—they won't even look at that picture. The one fella said, 'If the phone rings again, I'm goin' out through the wall!' They don't go for that stuff."

"You mean the phone was completely melted, so there was no way it could have rung?"

"I imagine there was a ring left in it and somebody dialed that number. It did ring about four times. One of the fellows that was in the house picked it up, but nobody was there. When you're looking at this stuff, and the house is all burned, and water is dripping, and pieces of sheetrock are hanging around, and the phone rings and you look and there it is—on the table, all melted!"

Donald got busy with customers, and I looked once more at the unusual picture. Stewart's son, Donald Jr. came over, so I asked him if he believed the story about the ghost.

"Yes, I do."

"Did anything ever happen there to spook you before the house burned down? Did you ever hear noises?"

"It was an incredibly silent house. Very silent. You take an old house like that, you expect it to creak. This one never did. Nothin'."

"When was it built?"

"Eighteen sixty-something. We've got the plaque that they put on the front of the house. It was a really nice house. It was strange that you couldn't hear nothing goin' on outside. It was very silent. That was the only room that didn't burn in the whole house. And the only thing there was that picture on the wall. That room looked just like it had when we walked out of it. There was a little bit of smoke. We had two doorways and the fire went to both doorways and stopped on the outside of the casing. The inside of the casings toward the bedroom was fine. It was awful spooky. February seventh, three years ago. Very silent house. You couldn't hear the rain. This wasn't the original plastered wall 'cause we'd had it done. It was sheetrock and lavender paint. You wouldn't even know the wind was blowing."

Before I left the store that day, I had Donald Sr. and Donald Jr. stand out front for a photo. Donald Jr. held up the round picture, and while I was still unable to see what they said they saw, I took the photograph and then a close-up shot anyway. It wasn't until September that I developed the film, but when the prints came back, there was that old sea captain just as clear as could be!

# CHAPTER 28

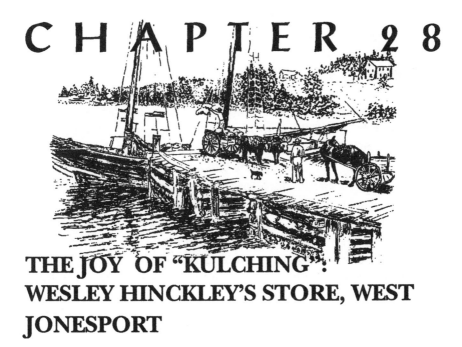

# THE JOY OF "KULCHING": WESLEY HINCKLEY'S STORE, WEST JONESPORT

A man named Horace, I was told, could tell me all I would ever want to know about an old country store in West Jonesport. I followed a driveway near the old store building, past a white Cape Cod house that appeared empty, onward to a larger white house dating from the Victorian Period. From the street you hardly noticed the large house because the Cape Cod house obscured the view. It was a quiet setting—a little world in itself. The driveway circled around the front of the house which was nicely landscaped with roses, delphinium, and other flowers. I knocked lightly on the elegant front door, but no one answered. I tapped again. And when I had walked several paces down the path I heard someone trying to open the door.

Horace was a very old man, badly bent over. It must have taken him a great effort just to answer the door. And although he had no idea who I was—I had just dropped by unannounced—he invited me in as if he'd been expecting me.

"That fellow painted it in black and blue," Horace said, when I told him I was interested in the history of the old country store nearby.

"You see what I have to look at?"

"Terrible," I said.

"The more I fight with him, the more he grins and laughs," Horace continued. "Doesn't pay any attention to me. It's disgustin'! Down here we have so much fog that it's gloomy and desolate, so they paint in bright colors—tan, or pale green, or something cheerful. But he specializes in bla-a-ack (Horace had a way of drawing out his syllables so that black came out bla-a-ack.), dark brown. Oh, it's awful. This town's never seen such messes!"

We were seated in a small room—antique furniture, wainscotting, old pictures hung on papered walls. A dark, elegant desk—very old—covered with books and papers, stood against the front wall between the doorway and the window. And through that front window I could see a tiny hummingbird lighting down on the delphinium.

At first I thought that Horace was just a cantankerous old man, but what I had taken for grumpiness, I began to appreciate as his dry sense of humor. He continued to grumble about things the new owner had done to the old store building. "The law required the owner to have a fire escape," Horace said. "I think they're going to use it for an entrance and an exit. They'll be dogs and cats and young ones and old trash and clutter and culch piles— just like anybody has behind their house."

"What do you call it? Kulch? You mean clutter?"

"I presume it developed from cull, to cull out, to pick out," Horace explained. "Some say 'weeding.' Well, I think a better word is kulch—K-U-L-C-H. Because you cull it out and there's a difference. Weeding—you throw it away. Kulch—you save it. It's something you have no immediate use for. But you think you might need it in the future. It's your typical Yankee. And therefore you say, 'Well, that might come in handy for something, so I guess I'll save it.' There are pieces I've cut out of *The Ellsworth American*, and I've got stacks of them."

There were newspaper clippings on the floor, on a chair, and piled on the antique desk. I had caught him in the act of "kulching." In fact, that's what he had said when I first entered the room, only I hadn't understood what he meant. I was impressed with, and curious about his interest in words. (I later learned that Horace had been a teacher and museum curator.) I also appreciated his need to kulch; because as a geography professor, I kulched all the time. I was always clipping and saving articles from *The Christian Science Monitor* and other newspapers. And on a file cabinet in my office are several manila folders labelled: "Africa," "Asia," "Europe," "Latin America," "Global," and "Writings;" each overflowing with kulch.

Old Yankee ways—The New Englander saves everything, uses it up, wears it out. The Mid-Westerner, on the other hand, doesn't use it at all. People in the Middle West seem intent on preserving their most precious possessions. They'd rather keep it in the box, so-to-speak. A friend in North Dakota saved his money for years, then paid cash for a brand new sports car that he only drove on calm, clear days. He never let his wife drive it. He didn't even drive it to work for fear of it getting hit in the parking lot. In a small town in North Dakota? Yep. And as soon as he had purchased the car, he and his wife moved to another house. "Why did you suddenly move?" "Well, we needed to get a house with a garage—for the car." "Of course." Another time, he told me about an expensive hunting rifle he owned. "I've never fired it," he whispered with a smug grin on his face. The Yankee, however, might boast of owning an old Winchester lever action rifle that his grandfather had used years ago to get his deer.

Southerners are different still. If at all possible, they want their possessions to be new also; but unlike Mid-Westerners, they'll use them for a while, then trade them in. It matters little if they can afford to "trade up"—they'll finance it. Indeed, many Southerners will finance almost anything—by the month, or even by the week. Compared to Downeasters, Southerners seem more status-conscious. One has to keep up appearances; one has to maintain one's social position. A friend in South Carolina recently said to me: "That's no car for a college professor to be driving." He was referring to our 1975 Dodge Dart, that I sort of felt was becoming a classic. He said: "You've got to trade up."

Horace said, "One of my relatives talks about clearing out the attic. It was full of everything, same as this one is. They said there was a shoe box—everything was orderly—put away and it was marked. And it said, 'Contents: Pieces Too Short To Use.' (Horace laughed a slow, deep laugh.) I had a piece of string the other day and tied it up and had a ball that big. (He held up his large hand, and with his thumb and index finger, described the size—about two inches—of the ball of string.) If I need to tie up something I'll have it. Oh, when I go visit my nieces and nephews—the younger generation—at Christmas-time, these magnificent wrappings, beautiful expensive paper—they tear it all to pieces. I fold it up, save it, and put it away. And all of that ribbon—yards and yards of it. Oh, what a waste!

"And no wonder we're the most wasteful nation in the world. A Frenchman told me, 'A family in my country could live on what the average American throws away.' I have an aunt who saves any food that's left over. She got a butter chip off the cupboard and she put a slice of cucumber on it and put it in the refrigerator—one slice of cucumber. And I said, 'Throw that out, it will clutter up the refrigerator.' 'Oh, I guess I won't. I'll come in later on and chop that up and add a little potato and a bit of onion and I'll have a nice little salad.'"

Horace was in his nineties. His legs were worn out. The fluid in his knees had dried out and he needed periodic injections with long needles. "And my back is worse," he said. "It has two curls in it now. The doctor says I should get fitted with a brace. Well, I said, 'I'd rather not, because I had a heart attack seven years ago.' And I have to use a pacer, and it's seven years old and I think it's wearing out. But I don't want to change it because I think it's wearing out. But I don't want to change it because I think there's still some good in it. When they put it in, I asked the doctor, 'If I die, can they take it out and let someone else use it? Put that in the ground when it costs fourteen hundred?' He said, 'Would you want it from someone else who had it?' I said, 'I would. Clean it up and oil it!' He said, 'What about false teeth?' And I said, 'No, I guess not.' I said, 'You could take them out and put them on another. It might be alright.'"

Horace said that a relative had wanted to take him to Rhode Island so he could visit old friends in the town where he had lived for thirty-five years. But he didn't want to go. He said, "Because I have my routine and it upsets me to think about it. And I've got my own bed and I know just where the hole is in the mattress. And I know just how to fix the foot. And I know how to come downstairs backwards 'cause I fell downstairs once. There's a woman who comes to clean for me once in a while, and she had put Lemon Pledge on the stairs. And I had on woolen socks and I put one foot on the first step. And I said, 'Here I go, Horace, good-bye.' You know, as kids, on rainy days, we would come down the stairs, bump on our tails. We thought that was fun."

He began to tell me about his childhood; about the Passamaquoddy Indians who came each summer, camped in tents by the shore, picked sweet grass, killed seals, and cured the skins. Horace said, "Their forebears before them—the Indians used this area to get away from the heat. Oh, it's rich in arrowheads and artifacts on the islands around here."

Horace showed me some Indian wampum—tiny circular colored shells, strung on a fiber; and a miniature birch bark canoe with two tiny snowshoes inside, and said, "I got that as a Christmas present when I was five years old. Indians used to make them down at Pleasant Point (Indian Reservation near Eastport). And they'd come around and sell them for little or nothing. I think the boat was probably ten cents. My mother would always buy them.

"So we played, catching minnows; played the way kids used to. We didn't have anything else to play with—just what we picked up, and what nature provided. And Frankie, an Indian boy, and I were chums. And I cut my hand; see that big scar right there (And he showed me his large hand again.), on a piece of gla-a-as. And I ran in the tent crying and bleeding. Of course, I thought it was cut off. And Frankie's father grabbed a handful of alder leaves, crushed them all up, and he held up my hand and put the leaves in there. Pressed it and held it, and I looked at him, and his mouth was going. And he was making some kind of incantation. And he held it there quite a while, and took his hand off and the blood had stopped. And I've learned since World War II that it was chlorophyll. And it cured it. What is it they call it now? Even the Indian—he knew it—Indian medicine. What is it they call it? Everyone takes it to offset poisoning."

"Penicillin?"

"Penicillin—the chlorophyll from the leaves. They knew that before we did."

"What do you think of Jonesport now, compared to when you were growing up here?"

"Oh, it's changed a great deal. Oh yes, when I was growing up we didn't have any of the conveniences we have now. We didn't have any of the problems—the sewer problems—either. They're having a sewer problem now—they say that everything in Jonesport is poisoned. All the water is poisoned and all the air is poisoned and all the clam flats are poisoned."

"Is the town water bad? Can you drink it?

"There's nothing the matter with the water."

"But the state stays it's bad?"

"They say, 'Don't use that well, the water's not fit to drink.' People drink it and it doesn't hurt them a bit. Generations and generations—they survived and had nice comfortable homes. My father built his house and brought up six children; brought up eight children from other relatives. A disaster would happen in the family and they'd swap the children around—parcel them around, you know. We always had somebody living with us—a cousin, or a relative of some kind. And my grandmother was the matriarch. She was the boss over my father and my mother. She was the boss over my aunt and her husband. But she didn't want to be. But if they had any question or family problem that came up—she was the one to settle it."

Horace began talking about the way houses and roads were situated in the past, when people traveled by water instead of land. He said, "The people who owned the two most expensive houses— the road went behind their houses. Then it got fashionable to have the town road go in front. Before that, you mustn't have a town road in front of your house. You would have a front field that went to the shore. That was the style. That's why you see so many lovely old fashioned homes that have a field right to the shore and the town road behind. Because everybody traveled by water. They went by boat. We went by boat up to Columbia Falls from Jonesport. There was an Indian trail through the woods which later became the highway—now Route 187. (The road that I had traveled down that morning had now taken on a larger meaning. I thought of Indians rambling on foot over hills and valleys; of white settlers plying the bays and estuaries in their sailboats.)

"Where the bridge goes over to Beals Island, there was a big steamboat wharf with big store houses on it. We kids lived there, and we would get in skiffs and go sail around and fish and catch skulpins, flounder, pollack and everything. And we'd go up on the shore and gather up crabs and boil them. We lived there— down around there. And they had these big drays—we called them—great big horses. And they would haul the sardines, and fish, clam chowder, and the big kettles of salted fish from the factories and different places where they manufactured it, to the steamboat wharf. They were shipped to the cities—New York, Philadelphia, and everywhere.

"And the salt, the big bundles of one hundred and two hundred pounds of salt fish that went to the West Indies to the Catholic countries where they had fish on Friday in those days. And it was heavily salted. And they'd pack that. And they'd bring the supplies—the people'd come to the boat. Every Saturday night the boat would come in. And everybody'd flock here. People would come to see who came on the boat. 'So and so came last night and so and so is going.'"

I had seen lots of pictures of wharves and schooners in the old days, but I really had no idea how it "felt" to be on the wharf when the ship came in. Horace had a way of bringing it all back; it soon became easy to visualize the entire scene; of Downeasters going down to the sea in ships. Horace said, "And when they'd go—and we'd see them when they went with their big trunk and their valises in their buggies. And all their city clothes—their pretty hats, coats, and dusters. There'd be someone there to meet them.

"People would take the boat if they were going to Portland. Sometimes when someone was sick and was going to the hospital for an operation their whole family would come with them to the wharf. And they'd all sit up and cry because they were going to the hospital."

Horace asked me if I had ever seen an orange crate. He said the crates would often get broken open and people would salvage those, and candy pails—wooden pails—that they'd use for washing clothes and floors. "They were dandy," Horace said. "And the bananas would come in big crates with hay—all packed in hay. And sometimes in the hay would be some of these insects from the West Indies. And the seeds—that's how a lot of different plants and insects and different pests got into the country. And a box of oranges would get broken open; they'd roll all over the wharf down there. We boys would run and grab those oranges, stick them in our pockets. And we wore blouses in those days, and they had elastic around the bottom, and they were buttoned up here and our mothers made them with a collar on them. And a little ruffle maybe; make them fancy. And we'd stick them (oranges) in our blouses all around in our pockets—all the oranges we could get hold of. But the candy pail had a wooden cover on it, and they had wire holding it. They never got broken open; unless in transportation, they'd fall off and all this candy would fall out on the wharf. Whether the horses had been there or not—didn't make any difference. We'd pick it up anyway!"

"Was that old store in your family? That old general store?" I was trying to bring Horace around to the subject of the country store.

"It wasn't in my family. My father's cousin owned part of it at one time. But it had stagnated. Because at the time there were changes—chain stores. Big supermarkets began to come in and the old country stores sort of went out of existence. But there wasn't anything special about it. It was an average country store. There was Wesley Hinckley was the one who brought it to its peak of prosperity and perfection. (Such an interesting way of putting it.) And before that, Newell Runry had it. (Just that archaic name itself conjured an image of an old-time storekeeper in his apron.) And I have a letter he wrote in 1873 to his chum who was my uncle, who lived down in the South. The letter was quite interesting. He was just a young man, and he said: (And Horace recited the following from memory!)

> I'm keeping store tonight. We've had pretty good trade (An old expression—if they were busy they had a pretty good trade.) The shops are all closed now. (Because the lobster factory was closed, and the sardine factory and the blueberry factory.) (And he said) I haven't been to any dances lately. You come home and we will go. But I haven't slaughtered the hog yet. I'm waiting for colder weather. (This was written on the twenty-third of November.) (And he said) I've hauled up my boat. (And then he said) I wish you'd come home so we can go to dances. (They used to go to Milbridge, Machias, everywhere then.) I haven't had my dancing school open, but it will open before long.

"They used to go to dancing school in those days. They would go to penmanship school and spelling and singing school. They taught them reading and music. They'd have organized classes to beautify their penmanship. I've got some calling cards that he used to write—all the flourishes, the flowers and everything. They had these schools because they didn't have T.V. He was just a young man when he wrote that. But he was married, and my uncle was there in New York on a vessel. And my uncle said he'd be glad when he came back. And he told him about the vessels, how they gradually would be bringing the ships home and put them in Alley's Bay for the winter. Then in the spring they would take them out and start on their coastal cruises. It was mostly to the West Indies and around there. They didn't go far overseas in those small vessels. But they'd go to the West Indies, then go to the Gulf States and Mexico.

"But bringing up the old-time country store again—when Wesley Hinckley had it, he had the counters all varnished, and they were inlaid with moldings all around them, and every morning the varnished counters were all dusted and polished. The showcases were cleaned. And in the showcases were the handsome dishes, you know, that had the handsome gla-a-as. And there were showcases where all the penny candy were put in. There were pails for penny candy. And the candy came in cartons to fill the candy pails. This one was orange, lemon, and chocolate. They were made in molds. There were French cremes—twenty cents a pound."

"I bet they were good."

"Yes, and soft inside. And the penny candy: I can remember that. You could get six pieces for five cents, and each piece was equivalent to a thirty cents a piece now. There was taffy, lozenges, and the marshmallows—and in my time, the marshmallows were made in the form of the battleship Maine." Horace mentioned other candies with names like "Poppsie Grandpa," "Buster Brown," and "Buster Dewey," and I was impressed with his ability to describe each in such minute detail. But then I too remembered certain candies that my father had brought me as a child. So often, it is memories of events and things and places of our childhood that we recall in such vivid detail later in life.

Horace said, "There was one woman, she couldn't count, but she'd say, "I'll have one of these and one of those, and one of them. And one of them and one of those and one of these.' She would get her five cents worth—that was six pieces." Horace mimicked the woman in the store. And with his large hands, he gestured towards an imaginary country store and said, "On the eastern side was where the shoes were kept, and the rubber boots hanging up, and jewelry in showcases—studs, things of that kind. They didn't have any bolts of cloth as I remember it. It was mostly clothing that people needed for work, like overalls and frocks. And they had ladies wrappers; it was a house dress, all machine-made. Women would buy them for their ordinary work. They were fixed up fancy. They had cases for jewelry and then ladies hair combs in sets—they'd wear in their hair, had side combs and back combs, the barrette. And they'd have diamonds set in their barrettes. I'd see them and say, 'Oh, don't I wish I had money enough to buy a set for my mother for Christmas.'"

"I bet they were pretty."

"They were—and that was the style—to have a set of combs. And they'd stand them up.

"And the hardwood floor was always swept and oiled. And over in the middle of it was where they had the potbellied stove. They'd put coal in that, and then the counter back of that is where they had the scales to weigh everything and where they'd cut off the salt pork. The salt pork came in big barrels. It was packed with great chunks of it and they'd take it out with a big hook. They'd cut it off. And they had brown paper—a coarse brown paper. They'd tear off a strip of that and put it on the scales, and put the pork on it, fold it over, tuck it in, pull on the string. (Horace used those large hands of his to mimic the storekeeper as he worked. I felt as though it was I who had ordered the salt pork.) The string was kept in an iron ball attached to the ceiling and it would hang down there. And then put up orders; they'd call it. If you were in there you'd wait for it at the counter, and you'd tell them what you wanted and they'd run around and get it and tie it up for you."

I had been studying country stores for nearly six years, and while I understood their locational characteristics and the reasons for their decline, I never really knew what they were like during their heyday. But Horace had had a personal attachment to this country store, and he had the unusual ability to convey that experience to me. He said, "I'd have a list and say, 'Now I want a quart of yellow eyes.' A quart of yellow eyes would be yellow eyed beans. They'd go to the barrel where they had the yellow eyes and dip in with a scoop, put them in the bag (And here he made the sound b-r-r-r-r for the beans flowing into the bag, while he demonstrated with his hands how the storekeeper would have done it.), weigh them on the scale; he'd look through his glasses and say, 'Ah, huh.' Then he'd take some string and tie it around them and that would be one order.

"And those raisins—they came in layers in pretty boxes with a lace paper doily folded over them. Those raisins would be just as they grew on the stem. And then dried and pressed and put in these boxes. The kids would have to stone the raisins; you know, break them open and get the seeds out. Nobody used seedless raisins because they hadn't been developed at that time. In those days they were pressed hard together. You'd take them apart and soak them on the stove. They would come apart. Oh, those are still good when you can get them.

"Well, we had the raisins and dried apples. They (apples) used to come out on strings. That was a long time ago. (He didn't say how long, but assuming he was a boy of about ten years old then and he was now ninety-two, this would have been around 1906.) The apples were dried first and then put on strings at the factory. And they would put them in boxes—pasteboard boxes—and you could buy these boxes of dried apples. You would soak them and they'd all plump up, and you'd make pies and sauce out of them."

Horace mentioned prunes and apricots, and then went on to canned goods with "handsome" labels on them. Women would save every one of those cans for the label. He said, "That made it pretty to put them on the window sills. On the outside you'd see these handsome pictures of peaches and maybe there'd be pictures of a pretty girl and past events to make it attractive. They'd plant geraniums and set them in the window.

"So they had canned goods and lots of things in bulk. You'd buy things in bulk. My father always used to buy one or two barrels of flour for the winter. On the barrels of flour would always be a picture of a train at night, with the flames and the smoke at the head of the engine coming at you. And they had another called Purity Maid. There was a picture of a beautiful girl in handsome dress, holding flowers in her hand. And called 'Purity.' The old saying they used to say was, 'She was as pure as the snow, but she drifted.' Have you heard that?"

I hadn't.

"Well, they'd pile these barrels of flour in the rear of the store. They would have, oh, a hundred barrels. And this man, Wesley Hinckley, was so fussy, that if the men piled them in and they got the picture on the end of the barrel crooked, he'd make them take it all down and do it over until the picture was straight. If the girl was standing to one side or the engine was upside down, they'd have to change it."

The store had a wagon team, Horace said, and they would go to each house in the morning to take orders, come back and fill them, and then make deliveries in the afternoon. Home delivery was common until the 1940s. And today, only one store, the Alleys Bay Grocery on Beals Island, still makes home deliveries, two days a week. Horace said, "They'd come to the door and say, 'Anything this mornin'?' And my mother would say, 'No,' because we were so near the store that she'd often go herself. She'd want to go to the store, but she didn't like it. The women didn't like going to the store. All the locals would be there in the winter. See, there were two settees. These settees were varnished. Had red on the end—apple red. So this was where the men sat when the women came in. And then the men would look them all over—to see what the women had on. And the men would watch what they'd buy. They'd say, 'How can she afford to buy that White House Coffee in a can? They don't have enough money to afford that.' And, 'She bought 'boughten' cookies.' If you bought store-bought cookies—that was out of this world! It was a big treat. Now you buy them out of necessity. If you get a homemade cookie; well, that's the treat. But in those days there was a crock of cookies. They made molasses cookies and sugar cookies, plus some with coconut. There was also a crock of biscuits. There was always fruitcake for an emergency. And doughnuts. My mother had a big bean pot to put doughnuts in.

"They had all those things in the store on the western side, and candy was on the eastern side, with the frocks, the pants, boots, shoes, things like that. Then out back they kept the grains for animals and stuff they kept in bulk.

"My stepfather—he'd been down to the store. My mother, she'd say, `Where you've been? Down nail-kegging?' Some of the stores had empty nail kegs to sit on.

"My grandfather had a special seat on the settee. It was the end one with the arm on it. And if anyone was sitting on it when he came through the door, they'd get up. If they didn't get up, he'd say, `Now you jump up. You're younger than I am.' He'd sit there and smoke his pipe.

"And that was a hangout for people. They would come from sea; they'd just come from a voyage. They'd come in and everybody'd greet them. And they'd tell them all the news in town. Well, you'd hear so and so and such and such. 'Well, what do you think of that?' 'Uh, pretty caper, wasn't it?'"

"Pretty caper?"

"Pretty caper. Yeah, pretty looking caper. And they'd, well, hash it over. They'd extend their sympathy too, if someone had hard luck or anything. They'd all pitch in. And then they would always know if anybody bought a piano, or an organ, or had something big to move. 'Will you give me a hand? I want to launch a boat.' People were always coming for help. They still do, over on Beals Island. The lobster boat; well, everybody goes to launch it. And there used to be, over there, a quartet, and they used to sing. Oh, beautiful singers, these men. They'd sing hymns or songs while they're launching the boat. It was quite an occasion.

"There was a spittoon right near the stove—to spit in. And when it was full, they'd spit and it didn't always make it. And there was sawdust in the spittle. And we kids—they'd give us a Needham (candy) if we dumped the spittoon and washed it out and put it back in. We'd take turns—the boys would—bringing it out behind the store, dumping out what was in it, and washing it out.

"They also had kerosene, and the man would come with a great big kerosene truck—great big brass horses—these handsome horses. And they'd give us ten cents to hold these horses."

The mention of kerosene brought Horace back to his child-hood chores; to an upbringing very different from that of today's children. He said, "We always had a five gallon kerosene can that set up on the bench up there. And one of the things we'd have to do before we went to school was help mother fill the lamps. My mother had two girls, but the oldest one had asthma. She was sickly. She didn't do a lot of work, but she did what she could. She'd love to. She died when she was only thirty-five. She was one beautiful girl. And the other one—the youngest—she was too little. So it was between these boys—we had to work. We had to wash the dishes. We had to learn how to cook, wash the floor, cut the kindling wood, split the wood, lug it in, take care of the yard, do everything—clean up the cow, feed the hens, gather the eggs— we had chores that had to be done before we went to school.

"We had to put the wash water on the stove and hang up the clothes line. Get the wash bench ready; put the tubs on it; fill the tubs with rinse water. Then my mother did the washing. (He said all this in a sing-song fashion, mimicking the sound of scrubbing on a scrubboard.) I remember my grandmother was very fussy about her clothes, because there was a public view. So the sheets went in front and the nonmentionables went in back. It would be immodest to stretch them all out on the line. Everything had to be just so—the size of the towels—the long ones, the medium, the short, and then the wash cloths."

Horace said that even the rags were washed. They were spread out on the grass to dry. The privy was also washed every week with boiling soapy water and left to air out. Just hearing him describe the weekly work routine was making me tired. It was easy to see how one might have wanted to run away from home and go off to sea.

Once again, Horace returned to Wesley Hinckley's old store. It was as if he had wanted to re-live it all once more; to get down every detail, no matter how minute, so that it might be passed along. He said, "He had a steel ceiling—that was something in those days. And he had beautiful hanging lamps—big brass lamps on a chain. They were all pulled down, and they were filled and cleaned every day. And he had a little office, and his safe was in there where he kept books. And he would always say—the old saying—'Charge it?' My mother never ran an account, but most of them did. Payday was Wednesday down at the factory and they would come in on the next day. They couldn't go Wednesday because they had to work. In the factories in those days you worked from seven to twelve and then from one to six—when I was a kid. There were no laws against it then and all the children worked in the factory. I can remember looking out in the summer—these pretty summer days—and saying, 'Oh, don't I wish I could go play for a minute.' I couldn't because I had to wait on the packers. You'd get ten cents an hour, and I'd work ten hours a day and I'd get a dollar.

"And the money that I made working in the sardine factory, I kept in a bank account in town. So I'd make my journey down there to take this dollar down and put it in the bank. The bank book—Oh, that was the most wonderful—that was next to the Bible. And I got to the huge amount of nine dollars when the bank failed. Of course, the people in town who had regular money—I know my brother, he was eleven years older than I was when the bank failed. He was planning to go to the University of Maine, and had the money for his tuition he had saved over the years. And he couldn't go to college and never did go."

Horace really had told me all I'd ever want to know about Wesley Hinckley's old store. But it was the last story, about his brother, that lingered in my mind as I walked down the path past the roses and the delphinium and out into present-day Jonesport. The story left me thinking—about my father; about his influence on my own education many years ago. My father was a shop foreman in a General Motors plant. He started working there when he was seventeen and had worked at General Motors for thirty-one years when he died of a heart attack in 1966.

Although my father read voraciously, I don't know if he ever wrote a line. I never saw his handwriting. But he loved books, and on Saturdays when I was growing up in New Jersey, my father and I would take the train from Millburn to Newark, where he would rummage through second-hand bookshops. He was the sort of person who seemed most at home leafing through old volumes by Charles Dickens'. My father taught me how to read. It was as if he just couldn't wait for me to start school. He used to take me to the library on Monday nights; and every evening, after he had gotten home from the plant, he would sit in his easy chair with the dog at his feet and his pipe lit, and ask me to bring him my school papers. My father had always wanted me to become a teacher—I think— because he wanted to be one himself. But like Horace's older brother, my father never had the money nor the opportunity to go to college.

# CHAPTER 29

## NOON RUSH AT ALLEY'S BAY GROCERY

B eyond the wharves stacked high with lobster pots, a boat named the "Jeremy Wayne," and the Advent Christian Church, stands an unpretentious wooden building that looks—well—bumped out in places. Once a one-room school house, Alleys Bay Grocery, the only surviving general store on Beals Island (population 600), has undergone some creative remodeling since Nancy and Maurice Hamor moved down from Winterport two years ago. They've enlarged the structure, and added an upstairs apartment, but once inside, you immediately realize the store's atmosphere hasn't changed a bit.

"They sit just like they used to," said Nancy. "Archie Alley (age 90, the island's oldest resident) is our main sitter. Then we have Isaac Seavey. He comes and he sits. Usually at nighttime there's ten or fifteen of them. They come and they all sit around, which I don't mind."

The Hamors were carrying on a long tradition. An article on the Alleys Bay Grocery (then Don Beal's) in the October 9, 1982 issue of the *Bangor Daily News* had emphasized the store's friendly surroundings:

ALLEYS BAY - It doesn't make much difference if the weather around Pig Island Gut here is clear or thick dungeon fog or blowing a living gale, something is always brewing or stewing around the front counter at Don's General Store.

The dozen or so locals who frequent the front counter area at night, leaning and hanging on the store fixtures, are considered no hindrance to business.

"The only thing you say is 'excuse me' and you reach for what you want," explained a young woman shopper who indicated she enjoyed the homey gatherings.

"It was wall to wall here the other night," another patron inserted.

"We have a lot of pot bellies around," a clerk said, "the only thing we lack around here is an old pot-bellied wood stove.

"You wouldn't dare stand around in some of the other stores. You're expected to get your stuff and leave. We think it's great. Really there's nothing to do in the evenings . . . there's nothing on TV.

"You can hear anything you want to hear. Like who are going to have babies and who aren't."

I was standing in front of the counter talking to Nancy and to Warren Peabody, the store's clerk the past twenty-two years, when an old man came in.

"Do I know you?" Archie asked, extending his hand.

"I don't think so," I replied, "but I've heard a lot about you. You're quite a famous man down here."

"Oh yes," Archie laughed.

"Is that your chair?" I pointed to the padded one in the middle of three.

"That's my special seat," Archie said. He patted the chair next to his and offered to buy me some ice cream. Meanwhile, customers came and went.

"How we doin', Grampy?" said a husky man in hip rubber boots.

"Hi, Uncle Archie."

"Yes dear," Archie replied to a tall, thin fisherman. "How long before you get your new boat?"

"Next year," the fisherman laughed.

Archie had a small thin face, eyes the color of a calm blue sea, and light features. His hands were large, and I thought of those hands hauling countless lobster traps over the years. It was evident that Archie had built up considerable respect in the community as everyone who entered the store spoke to the old man. I began to feel like his special guest. It was nearly the dinner hour and the store was jumping.

"He can handle it, that fella," Archie said of Warren. "He's been here for a long, long time. Oh, they wouldn't get no better. It's worth something to have somebody you trust. Nearly everyone on Beals Island is an Alley, a Beal, a Norton, or a Carver. And judging from the ruddy appearance of the patrons in the store, the island has an abundance of people with blond or red hair and freckles.

"You must be related to everyone on Beals," I said to Uncle Archie.

"I am."

"Everybody around between here and Jonesport," Warren added.

"So you must be a great grandfather?"

"I am, a number of times. And a great, great grandfather too! Ayuh, I've got a little lively one. He stands about this tall, don't he, Warren? He's just a small fella. And I'll say, 'Can't you stand for Grampy?' He's not very old. I think a lot of him."

"But I feel something about those islands out there," my friend, Josh, had said after he had sailed his boat down the Maine coast. "And it's like it's more behind the times, and that's good. And the island people are still island people."

I too got that sense when I talked with Warren and Archie. They were different—refreshingly different—like characters out of an old movie, say, from the 1930s. Warren might have been a middle-aged British actor, his thick graying hair slicked back, a slight lilt to his voice. Archie was the old lord of the manor. These men had nothing to prove. You knew they were as solid as an English castle. They had always been here; they would always be here. And you were comfortable with them because they were always at ease.

I asked Archie if he remembered when the store building had been a one-room school.

"Oh yes! I was right here and helped move it. Moved it in the night on a scow. We had to do it at night because we were busy tending our traps during the day. It was my schoolhouse down to

Slate Harbor. I lived in Sand Cove and we used to walk over and go to school. Viola Crowley was our teacher. We moved it up from the Flying Place (a narrows between two bays where flocks of sea birds are said to fly past). I towed it up with my powerboat."

Once there had been five general stores on Beals Island. The bridge to the mainland was completed in 1958, however, and islanders began buying cars. And like people everywhere else, they soon got into the habit of shopping in supermarkets, rendering the old stores obsolete. When I last visited the island in 1985, there were two stores still operating. But, Carver's General Store—just over the bridge—closed soon after, and Don Beal, then owner of Alleys Bay Grocery, decided to put up the FOR SALE sign.

"Don couldn't make a go of it," Warren explained. "See, he teaches at Narraguagus High School. You can't teach school and run a business at the same time. He might be in fifteen to twenty minutes when he come from school and that was it. You've got to be around."

Richard Carver, the owner of Carver's General Store, had told me in 1985 that country stores were "dying off." In 1988, he explained, "We got out of it because we weren't making any money." So I asked Nancy why she and her husband had bought the Alleys Bay Grocery.

"My husband was very dissatisfied with the job he had, and we had joked about this store for about two years. We came down to work on our island which we have down here. And he came home one night and said that he found out the store was for sale—and he wanted it. He said, 'I want to move down,' and I said, 'fine.' He has family down here. And I think that's one reason we were accepted. Oh, I know we would have been accepted regardless, but because of the family, I think we were accepted more quickly."

Country stores change hands frequently. The Gouldsboro Grocery, for example, has had fifteen different owners that past three decades. I wondered how Nancy felt about their decision now.

"Oh, we think it's nice. Of course we have Warren; he's been loyal to us; and then we have Judy, his cousin, who works for us part-time. And sometimes the four of us are right out straight."

"And I'm the overseer," Archie added. "You're livin' right now in God's Country."

"Every part of Beals is God's Country," Nancy exclaimed.

I asked about the lobster fishing. It was slow, everyone agreed, but it would start picking up in August. "I understand the clamming is not too good now either."

"No Sir! Everything is ruined," Archie responded. "Everything is dug up and gone! Why when I was a clam digger you could go anywhere. There weren't no law. Not 'til the last of it. You could go anywhere out of town and dig—up around Steuben Bay and places like that. You've got to buy a license from each town now. Yes Sa', Yes Sa', it was no job at all to dig twenty-eight bushels of clams."

"Twenty-eight bushels of clams! In one tide?"

"Ayuh, one man, one man right here!" Archie boasted. "In Steuben Bay. Of course we got nothin' for 'em—fifty cents a bushel."

"What year would that have been?"

"Oh land. That was way, way back. Way back. Hadley Beal, Riley Beal, Charles Edwards, my brother, Darris, we was all there together. Sold right up there. We took 'em to Wyman's factory in Milbridge. Fifty cents a bushel, and a big bushel too!" (It was hard to tell when this was, because Bill Crowley had told me he got thirty-five cents a bushel in the 1940s. Perhaps Bill had meant the 1930s; maybe Archie was in the late 1930s or early 1940s.)

"Was that before or after 1900?" I joked.

"After," Warren said with a grin.

"After, because I went in the service when I was eighteen. I was in the Coast Guard nine years. I spent a lot of time around Portsmouth, New Hampshire. Oh, I've sailed up and down the coast a good many times. Carrying sardines. There was a factory here years ago and two other ones before that. All gone now. The nearest sardine factory to us is Machiasport."

Archie was atypical of Downeast lobstermen, not because he was ninety years of age, but because he had been many places beyond Beals. Lobstermen are among the most provincial people in Maine. They fish their own waters, not because they are unwilling to go elsewhere, but because the adjacent waters are already the territory of someone else. Lobsters are found close to shore, so fishermen harvest their own harbors. They become provincial out of necessity at first, and as they become more and more secure in their respective communities, they tend to stay put. A friend in Prospect Harbor told me a story about his neighbor, a retired lobsterman. The fisherman and his wife decided to take a trip. They hadn't been many places and now they had the time to travel. So they packed their car, left town, and stopped first at Ellsworth, twenty-five miles from home. There, they went to see a movie. And when the movie was over, the lobsterman's wife excitedly said, "Where are we going now?" To this the lobsterman replied: "I don't know about you, but I'm going back to Prospect Harbor."

In his book, *The Lobster Gangs of Maine*, anthropologist James M. Acheson, suggests that lobster fishing is monotonous, that hauling traps every day has "all the interest of a paper route." Acheson believes that outsiders like to paint a romantic picture of lobstermen as rugged individualists because they want to think the world still contains such people. Lobstermen are actually highly dependent on each other, on banks, insurance companies, mechanics, and the Internal Revenue Service. Successful lobstermen are responsible small businessmen. Sort of like farmers in the Middle West: lots of money tied up in equipment and machinery; mountains of debt; tied down to home. About as stifling as being a country storekeeper, I thought.

"So it's mostly lobster fishing and clamming here now?" I asked Uncle Archie.

"Ayuh, that's all there is. That and musseling—they drag mussels (quahogs), wrinkling—whatever they can do, they do it." But the clamming on Beals had gotten so poor that Carver's Shellfish Company had been importing Maryland clams. "Our clams taste better to me than those Maryland clams," Archie said. "Oh, it's awful, awful clamming. They're trying to seed them in again. They used to sell them by the bushel, but now they sell them by the pound. If I can't dig 'em, I'll go without 'em."

A young woman entered the store. "Now that's a lobster fisherman," Archie said, loud enough for her to hear. "Oh yeah, she goes right out with her husband."

Another woman entered the store. "Now that's a sardine worker," Archie said of her.

"And a mother," she added.

"Of three," Archie interjected.

"And a carpenter," she continued.

"A jack of all trades," Archie joked, "And good at none!"

People continued to enter the store. One man bought ice cream for his dog. "What flavor?"

"Oh, it's vanilla," the man said as he went out.

"What kind of dog does he have?" I wondered.

"Oh, it's a small one—Chihuahua or something," Warren said.

"I bet it's a fat one."

I wondered how people on Beals felt about developers coming in and buying coastal property.

"They'll soon own the whole of it," Archie joked.

"You go down the island, you'll find out," Warren explained. "There's plenty moving in." He pointed with his index finger and said, "You'll see a road here, road here, road here."

But Archie saw another side to the development issue.

"The more out-of-staters come down here, that lowers our taxes."

"It lowers your taxes maybe, but it also takes our land from us," Nancy argued.

"Down the lower end of town, where Warren lives, they've built some monstrous things down there," Archie added. "And all that takes money. It cuts us little fellas down on their taxes."

"Do they put up NO TRESPASSING signs?"

"Yes, they do," Archie admitted. "They don't want anyone on their land."

"It's not good," Warren added. "When strangers move in and won't even let you walk by their land. We always could go wherever we wanted to."

"They're gonna take over," Archie said.

"Where are the island people going to go?"

"Underground," Archie joked. "They're buying up every place they can get. And over to Jonesport it's full of them."

"What's the attraction?"

"I don't see one thing," Archie said.

"Well, they'll get tired of it," I suggested. "If we have many more foggy days like this, the weather will drive them right out."

"You know, they love it," Warren said. "They love it. When I was over at the harbor yesterday afternoon, the sun was out and just as nice and warm over there. Next thing I know the fog's rollin' in. When that ol' sucker rolls in it gets some cool!"

Warren had lived on Beals all his life. He knew the weather was just plain lousy. Indeed, Downeast Maine has one of the dreariest climates in the whole United States. The trees down here aren't fully leafed out until the middle of June. Then it usually rains on and off until the middle of July. We usually get a heat wave about then, and that's when the mosquitoes get so thick they sound like sirens outside the camp screens at night. It stays warm until the full moon around the second week in August, when the nights turn cool and starlit, and you know that fall is fast approaching. That's when the BLUEBERRY RAKERS WANTED signs are replaced by notices for brush pickers and Christmas wreathmakers. The fall colors peak around October the fifth, and all lies dormant until the peepers start up in May.

Many outsiders who move here and rave about the cool foggy summers soon get tired of it. "Oh, we're moving to Montana," a neighbor recently told me. They had moved here from out-of-state and opened a bed and breakfast. But when the tourist season doesn't really begin until July, and then it's foggy much of the summer, it's easy to see how one could get frustrated.

The Alleys Bay Grocery is unique in at least three ways. First, they still make home deliveries to residents of the Beals/Jonesport area two days a week. Customers simply phone in their orders to be filled and delivered at no extra charge. "We don't make much money at it. But it helps people," Warren explained. Second, they still carry people on credit. "Most of them pay us. There are a few that don't," Nancy said. "That's part of it. You have to set a limit on what they can charge at times." And finally, they don't sell alcoholic beverages. Beals is still a dry town, and until Don Beal, the previous owner, ran the general store, they didn't even sell cigarettes.

"I guess not too many people leave the island," I said to Uncle Archie.

"They come back. When I was in the Coast Guard I went around to different places. I like it home here best."

"You wouldn't think of living anywhere else?"

"I wouldn't want to," Warren replied.

"Most folks stay right here then?"

Uncle Archie smiled and said, "That's why they call it Alleys Bay."

# CHAPTER 30

## HE RACES HORSES: STANHOPE'S GROCERY, JONESPORT

Mr. Stanhope has eleven horses—harness racing horses— he drives his own. How exciting that must be! But he said, "Awful disappointing—most of the time. That's not a sure thing, you know. The fastest horse don't win the race."

Mr. Stanhope asked me what I did. I told him I was a college professor. He said, "Oh, good. You're the best looking college professor I've ever seen. How did you ever get into—being this college professor.

I told him it was a long process—that it had taken me about ten years to earn bachelors, masters, and doctors degrees. Mr. Stanhope said, "Yeah, you could have been raising the devil all them years."

Unlike most of the people I interviewed, Mr. Stanhope, owner of Stanhope's Grocery in Jonesport, seemed as interested in me as I was in him and his store. Stanhope was an amiable sort; he was easy to talk to, if not always easy to comprehend. I'm not sure of his age—late middle, thereabouts—but he had a lot of life left in him.

The last time I was in this one room, non-descript little store, it was called Ma's Gameroom. "She (Mrs. Lorraine Stanhope) runs the business," Stanhope said. "I ain't here half the time." Indeed, Lorraine had been running the little convenience store with the game room attached for more than twenty years. "The game room was good for a while, but now hardly anyone comes in to play," Lorraine said. "I don't enjoy it. My husband plays horses. He has colts for harness racing."

I said to Mr. Stanhope, "How did you get involved in harness racing?"

"I do it 'cause my father done it."

"You must like it. Is it profitable?"

"You can't make a nickel. But we've got that stallion and he pays the way for the other horses. He wins every year. I've got eleven horses."

"Stallion?"

"Yeah. We have the best producing stallion in the state of Maine."

"Do you really?"

"Yeah. We bought him in Ohio four years ago. Went down to a sale in Ohio and he was crazy. And that's how come we bought him."

"They told you he was crazy?"

"Yeah. He was unruly—terrible. The way I got him in the trailer— I got some of these A-mish boys down there. We set up with the A-mish. They thought we were stupid. We went along and they were setting up, oh, six, eight feet high, and we went and sat right up there with them. The other people thought we were crazy. It was all A-mish. That's where I did my bidding from. We brought him up here and we had the fastest two-year old filly in Maine last year."

"So, you go up to Bangor every weekend for the races?"

"No, I go up every couple of days. I have my son up there to take care of the horses."

"When does the season start?"

"It's almost year-round. Start in Lewiston in the middle of February and it runs 'til next week before Christmas. If my wife didn't work in the store—I couldn't do it. She puts in some long hours."

Stanhope's avocation surprised me. I didn't expect to find anyone in Washington County interested in harness racing.

Jonesport was famous for its lobster boat races, but this was something altogether different. And then I though, well maybe I don't really know this town. Perhaps there are many people here who do this sort of thing. I asked Stanhope if many people from Jonesport went up to the races.

"No, they don't go nowhere."

"What do you mean?"

"Do you remember when Jonesport/Beals played in the state basketball tournament in Augusta? It was about seven years ago. People came in here and they wanted a road map to see if they could find their way to Augusta. It was when they had that championship basketball team two or three years in a row. The first year they went, a lot of them young people had never been there before."

"Young people?"

"Young people. Yeah, they didn't go nowhere. They'd go as far as Bangor. What would they want to go anywhere else for? You've got everything right here."

"Would you say that they were unusual?"

"No, no. They were young, smart people. They just don't run around all over the place. They stay right here. I think that people in Washington County—they stay right down in here. They don't go anywhere. No. Well, you stop and think—you drive an hour to get to Ellsworth. You haven't gone anywhere when you get there."

"Do you suppose there are any people in this town that have never been out of the state?"

"I'm going to say there's probably some older ones here that's never been out of the state of Maine. Aside from going to the horse races, I've never been out of the state of Maine."

"But you went to Ohio to buy horses."

"I went right down and straight back. I didn't look around to see no scenery or nothing.

"A lot of these people—where the drug store is right now—I know a fella worked in there. He and his wife never had been to Bangor until they both wound up in the hospital, and that's where they died. They was born here and they died here."

# C H A P T E R  3 1

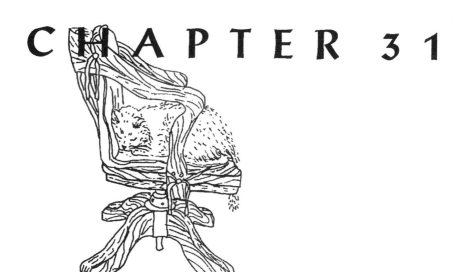

## ANOTHER SIDE OF BEALS:
## CARVER'S GENERAL STORE

Even a little place like Beals is complex once you get to know it. I had always thought there was just Beals Island, a foggy village across Moosabec Reach from Jonesport. But when I looked more closely at my map, then drove around Beals a bit, I began to sense a bigger, more diverse community. You cross the Reach to Beals alright, but then you drive across the Flying Place to Great Wass Island. The Alleys Bay community is a couple of miles beyond Beals Island; it's actually on Great Wass.

And when I talked to Richard Carver in his former country store—now converted into a shellfish and heating oil business—just beyond the bridge, on Beals Island proper, I began to see Beals from a different perspective than I had from Alleys Bay. It was partly the result of opposing viewpoints: the former store owner, Richard Carver, versus the on-going store owner, Nancy Hamor. Carver felt that country stores were obsolete, while Hamor saw them as viable. But my enlightened view of Beals was also shaped by its geography. At Carver's I was just over the bridge—scarcely on the island—while at Alleys Bay, I was a good two miles farther along and could "feel" the increasing insularity with every turn in the road.

With Richard Carver, I went back to the building of the bridge in 1958, to learn how the island had changed over the years so as to have rendered his general store obsolete.

"Everybody bought a car," Richard said, when I asked what difference the bridge had made. "Well, the first time people bought cars was when they put the car ferry over. We didn't even have a car ferry. And there was like two pickups and a couple of cars."

"Is that why the houses are so close together on Beals—because people walked everywhere?"

"Well, you see, land didn't have any value because everybody got their living on the ocean. So what probably happened—Dad had a piece of land and you put your house over there. And they didn't care if it was crowded—it wasn't like Aroostook County where everybody's got to have two-hundred acres. They divided it up on the road so everybody got so many feet on the front. It wasn't because there wasn't any land either. Because back then, when most of these places were built, there was plenty of land. But what they were worried about was having a place on the shore where they could have a wharf."

"Stonington's that way too," I said.

"Yeah, many of the people in Stonington came from here— Alleys, a lot of Faulkinghams."

"Why did they move there?"

"I think they thought the lobster fishing was about over. Which it was. It got crowded here as far as fishing goes—very crowded. There's a lot of lobsters here, but there's a lot of lobster fishermen. There's an awful lot of lobster pots."

Beals does seem densely populated, but its density is misleading. Most of the island is still woods. It seems more crowded than it is because most of the houses are clustered around the wharves. Beals has a human scale, which gives it a sort of intimacy.

I asked Richard if he really thought lobstermen were independent. "It's about the only thing left where two people can go in a boat and make a real good living. Other than that, you've got to have a big boat, big crew. It's still an independent way of life because you get what you put into it. You get up in the morning and say, 'It's kind of foggy, I don't think I'll go.' You won't make any money that day, but maybe you wouldn't have made any if you'd gone. There are lobstermen who do very well."

Carver had been in the country store business for forty years when he finally gave it up a few years ago. He didn't look that old, so I said, "You must have started at quite a young age."

"I got a driver's license when I was fifteen, and my father and mother had a store and I was able to work when I was fifteen. We had a store down on a wharf. We used to do quite a lot of business because people were sailing in boats and they'd come in and buy their groceries and gas. After the bridge came in we moved the store up here. It got so that there weren't many people travelling by water. Of course, you had to go by water to get to Jonesport and back so we had it on the water until the bridge."

"Why did you get out of the country store business?"

"Because I had other fish to fry. And I wasn't making any money."

One of Carver's sons ran the fuel oil business; the other son ran the shellfish business. His daughter taught school in Jonesport. She liked it, he said, and he had encouraged her to pursue a teaching career, rather than take on the country store. Carver could have sold the store to an out-of-stater: "And got a good price for it." But he didn't; he said, "I don't want to classify all out-of-staters as being dumb, but those who buy those country stores are dumb." And I got the feeling that—because Carver knew the country store was a losing proposition, his conscience would not permit him to sell it at a profit to some unknowing out-of-stater. Instead, he had remodelled the store building to be used as offices for his heating oil and shellfish businesses.

"Lobsters and clams?"

"Lobsters, clams, mussels, quahogs, crabmeat—I've got a plant down the road. We've got ten people cutting."

I changed the subject and asked Carver if most people born on Beals stayed here. (I had asked the same question at Alleys Bay and wondered how Carver would respond.)

"I think most of them do. I mean, they might go into teaching—things like that, but they teach locally. My kids—all three of them—when they were in high school, they didn't know what they were going to do, but they were going to go away to school, and they were going to come home twice a year and all this baloney. And my oldest boy, he went to South Portland to school and he was so homesick the first week, he almost quit."

As we talked, I noticed a large, framed photograph on the wall next to Carver's desk, of him and his wife standing in front of a building on a city street. The scene didn't look like any place in New England; it looked like Europe.

"That's Pat and me in front of a beer restaurant in Germany."

"When were you over there?"

"Last October, for the World Trade Food Show. We're going to Paris this October. They're going to have the same thing there. We pass out stuff like pickled corn, and smoked mussels, and smoked scallops—stuff we never want to sell."

I had thought of Carver as just another down-home Beals Islander, hardly a man who jetted around the world. "I didn't realize you did anything like that."

"Oh yeah. Well, the Maine World Trade Association is looking for people who have the time and energy to do it. We have booths and all."

"And you're exporting overseas?"

"No, I just go over on vacation."

Carver had even been to Japan, which he said was too expensive and too crowded. He liked to travel, however, and said, "I like to go every six months for ten or twelve days. We went to Tokyo and went on the Bullet Train—had a rail pass."

The Carvers didn't travel when they had the country store, however, and I assumed they had deferred their urge to go places all those years. "I had to laugh though," Pat Carver said. "Two or three weeks ago, Richard and I were riding around and everyone had strawberries. And he kept saying, 'Stop, so I can get some of these.' There was one place that had them for ninety-nine cents a quart. And I said, 'What for?' And he said, 'I can take them home and sell them for a dollar and a quarter.' I said, 'We're not in that business anymore.'"

"It's in the blood," I said.

"Yeah, he likes to be wheeling and dealing, I guess you'd call it."

Still marveling at the Carvers' recent travels, but also thinking of the provinciality of islanders and fishermen in general, I asked: "Do many people on the island travel very much?"

"Oh, I think so," Richard said. "They're always going to Disney World. These little mini-cruises—they go for a week or three days. It's all packaged up now—cheaper than the devil."

"Outsiders have this perception of Downeasters as people who stay put and never go anywhere. That's no longer true?"

"I don't think it's true anymore. It's like anywhere else. I'll admit that everything starts in New York and works this way, but I still think this is a big misconception of Washington County."

Carver was indeed a busy man; the phones were ringing, people kept coming in the door. He had people to see, places to go, and I didn't dare keep him any longer. He had shown me another side of Beals.

# CHAPTER 32

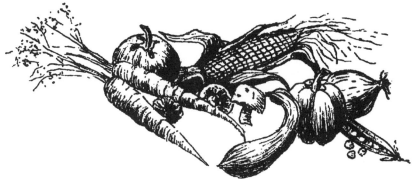

## TOM SELLECK STOOD HERE: WOODWARD'S GENERAL STORE, JONESBORO

W as it true? Had Tom Selleck, star of the popular television show, *Magnum P.I.*, really set foot in Woodward's
General Store during the spring of 1988? I had finally
made my way to the little village of Jonesboro, where I hoped to
solve the mystery, and draw some conclusions about the future of
Downeast Maine.

I still thought of Woodward's as the Look Brothers' Store. It
had been a family-owned business for seventy years when Califor-
nian Phil Albee bought it in March of 1985. What I knew of Albee
and his store I had got from an article in the March 12, 1985 issue
of *The Bangor Daily News.*

> Although the nearby Chandler River community bears
> little resemblance to Catalina Island, California, where
> the Albees first met on board movie actor John Wayne's
> yacht, the quiet and friendly little community measures
> up pretty close to exactly what the Albees have been
> searching for.
> 'It is quiet. And we both like people,' said Albee, 28.
> The California native and businessman explained that
> he once built, owned and sold a trucking business; be-

came a boat captain in the Merchant Marine; sailed around
the world; and met Terry, 24, on John Wayne's yacht, a
136-foot former World War II mine sweeper. The couple
married three years ago.

When they came to Jonesboro, they liked its people and
were attracted to the country store that overlooks a portion of Chandler River.

The couple said they plan to make a few minor changes
in the store over a period of time, including the installa-
tion of an old potbelly stove and some chairs where
people can stop and chat a while. 'We want this to be a
people store,' he said.

The arrival of the Albees was a turning point for the old Look
Brothers' Store. They phased out the clothing and hardware,
making the transition from a general merchandise to a convenience grocery store. The Albees were also the first owners to sell
beer. According to Joan Look Brown, the daughter of Leona
Look, who had run the store for fifty years: "It was a dry town. It
was election day 1984 when they voted. So we were able to sell
beer. My uncles were very much against beer and drinking. I
wonder if they would have it that way—if they would even have
sold it? It was mostly family that worked here. We worked three-
hour shifts."

The Albees only stayed about a year; then Bill Woodward, a
salesman from southern Rhode Island, bought the store. When I
stopped in, during July of 1988, Woodward had just sold the store
to another out-of-stater. I thought it interesting that Joan had
continued to work in the store despite the changes of ownership.
It made me think that this old store had a mind of its own—that
it didn't run properly without a Look behind the counter. I never
got to meet the incoming owner, but at least I had a chance to talk
to Bill Woodward.

"I've had it," Woodward said.

"Why did you buy it in the first place?"

"Oh, I had a son who needed to be straightened out a little bit.
(It was Woodward's son, I later learned, who had met Tom Selleck.)
You know, get out of the fast lane, so I brought him up here.
That's all I wanted to do and it's been fine. He'll be a senior at
Washington Academy this year and I want to spend some time
with him. We've spent three years in this store."

"You live above the store?"

"Yeah, we have a little apartment." The store building was over a hundred years old. It was a traditional gable-front structure with a lot of charm. The building had originally been the property of the Bodwell Granite Company before the Look family bought it about seventy years ago. I wondered what Woodward was going to do now.

"I'm helping three brothers who have a sawmill here in Jonesboro. And we're making models up here on the hill—cedar log cabins. We have one going up in Bucks Harbor now. But as far as the store business is concerned—I kind of think it's an endangered species. Too much competition, and your fixed expenses are hitting you in the face all the time. The power company's rates are outrageous. My liquor license costs as much as say, Shop 'N Save, that probably sells three hundred times more. There's no adjustment for the small businessman in Maine. He's just got the deck stacked against him. And in this town there are three convenience stores—you've got competition on both sides."

Sooner or later I had to come around to the Tom Selleck story. Was it true? Had the big man actually set foot in Woodward's General Store as all the newspapers had reported? It seemed like nearly everyone Downeast had either gotten a glimpse of Selleck or else they knew someone else who had. "Yeah, I think that was him who went by in a jeep one day," a friend in Steuben had said. "I think it was in March. He was wearing sunglasses and a baseball cap." In March? Indeed, everyone and his dog had laid eyes on the big man, except Woodward.

"My son was here. It was in April."

"April tenth," Joan said.

"Usually Sunday mornings it's my son's responsibility to open up," Woodward explained. "Apparently he (Selleck) came in, bought a few things, introduced himself. Talked to my son who is kind of blase—like I am—no big deal."

And that was all there was to it. Joan said, however, that patrons had since come into the store wanting to know the exact spot where Selleck had stood. "Tom Selleck stood here? Wow!"

"I think he bought down on Bucks harbor," Woodward said. "I think he came up to look at some property in Jonesboro. I think that's the extent of it. He's got a place in Bar Harbor. He's an avid sportsman. Big duck hunter and fisherman. Same things I came up here for. I didn't come up to buy a general store. I came to look at some property that one of the developers had advertised. It was totally bogus."

"How do you mean?"

"They had it so orchestrated. They screened me—found out I was single. So they had some bombshell meet me. She wasn't even from Maine. She didn't know the area any better than I did. So I decided I was going to have some fun with her. So I put her through the paces. I made her get her shoes dirty and show me the lot. They have this really good ploy. They've got a partner parked out in front, see. He's in a jeep with this other bogus couple. He says, 'Well, we just sold lots G, H, J and K. Well, you can show him the other lots, okay.' Like sure—they just sat there and wrote this check out, right? I thought: This is getting ridiculous. I said, 'Thank you very much,' you know, after coming all this way. I just happened to drive down to Milbridge—there was a realtor there. I said, 'Gee, what have you got listed?' Stayed the night, my friend and I, and said, 'Gee, you know, this would be a great place to bring my son to.' And he wanted to kill me when I brought him up here. His first year was tough, but he's adjusted pretty well."

It was easy for me to imagine what a difficult adjustment it had been for Woodward's son. My mother and I moved to Steuben permanently after my father died in 1966, and it took me much of my sophomore year before I was accepted by my classmates. They had gone to school together for years; it was hard to be the new kid. Sumner High School was terribly cliquish back then, and unless you were an athlete—and in eastern Maine being an athlete meant playing basketball—you were a "dub." It was okay to be a dub if you were in the general or shop course—little else was expected of you—but if you were in the college-bound course, like I was, you were expected to play basketball, or at least be an avid supporter of the team. I was neither. I had a miserable sophomore year.

So while my classmates practiced basketball after school, I spent my winter afternoons outdoors in the woods, hunting rabbits, or down on the bay—my favorite place—rowing around in my old leaky skiff, or tramping along the shore. I often carried my rabbit gun—an old 303 Caliber British Lee Enfield. I used steel jacketed military ammo which made a small, clean hole in a snowshoe hare. I haven't hunted since high school. Just the thought of killing a rabbit makes me cringe now, but those were difficult years for me—especially without my father—and hunting seemed to fill a void.

In the fall of my junior year of high school, I bought a second-hand outboard motor in need of repair. I couldn't seem to get it running, but my friend, Dickey, who was in the shop course at Sumner, said he could fix it. A few weeks passed, then Dickey was quite certain "She'd go." "Let's take that beauty down the bay and try 'er out," he said. "She'll go like a bastard, you just watch!" My excitement was building, but before we departed for the bay, I grabbed my Enfield rifle. It was November—deer season—and I had got in the habit of carrying the big gun.

I remember my anticipation as we filled the gas tank, then began to pull on the cord. "Let me start that beauty," Dickey said. "Stand back! Stand back!" Dickey said, as it started to sputter.

"Let's go all the way out to Lobster Island," I said in anticipation. It sputtered again and then suddenly the five horsepower motor started. Dickey threw it in drive, but nothing happened. The propeller turned, the water churned, but we just stayed there. "What's wrong?" "Just a minute," Dickey said, his face had grown serious, stern almost—a look of genuine consternation. He turned the throttle wide open and the water churned, but we still didn't go anywhere. The engine hummed louder, then louder still; it began to shake, to vibrate. There was smoke all around us. "Geez," Dickey let loose with a string of good ol' Downeast cuss words. Then he said, "I forgot to put the governor on 'er! She's gonna explode!" We rowed furiously, jumped out of the boat, and ran up on shore. "She's gonna explode!" Dickey screamed.

"Stand back!" I yelled. The Enfield did not let me down. There was a flash of light, and then an explosion. A flock of ducks, their wings flapping frantically, ascended from the grass on the opposite shore. Dickey jumped up and down and shouted, "You blew 'er all to Hell! You blew 'er all to Hell! We both doubled over in laughter—two dubs raising hell—and then all was silent. We rowed the gray skiff out into the channel, unbolted the motor, and watched while it disappeared into the brackish water. So irresponsible! So much fun!

"What's this I hear about you shooting an outboard motor?" a teacher asked me the next morning at school. Dickey was not one to let such an "achievement" go unnoticed. And kids who never seemed to leave the inner sanctum of the automotive shop suddenly began to acknowledge me. Some even sought me out. "Hey, Big Al, heard you blew an outboard motor all to Hell! Ain't that wicked!" Indeed, just a single bullet fired into the belly of a live outboard motor had instantly transformed me into a Downeaster.

"Yeah, that first year was tough," Woodward said. "Then last year he met a girl—that made a big difference. He got into snowboarding, which is a new fad. And that helped him through the winter. Next year I'll buy him a little pickup truck. He'll be able to ride around, have a little fun."

"Yeah, make a Downeaster out of him," I said. We talked some more about the developers and the effect they were having on the local area. And then Woodward said, "There's a certain percentage of people up here who won't change. They dig just enough clams to buy beer and to get gasoline for their truck. I don't think those people should be disturbed. Why should a family who has lived on the shore a couple-three generations have to pay higher taxes because somebody came in and bought some property at an outrageous amount of money? That's just not fair. It ought to be okay to tax the people who can afford to pay, but don't try to raise the guy's taxes who is trying to make a living digging clams."

Like most country store owners, Woodward had become bonded to the local population. At times, he sounded like a native Downeaster. He identified with the average person who struggled every single day just to stay ahead. Jonesboro was indeed a difficult place to make a living. He said, "It's just not consistent enough. The whole Washington County area—inconsistency is the word. All they have to do is talk about rain in the forecast along about Wednesday and you'll see the traffic slow down.

"I want to work five days a week. I want to go fishing on weekends. This seven days a week is just too much. And you go away on vacation and you worry about it. Every time you're not here—it's just a hard situation."

But Woodward was going to miss the daily contact. He told me about one of his most colorful customers. "He's notorious. If you tell him you saw a deer, he saw six. 'Shot a bear this morning—wouldn't believe it. Just as I shot him a big rock fell on him. You'd never be able to find him.' That type of thing. Anyway, apparently he was out wreathing—getting his greens for wreaths—and he heard this coyote. He said, 'I looked over and there he was. I didn't think too much of it. One coyote didn't bother me.' He said, 'I looked over and there's another one. I looked around and there was six of 'em! They had me surrounded! I didn't have my gun. It was in the truck. So I climbed up a tree. I looked, and I had my big knife with me. I took this alder and I slashed it on the side. Threw it and hit that lead dog. I came off of that tree. I beat it to the truck. Sweat ran right off my eyes—right off my back! I had my gun. I could have gone back and got all five of 'em probably. But I thought better of it.'"

# CHAPTER 33

## GIVE THE DOG A BONE:
## JAKE'S PLACE, JONESBORO

J
ake's Place, a general store and luncheonette on Route 1 in Jonesboro, was named after a dog. "Her name is Jake," Ginger Chamberlain, the proprietor said. "She's terribly abused and neglected. Ha Ha. Customers will come in and talk to Jake before they'll talk to us. Her mother was Old English Sheepdog and her father was whatever got over the fence." Jake was indeed a pampered pup. Regular customers routinely brought her biscuits. "She just about wags her whole back end off," Ginger said.

Bob and Ginger Chamberlain had moved to Jonesboro from southern New Hampshire two years ago. Their's was a familiar story. "We just wanted to get away from the rat race," Ginger explained. "Bob's been in sales all his life. I had never done anything like this. I worked at Raytheon, in the engineering department. The day we passed papers, Bob and I stood here in the store and looked at each other and said, 'What did we do?' And then we spent six weeks ripping and tearing, and painting and papering, and cleaning and fixing. There was yellow and brown and orange striped wallpaper and brown paint everywhere.

"That was January and February—we had all these signs in the windows: WATCH FOR OPENING UNDER NEW OWNERS. We already had people coming in here. A woman came up to the door one day and she opened it, and I'm over there painting the ceiling, and Bob's ripping out walls, and she said, 'Oh, I guess you're not open yet.' I said, 'No mam, we're not.' Well, she says, 'You are going to have some ice cream, aren't you?' It was about eight below zero!"

"So you've retained the local clientele?"

"Retained and regained some for one reason or another. We like it here and we try to fit into the community. We're not going to get rich. Some kid will come in and want candy and doesn't have enought money. He usually winds up getting the candy.

"When I went to give my notice to my boss, I said, 'I'm going to Maine.' He said, 'So—you've been going for two years.' I said, 'Yeah, but this time I'm not coming back.' He said, 'You can't do that. You've got eighteen years in the company!' I said, 'yeah, and I've got seventeen years to go before I can retire—and I'm not going to live that long. Good-bye.'"

Jake's Place was jumping the day I was there, and I couldn't help but notice the huge portions they served. Bob said, "We tell our people that work for us—'When you're making sandwiches, if there's any question about how much stuff to put in it, you put in more.' We don't want anybody going out of here with a portion they feel wasn't worth it. Our hamburgers are a little better than six ounces. They can brag all they want about their quarter pounder—ours are bigger."

# C H A P T E R  3 4

# A BUNDLE OF STICKS:
# BRIDGHAM'S STORE, JONESBORO

B ridgham's Store on Route 1 in Jonesboro was my last stop. The next town was Machias, the county seat, a place I no longer thought of as "country:" hence, no country stores there. So, it was at Bridgham's that I hoped to draw some conclusions and to gain some insight into the future of the Downeast region. It was a tall order, but Ozias Bridgham, a graying school superintendent and country store proprietor, was a man I could count on for information. Bridgham was probably in his sixties; he had a dry sense of humor and was a good talker—we had talked before—who knew the store business and area well. As usual, I began with the country store and said, "The last time we talked, you told me you bought this business for something to do in retirement."

"Well, I think we originally bought it for that purpose. How long we keep it depends on a number of things. As we grow older, this type of business becomes difficult to maintain. It takes a lot of hours to run a general store in a small town. We're here at five-thirty in the morning until seven o'clock at night, seven days a week. That's the only way you can make it work. You have to fill in what everybody doesn't get at the supermarket."

"Why do you have to open at five-thirty?"

"There's a lot of business between five-thirty and seven. It's probably the busiest time of the day, really. People going to work—carpenters, people who go into the woods, workmen—many of them pack their lunch right here every morning, with Italian Sandwiches, sweets, a drink, cigarettes—necessities for the day, and gasoline and oil, things of that sort. So basically, what you do from five-thirty until seven is get everybody off to work. And it is a very busy time of the day. That's my shift because I'm an early riser. I'm over here at five-thirty every morning."

Bridgham said they had made many changes in the five years they had owned the store. They had gotten into movie rental, installed a walk-in cooler, and were instrumental in getting the town to go wet for beer sales. Jonesboro had been a dry town since the 1930s. But like many of the proprietors I had spoken with, Bridgham felt that government regulations were making it harder for small stores to survive. In their own case, they would probably have to enlarge the store to carry many of the items that people normally purchased in supermarkets in order to make a "real living" off of it in the future. He said, "Maybe looking at a different product mix and make it so it has real possibilities. I really think that's what it's going to come to because the area is growing. It's slow, but it's growing, and I really think there is a way to make a reasonable living in a small store. But the small stores have to change."

"Do you want the area to grow?"

"It's inevitable. Change is inevitable. It's already changed a lot in the last five years. We've had a lot of people buy land. The price of real estate has skyrocketed. And we're just beginning to feel the impact on Washington County that southern Maine has, and that's a pity. But it has started. Some of the good things might be—I'm sure it's going to boost the economy eventually. It's going to increase the tax base because people who have bought land are going to eventually build on it. If you can afford to pay forty to sixty thousand dollars for a house lot, then you can afford to put a house on it.

"I think the things that are going to become problems—the native has been priced out of the land. It's just a shame—the youngster whose father and grandfather had large pieces of land have cut a piece out and sold it. Now it's gone. And you can't work in the woods, dig clams, or be a laborer around here and get minimum wage and pay forty to fifty thousand dollars a house lot. So the local person is already priced out of the housing market—that's set. The other big problem I see is going to be re-evaluation of the tax structure. And that is going to be a burden on some people. I think what's going to happen when it's balanced—when it's reasonably equitable—the person who is going to hurt the most is probably the elderly person living on a fixed income, who all of a sudden finds their taxes doubled, tripled, perhaps quadrupled overnight. And they may not be able to afford to live in the home they've lived in all their life. So the revaluation of the tax structure is going to be a horrible problem. The local—the native—is priced right out of the housing market now."

I tried to think of people I knew—friends around my own age, thirty-eight—who owned land. But hardly any of my friends had much property. One owned four acres. He said, "I tried to buy a wood lot, but couldn't afford one." Another friend had once owned several pieces of land, but now had nothing. The taxes had gotten too high. In my own case, I still have the same half acre that I bought years ago, but it's now assessed at seventy-five times as much as when I bought it, and the taxes doubled from 1987 to 1988. There was still plenty of vacant land around, but nobody seemed to know who owned it anymore. The acres of woods and miles of shoreline were usually owned by faceless out-of-staters and speculators who rarely set foot on their property.

Landownership may indeed mean power as some have said, but more important, it is the difference between rootlessness and a sense of place. During the fourteen years that Linda and I have been married, we have lived in seven states. And although we were renters, and not owners, in six of those states, we've never felt rootless because we've always had our camp in West Gouldsboro. In a sense, my teaching job has always seemed like nine months at sea, while the camp has been our true home.

I said to Bridgham, "But don't you think with these prices rising the way they are, that people coming to retire here are going to say, 'Wait a minute, I can't afford that. I'm going to stay here in New York or Massachusetts, whatever?'"

"It's going to level off like everything else. And I think you'll find it hasn't reached its peak in this area. But I think it's beginning to slow a bit. It's gone from here to there very quickly. But I think we're at least five years from a real leveling off. Because if you compare land here with southern Maine, there's still quite a difference. And it's going to balance. You watch what's happening. It's just push, push, push going up here. Next, it will be New Brunswick. And it's just not going to stop. It's not going to stop in Ellsworth or Harrington or Columbia Falls. There's just too much land. The big grab has been for shore property. Everybody wants to be sitting on salt water. That's gone. But there's tremendous acreage out here (inland) that's good building land. So if you can't get the best, you start with the next best. So even though the shore property is gone, the movement of people from Massachusetts, New York, wherever—from outside—is nonstop. It's just going to be—pick up the best of what's left. There's a lot of it. You look around Maine; it's still ninety percent unsettled. The movement of people has just begun to scratch the surface.

"So I look for moderate growth. It's still going to be a struggle. If you're going to survive in Washington County, you're still going to have to put together a bundle of sticks. You can't do any one thing. It's like running the store—you can teach school, you can do a little of that, you put everything together, you can make a living. But there are very few people who are fortunate enough to say, 'I do one thing and I can make a living at it.' Because that's not the economy. It's self-employment, it's imagination, it's a lot of individual capabilities where a person can put together three or four things and total it up and make a good living. It's going to be that way for quite a while—long after I'm gone before it's going to change."

"Yes, I guess most people Downeast still work the seasonal round—brushing in the fall, blueberry raking in the summer."

"Right. Find something to pick up the slack. You see some things emerging because of the vocational schools. Boat building is going to be one of the areas that I think is going to be open to people who want to do it. And I mean a backyard operation, but I don't mean a shoddy one either."

"Working boats or pleasure boats?"

"Small boats, pleasure boats, wooden boats:  There is still a market for wooden boats, fiberglass boats, that can be turned out with a one, two, or three person operation.  I think you're going to see those come on a little stronger in Washington County.

"I also think we're seeing a lot more interest among young people in—how should I call it?  Cooking?  Food preparation?"

"Culinary arts?"

"Yes.  And I think that's a natural for Washington County because with people coming in, you're going to see more and more need for that.  So kids can get employment without leaving Washington County.  Or the ones with enough drive can always set up their own business.  And I suspect you'll see people going out on their own.  And here, that adds up to, 'I run a little take-out in the summer, and I do a little wreathing in the fall, and I do this in the spring, and I get by.'

"I think—basically, here, we like our open spaces.  And I think change is difficult.  All of a sudden there are new faces.  It's a jolt."

As part of his retirement, Bridgham had accepted a three day-a-week, one hundred and sixty day-a-year position as superintendent of schools for the town of Lubec, farther Downeast.  He had been a full-time superintendent in Machias for many years, but wanted a change of pace.  I wondered if people's perceptions of education in Washington County were changing, so I said, "There used to be almost an anti-intellectualism here.  Many people just didn't think there was a need to go beyond high school.  Is that still true?"

"Oh, I think it's changed.  Society has changed.  We're in a technological revolution and times are different.  Fifty years ago, your grandfather or your father taught you how to fish lobsters.  That would do you.  You bought your boat.  You built your traps.  And you got your vocational education from your family.  And today that doesn't prevail as much because we're getting into a society where most people are going to have to be retrained several times during a lifetime.  And you can't do that by the same method you used to use.  So I think people began to realize that if you're going to survive in the world you have to have tools.  And number two—you can't rest on those laurels, you have to keep upgrading and retooling while you're a member of the work force. Read the newspaper today and look at the jobs. There's no place for the unskilled worker.

"Here again, let's go back to some of the problems we talked about in the area. The tourist industry is facing it right now, in Mount Desert, where they just can't get people to work. And the problem is you can't put someone to work full-time; and for the wages they can earn for that skill level, they can't survive. They can't rent a place. They can't buy their food. So why work? They can't make a car payment. So you have a situation where an unskilled or semi-skilled worker cannot earn enough to survive. If you don't have a saleable skill then you're not going to survive. Not unless you have some assistance—foodstamps, whatever—the benefits that basically subsidize the person whose not skilled enough to make it on his own.

"My belief is that everybody ought to earn their own way. I got mine that way—why shouldn't everyone else? Basically, I feel we have gone way overboard on welfare—because there are people out there who are abusing it. I think we owe something to our elderly people. That's because I'm reaching that age. Here's something to make you stop and think—somebody made the statement: 'We're all of us aging right now.' And it's true. Not pleasant, but true."

# C H A P T E R  3 5

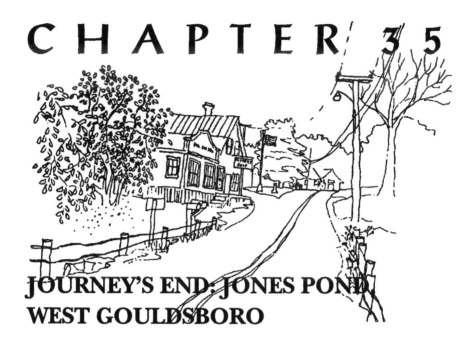

## JOURNEY'S END: JONES POND, WEST GOULDSBORO

On my way home from Bridgham's Store, I stopped at Steuben to fetch my mail. Although I had summered in West Gouldsboro since 1973, I still retained my Steuben mailing address. It was another symptom of my rootlessness; I'd had so many addresses the past twenty years; I wanted this one to stay the same. So I never changed it. I told friends in other states that my summer home was Steuben, Maine. Actually I haven't spent a night there since 1972.

Roger's Store was long gone, but around the bend, our old Cape Cod house was still standing. It was once again the summer retreat of people from out-of-state—New Jersey, I think. My mother sold it in 1972 and moved back to New Jersey herself. After six years Downeast, she had decided that Maine wasn't for her. She missed our family; she also likes to garden, and was tired of fighting the black flies.

So after the house was sold, the camp on Jones Pond became home to me. There is still no electricity here—no television, lights or phone—nothing. Nor is there running water. We rely on the pond for bathing, a neighbor's well for drinking water, kerosene lamps for light, a woodstove for heat, and an outhouse built in 1978 from boards scavenged from a friend's fallen barn. One board measures eighteen inches in width and has a knot hole for peering out.

"An outhouse!" a colleague once shrieked when I told her how Linda and I spend our summers. She walked off muttering something about each to his own before I could tell her how proud I am of that privy. It's such an improvement after my original wilderness outhouse—a hole surrounded by a lean-to of fir boughs. A balsam tree had stood in front for cover. If she had only known what it was like my first summer here in 1973. I was twenty-two then and still an undergraduate. I kept a journal that summer, and wrote mostly about the rain, fog, mosquitoes, discomfort, and loneliness. I suppose it was typical of a self-centered college student; to insulate oneself from the rest of the world; to think only of one's own misery.

I remember coming home evenings from my job in Harrington that summer, building a fire on the rocks below, and cooking hot dogs among the mosquitoes. Occasionally, I caught bass, drove sticks through them, and roasted the fish over the flames.

The camp was tiny then; just ten feet by twelve. It had a rough floor of random-width pine planks that had dried out over the years. There were cracks as wide as three quarters of an inch which invited hordes of mosquitoes. I had an old iron bed and springs, but no real mattress. I slept fitfully on a two-inch-thick piece of foam rubber which molded itself around the curves of my body as it swayed over the coiled springs. Later, I tried placing a four by eight foot sheet of plywood on the springs with the cot mattress atop it, but the bed rocked and rolled like a small boat in deep swells. An old picnic table but no chairs, a pine trunk for storing canned food, the makeshift bed, a tiny wall mirror, and a kerosene barn lantern with a red globe that gave off little light, were my only furnishings. There were no screens on the three windows which were nailed shut. The front door stood almost three feet above the sloping ledge on which the structure rests, and I had to climb up on a big granite boulder and hurl myself inside.

A child's idea of paradise; I had built the ten by twelve foot camp in 1966 when I was fifteen years old. My father was with me when I strung out the original chalkline. He had suggested I build it among the ruins of an old stone wall that runs along the bank. To my father, the camp would have been a teenaged boy's hut or hiding place in the woods. I doubt he ever imagined it as my future home. But to me, it was to be something more substantial; I envisioned myself living here permanently some day, so I built the camp on a ledge, a good seventy-five feet back from the pond.

To buy a piece of land in Maine, and to build on it my very own camp, had been my obsession since I was about twelve. My parents encouraged me; they loaned me the money, which I slowly repaid by mowing lawns. And in 1965, when I was only fourteen, I bought this half acre for less that 500 dollars.

We strung the original chalkline while on vacation in 1966, then my father retreated to his fishing rod, while I began digging the post holes. And during the next two weeks, I was able to set down the cedar posts, sills, joists, and floor of random-width planks.

My father and I went fishing the last night of our vacation. "Take one more cast," he had said, again and again that evening, as the sky changed from blue to orange to black. "Maybe we'll see some animals tonight," he said, as we drove out the dirt road in darkness. We stopped for an ice cream cone on our way back to Steuben, and that night he died. He had a massive heart attack. He was only forty-eight.

We left New Jersey for good that summer. We sold our house there, and my mother and I moved up to the old Cape Cod house in Steuben. And on weekends in the fall, until the snow fell, I worked on the camp. It was the only autumn I've ever spent at Jones Pond, and I remember sitting on the ridge pole, marvelling at the brilliant colors. It wasn't a bad place to be alone, and on many a fall afternoon in present-day South Carolina, I've sat at my desk and fantasized about flying home to Jones Pond. I got the walls and roof boarded and tar papered that fall, and that's essentially how the camp remained until Linda and I were married.

When we arrived in the summer of 1976, Linda insisted on some improvements. We covered the floor with linoleum, replaced the granite boulder with wooden steps, put screens on the windows, and tried to make the camp mosquito-proof, but it was still "wicked hard living." There was still no heat—you can freeze to death here in June—and the ten by twelve foot hovel tested our relationship.

We never have solved the mosquito problem, probably because we are surrounded on three sides by water. A wooded, bullfrog heath lies to the north, Fred's Cove to the east, then Bar Point, and finally the main body of the pond to the south. In the west, the pond empties into Frenchman's Bay, and in the morning and again at night, we can hear the departure and return of the Bluenose, the ferry to and from Nova Scotia.

In the late 1970s, we popped open a portion of the roof and built a four by eight foot sleeping loft. It had a window in front resembling a sort of funny-looking dormer, but it leaked like a sieve when it rained, and we were always hitting our heads on two by fours. Still needing space, we added a tiny sun porch in the early 1980s, but I installed the corrugated fiberglass roofing incorrectly and it flapped and fluttered when the wind blew, and it too leaked in the rain. And worse, the rounded hollows where the corrugated roofing adjoined the main roof made an ideal habitat for bats that seemed to thrive and multiply with each passing summer.

This camp and lifestyle represent the fulfillment—and persistence—of a childhood dream. As a youth, I studied the maps on my bedroom walls, dreamed of trekking to distant backwaters, and holing up in a cabin in the wilderness. My life became the dream. I eventually became a geography professor, yet squirreled away as much time as possible each summer for living at the camp. But our standard of living has been hand to mouth. I was in graduate school on and off—between teaching jobs—until the mid-1980s, and we muddled along in academic poverty. One summer, when we had got down to less than forty dollars, we gathered up all of our nonessentials and sold them at the Even Exchange. If we could hang on until blueberry season, we could earn enough money raking berries to get back to the classroom, which unfortunately, has always been more than a thousand miles from here. Still, the dream has persisted despite the bewilderment of friends and family.

In 1985, with a teaching job at a state college in North Dakota, but my doctoral dissertation still unfinished, we built a sixteen by sixteen foot addition with a wood stove and double hung windows with small panes and screens, and a real loft with skylights. Such luxury! I finished my dissertation that year, and we dreamed of further improvements.

The new camp opened into the old, which we had left intact for sentimental reasons. But the cedar posts on which it rested had rotted over the years, as had the sills, and some of the floor boards. The building dipped down on one end; and, of course, we still had the sun porch with the leaky corrugated roof and the bats in residence. And because of the many cracks and crevices, and doors and windows that didn't fit properly, the camp was still infested with black flies and mosquitoes—so bad were they that we slept under a net.

We tried to think of ways we might remodel and save the old camp. So many precious memories were housed in that ten by twelve foot shack; we just couldn't bring ourselves to tear it down. But there was no practical solution to the ravages of time or to the limitations of a tiny structure built by a fifteen-year-old with marginal carpentry skills.

Finally, in May of 1989, we pulled the old camp down. And what a task! Teenaged boys, I learned, love to drive nails. Some of those eight inch wide sheathing boards had five or six nails per stud. There were spikes and carriage bolts in every corner post and rafter plate. It was not built to be torn down—ever! It was all done according to the 1920 edition of the *Audel's Carpenters and Builders Guide*, that my father had picked up at a used book shop in Newark, and that I carried around with me my freshman year of high school.

In place of the old camp, we added another room, fourteen by sixteen feet, which made the entire structure now measure sixteen by thirty. The window at the end of the new second-story loft looks out over Fred's Cove, and it is from here that I write. I'm sitting on that same pine trunk that I used my first summer here in 1973; my feet are resting on those same random-width floor boards. We salvaged them; decided they were just right for the floor of the loft.

At the end of the summer of 1989, after we had pulled down the old camp, and fixed up the new one the way we wanted it, we changed our mailing address—from Steuben to Gouldsboro. After all those years, I was able, finally, to transfer the attachment that

I'd had to Steuben and to Roger's Store, to Gouldsboro; where, during every summer since 1973, I have gone up to Young's Store to buy my camp supplies. I had come, slowly, to rely on Young's, like I had relied on Roger's so many years before—for cold drinks and ice and kerosene—and for the sense of community it offered.

Perhaps there are no more real Downeast country stores—the kind that Horace had described with the potbellied stove, the spittoon, and the old men on the settee—but there are still many small stores out in the countryside—like Young's—that retain various functions of an earlier age. And it was these relics that provided me with a link to the past and a bridge to the future.

At first, these tiny rural stores had only stood as objects. They were wooden buildings in a land of fog, forest, and water. In time, I began to see them individually; each building transformed into a real place; its atmosphere shaped by its own special clientele, so that stores had a human quality. And when I thought of a certain store, I thought of its owner and the characters who regularly patronized it. And seeing those people, and listening to them talk—about clams and tides and worms—I began to understand the relationship between humans and the environment more clearly. Each country store and its patrons became another link in the ecological chain—no longer an isolated entity, but part of a larger whole.

And that was my method of travel and discovery during the summer of 1988, when I talked to Frances and Flossie, Colin and Horace, Archie and Warren. I moved about slowly; I entered places I scarcely knew; I forced myself to talk to strangers; and I listened and learned from them. Each encounter revealed to me how little I knew about places I thought I had known for years. Sometimes it seemed as though I were seeing Downeast Maine for the first time; it never failed to surprise and delight me.

A few summers ago, I had to leave Maine suddenly for a job interview in South Carolina. I left Jones Pond before daylight and drove the blackened miles to Bangor carrying inside me the dual anxieties of leaving home again and wondering what I'd find at the other end. But when the twin-engine commuter plane lifted off the runway I was awestruck. Nothing could have prepared me for the sight of sunrise over the bays and islands and peninsulas, and the emerald green hills of Maine. I had never seen its extraordinary beauty from the air before; my eyes misted over, chills went down my spine. We flew low, as the plane made a stop in Rockland, and I wondered what I was even doing on a southbound flight.

It is not at all surprising that grown men and women will take their clam hoes to the mudflats each day and accept what nature has to offer. Nor is it surprising that urbanites from out-of-state will "chuck it all" to move Downeast and buy a country store. What was unusual was my own direction. But—then—geographers always seem to wish they were somewhere else. And like old sea captains of a bygone era, I could only dream of coming home.

*May 1988 — August 1989*

# I N D E X

Raised in New Jersey and Steuben, Maine, ALLAN LOCKYER is a 1969 graduate of Sumner Memorial High School in East Sullivan, Maine. He received his bachelor's degree from Southern Arkansas University, master's from Western Kentucky University, and doctorate from the University of Northern Colorado, where he wrote his dissertation on *The Survival of Country Stores in Eastern Maine*. He is currently an associate professor of geography at Francis Marion University in Florence, South Carolina.